Groupwork Volume 6

In this series

Published Spring 2007

Groupwork: Volume 1
ISBN 9781861770554

Groupwork: Volume 2
ISBN 9781861770561

Groupwork: Volume 3
ISBN 9781861770578

Groupwork: Volume 4
ISBN 9781861770585

Groupwork: Volume 5
ISBN 9781861770592

Groupwork: Volume 6
ISBN 9781861770608

Groupwork: Volume 7
ISBN 9781861770615

Groupwork: Volume 8
ISBN 9781861770622

Groupwork: Volume 9
ISBN 9781861770639

Groupwork: Volume 10
ISBN 9781861770646

Groupwork: Volume 11
ISBN 9781861770653

Groupwork: Volume 12
ISBN 9781861770660

Groupwork: Volume 13
ISBN 9781861770677

To be published Autumn 2007

Groupwork: Volume 14
ISBN 9781861770684

A full contents list for volumes 1-13 will be found at the back of this volume

Groupwork

An Interdisciplinary Journal for Working with Groups

Volume Six

edited by

Allan Brown & Nano McCaughan

Whiting & Birch Ltd
1993
Reprinted 2007

Notes from the Publisher

Citation

This volume comprises, without any amendment, all material published in *Groupwork* Volume 6, 1993. It is advised that authors citing material in this volume should recognise this original date and journal provenance in the manner indicated by the house style of the publication for which they are writing, either by citing material as the original periodical article, or, if citing this volume, by clearly indicating the original date of publication of the material both in text references and in the bibliography.

Reproduction

For technical reasons, the typesetting files of some early volumes of *Groupwork* are no longer usable. We have therefore scanned early volumes in this series from the original journals. This inevitably results in reproduction which is less than ideal. Material is available in some other formats.

Editorial contact details

We have reproduced volumes in their complete original format including notes to contributors and advertising. It should be remembered that editorial contact details and manuscript preparation requirements have changed. Current contact details and notes for contributors are available at www.whitingbirch.net.

Published by Whiting & Birch Ltd,
Forest Hill, London SE23 3HZ

ISBN 9781861770608
ISSN 0951-824X
Printed in England and the United States by Lightning Source

Groupwork
An Interdisciplinary Journal for Working with Groups

Volume 6, 1993

Contents

Preface

Since its first issue in 1988, much interesting and inspiring material has been published in *Groupwork*. Most of this still says much of use to today's groupworkers. We are therefore delighted that back volumes of Groupwork will in future be readily available in convenient form.

Mark Doel and Pam Trevithick
Co-Editors *Groupwork*

GROUPWORK

Volume 6 Number 1 1993

Editors: Allan Brown and Nano McCaughan

SUBSCRIPTION, ADVERTISING AND BUSINESS ENQUIRIES
Should be addressed to the publishers, WHITING & BIRCH LTD, PO Box 872, Forest Hill, London SE23 3HZ. TEL: 081-699-0914 (Int'l +4481 699-0914). FAX: 081-699 3685 (Int'l. +4481-699 3685)

SUBSCRIPTION RATES
British Isles £32.00, North America US$65, Elsewhere £37.50
Special reduced rates apply as follows:
Individuals to private address: £16.00 British Isles, North America, US$35 Elsewhere £20.00. Special reductions available for members of AASWG and Groupwork Exchange Network.
Groupwork is published three times a year.

PAYMENT
Should accompany order. Cheque or banker's draft (made payable to WHITING & BIRCH LTD) may be in any convertible currency to the relevant amount. Direct transfer can be made to our Girobank account (no. 5440564). The following credit cards are also accepted: Access/Mastercard, Visa, Diners Club, American Express. Quote card number, expiry date and give cardholder's name and address if different from delivery address.

GROUPWORK is cited in: *Applied Social Sciences Index & Abstracts, Sociological Abstracts, Bibliographie Zeitscriftenliteratur aus allen Gebieten des Wissens, Social Work Research & Abstracts, Special Educational Needs Abstracts*. and *Studies on Women Abstracts.*

PUBLISHED BY WHITING & BIRCH LTD, LONDON. ISSN 0951-824X
Printed by Short Run Press, Exeter.

EDITORIAL

In this edition of GROUPWORK we include articles from Germany, Denmark and the USA, and are pleased to be so international.

Roselle Kurland and Robert Salmon remind us that there are cyclical fashions in practice methods and possibilities - Emmanuel Tropp's article 'Whatever happened to group work ?' in 1978 (*Social Work with Groups*, 1[1]) could be just as relevant today. Their paper identifies the difference between an aware use of group process as an agent of change or help, and the use of the group as a vehicle for the spectator observation of the interaction between the worker and a member. They indicate that the effort to find a common base for the practice of social casework, social groupwork and community work was a disaster for groupwork. Groupwork specialists were always a small minority on the faculty, and subsequently got squeezed out. 'Membership' they quote 'is a fundamental condition of all human life wherever it takes place and across all cultures'. The construction of mutual aid is described, as opposed to advice offered to an identified individual in trouble.

Their paper links coherently with the theme of the two papers given at the Groupwork Symposium last July by Ulla Habermann and Jurgen Matzat. Habermann's views are linked to Kurland and Salmon's - groupwork she indicates, is the practice also left behind in the professional scene in Denmark, in spite of an increasing number of self-help initiatives. She is intrigued by the difference between professionally led groupwork and self-help groups, which could be seen as posing a threat to the former. Habermann lays the decline in professional groupwork firmly at the door of its practitioners, as well as the effect on it of the political and economic context of social welfare institutions and of social work course curricula. Her paper is well organised around seven questions or issues she raises to account for this situation.

Habermann questions whether groupwork as a method has outlived its usefulness and is now being substituted by self-help initiatives. It is possible that it smacks too much of paternalism for the contemporary context. However we have to consider carefully whether we would label 'out of date' the work of those groupwork theorists in the USA of the 1920s, who saw groupwork as a basic training in citizenship. Habermann complains that contemporary groupworkers are adopting a Freire like view of 'empowerment' without much reflection on how this can be achieved. She concludes by stating her view that social groupwork cannot be replaced by self-help. Matzat also reaches this conclusion - but perhaps it could be said 'They would, wouldn't they?.'

Writing about self-help in Germany, Jurgen Matzat first classifies the different types of self-help groups and then discusses how self-help joining and participation can be therapeutic. He makes interesting connections between the natural and spontaneous helping efforts of peers and professional helping, which, he feels, is just a more thoughtfully worked out set of behaviours. Both authors conclude their papers by outlining what is the most appropriate involvement of professionals.

Georgina Ferraro and Julie Tucker attempted to organise mutual aid as well as professional helping in their group work with the siblings of children with special needs. This practice came about because some adult siblings had said it would have been helpful to have had some groupwork to help work out their feelings, when they had been children. The parents who were participating in programmes run by KIDS had also asked for some help with these children. The children were not required to have a problem to be eligible for the group - the experience of having a disabled sibling itself was the criterion of eligibility. The commitment of the members was almost total, and their parents were involved in the feedback. We think this is a rather rare example of groupworkers responding to a requested service from users, rather than the other way around.

The second practice article by T. Wing Lo complements his earlier contribution to 5(1). This is an analytical study of a piece of detached youth work, which blends and extends existing theory very effectively. The author uses theory to join with and influence the perspective of delinquent gang members in more pro-social directions, focusing in particular on the relation between group norms and group control. He is quite open about mistakes in practice that can occur in these risky interventions, as well as demonstrating a deep understanding of how to undermine the anti-social power of a group. Wing Lo teaches at the University of Hong Kong and writes from a Chinese cultural perspective. Some of his illustrations may have a controversial impact on European readers.

Adrian Ward, in his paper on the centrality of large group work in care settings, touches on the anxieties of workers which they tend to project into the users/clients. He writes from a psychoanalytic perspective, which considers that all groups may pose a threat to the satisfaction and containment of the two person relationship. Large group work, as Pierre Turquet postulated, poses threats to our identities - small group experiences relate to the threats posed by families, and large groups to the threat implied in our relationship to society. This article is a useful reminder of the underlying currents in human interactions, and implies questions about how these are navigated in the self-help movement.

Allan Brown and Nano McCaughan, Editors

GROUPWORK VERSUS CASEWORK IN A GROUP

ROSELLE KURLAND AND ROBERT SALMON

This paper identifies and examines the difference between groupwork and casework in a group setting. Examples of each approach will be used to illustrate the distinction. Steps that are essential to maximise the value and benefits of the small group and to ensure that groupwork takes place are described and discussed.

In 1978, the first issue of *Social Work With Groups* appeared. Receiving and reading Volume 1, Number 1, was exciting. Those of us who had lived for a while viewed it as an intellectual rebirth of a kind. Groupwork had its own journal again, and this would help the method have another chance to be born again and take its rightful place on the social work stage. Some of the articles in that issue are as relevant today as the day they were printed. Margaret Hartford's article, 'Groups in human services: some facts and fancies,' Ruth Middleman's 'Returning group process to group work,' and Emanuel Tropp's 'Whatever happened to group work?', each spoke of issues that remain important today.

Tropp had become concerned that schools of social work were eliminating or de-emphasising the teaching of groupwork as a specialisation at the exact time that there was a growth industry appearing and developing for groups. The statistics published yearly by the Council on Social Work Education for a ten-year period ending in 1976 were the realistic basis for this concern. Social groupwork was fading away as other disciplines and other professions were expanding the use of groups. Since a vacuum had evolved, it was to be expected that other forces would fill it. We would not be pleased with the results.

Both Hartford and Middleman discussed some of the results of movement in that direction. Hartford said:

> Another myth is that if a worker collects an aggregate, that is, gets people together in the same place and responds to them individually in the presence of each other, something significant and helpful will occur. It may and it may not. It may be good and it may be harmful for individuals in a gathering to observe a therapist responding to one and then another in sequence, but it

> is not working with the group and it is not maximising the full potential of having the group begin to work for itself. It is rather, doing what I call 'Aggregational therapy of individuals' (Hartford, 1978, p.23).

Ruth Middleman, in her article, discussed three issues that contributed to the lack of attention to a stance that maximised group process. In her view, at that time, one of the issues had to do with the continuing dominance of the helping person, and a therapy perspective that valued personality more than group theoretical constructs. The emphasis was on intrapsychic issues, and led to what she described as group casework, a hot seat pattern with the leader engaging in extended back and forth discussion with one group member while the others watched(Middleman, 1978, pp.16 & 22).

The 'aggregational therapy of individuals' that Hartford described and the 'group casework' or 'hot seat pattern' identified by Middleman are characteristic of an approach to groupwork that we call 'casework in a group.' Such practice with groups minimises the unique potential of the small group to help its members learn and benefit from the differences and diversity as well as the commonalities among them. Casework in a group is very different from groupwork. This paper will identify and examine the differences between the two. Examples of each approach will be used to illustrate the distinction. Steps that are essential to maximise the value and benefits of the small group and to ensure that groupwork takes place will be described and discussed.

Groupwork's presence.

As training in social groupwork methods and foundation knowledge about groups faded from the curriculum in graduate social work schools and therefore from the profession, caseworkers who may not have been trained in social groupwork methods at all often conducted groups. That they did so, and continue to do so, is in keeping with social work history. People trained in casework worked in groups with children and their parents as far back as the turn of the century, especially in hospital settings. This was even before the first group specialisation was started by Wilbur Newstetter in 1923 at Western Reserve.

Historically, some of the foundation beliefs in casework and groupwork are similar, and have shaped the current practice. Newstetter wrote:

> The underlying social philosophical assumption is that individualised growth and social ends are interwoven and interdependent; that individuals and their social environment are equally important (1935, p.297).

The dual focus he described is basic to all current models of social group work practice (Roberts and Northern, 1976).

Prominent casework scholars also emphasise a dual focus. Gordon Hamilton, in 1940, said: '...problems are both individual and social; a case is always a complex of inner and outer factors' (1940, p.25). In 1990 Mary Woods wrote: 'In our psychosocial approach, ecological systems and psychodynamic perspectives have become inseparable' (Woods and Hollis, 1990, p.9). Similarly, Francis Turner accents the dual emphasis as one of the generally accepted, fundamental points which comprise a common core for all casework practice. (Turner, 1974).

The generalised acceptance of a dual emphasis in work with clients may be one of the forces that gives impetus to the actions of the Council on Social Work Education, which from the 1960s on, moved:

> ...to find, elaborate and teach the generic and underlying pattern of regularity that presumably unified the direct practice method of social casework, social group work and community work. This effort was intended to define more sharply social work's identity as one profession (Middleman and Wood, 1990, p.6).

This effort, however, has been a disaster for groupwork. Since groupworkers always were a small minority of social work faculty, generic practice courses, by necessity, were taught largely by people whose expertise was in work with individuals and who had little or no social groupwork experience. The emphasis in such courses was on work with individuals. Birnbaum (1990) analyses the results in *Group Work, The Spotted Owl: An Endangered Species in Social Work Education*. In it, he describes the diminution of groupwork. To continue the analogy from the animal world, the situation was akin to putting a handful of guppies in a tank full of goldfish; the outcome was predictable.

Despite this, interest in groups has not died, and this is not surprising:

> When viewed from a membership perspective, one observes that all social workers and clients, as human beings, are members of groups. Those groups may be large or small; they may be dyads,

> formed groups, families, neighbourhoods or organisations. Membership is a fundamental condition of all human life wherever it takes place, and across all cultures (Falck, 1989, p.24).

Even in today's times, the use of group process was listed as the third most frequently used intervention technique in the study of 142 mental health programmes, and work with groups has emerged as a major modality for service delivery (Middleman, 1990, p.1).

The problem, however, is that what is identified as social work with groups often is not that at all. Gertrude Stein's phrase 'A rose is a rose is a rose....' resonates, and we know the rose when we see or hear the words. However, 'a group is a group is a social work group' is not true and it is not necessarily the same.

Konopka, in her recent paper on work with the emotionally disabled, commented that in the last 25 years groups have abounded with emotionally upset people and are popular vehicles for treatment. But, she points out, now groups frequently are boring, suppressing, and run by people with a need for power. Group process has been used to enhance conformity. Dissenters may be humiliated. 'Revealing' may be required, with punishment if refusal takes place. Konopka describes groups which are one-to-one treatment with the rest of the members acting as bystanders. She calls for a revival of groupwork with:

> ...its basic grounding in a philosophy of respect for the individual, the skilful and gentle use of the positive aspects of group process and the goal of enhancement of the individual's power and capacity (Konopka, 1990, p.14).

One can take heart from Konopka's remarks, and try to bring them to being. A revival of renewal of this kind of groupwork is possible and may be occurring now:

> Trends run in Cycles...once again there is interest not only in specialised fields of practice, but also by methods. Schools of social work once more are offering courses in social group work (Sundel, Glasser, Sarri and Vinter, 1985).

There has been a burgeoning of literature on social work with groups in the last few years. Politically, our efforts in expressing the need for greater collaboration, inclusion, and participation with both NASW and CSWE have been fruitful.

Differences between groupwork and casework in a group.

There are major differences between groupwork and casework in a group. Some of the differences are obvious, others more subtle. The worker who views each member only as an individual and who applies individual personality theories and dynamics without appreciating or understanding the impact of such concepts as group size, roles, norms, communication patterns, member interaction and influence, and group stages, to name but a few, is obviously practising casework in a group. Similarly obvious, the worker who allots time to each individual group member, in turn, to talk about progress on issues of concern, who allots time in round robin fashion and who does not maximise group interaction and mutual aid, practices case work in a group rather than groupwork. Groupwork requires the worker to engage in what Middleman and Wood have called: 'Thinking group (which) means considering the group as a whole first, individual participants second when initiating or responding to others.' (Middleman and Wood, 1990, p.97)

But sometimes group members can all be participating actively and groupwork can appear to be taking place when actually it is not. When, for instance, group members are actively engaged in aiding and offering advice to one member who has raised an issue or problem with which s/he is struggling, case work in a group can still be what is taking place. If, in such an instance, all the group members become 'caseworkers' in an attempt to help solve the problem of one group member, then this remains casework in a group.

In a pre-vocational skills group in a day treatment programme, Sara explains that she is nervous about going back to work. She tells the group that she's gained weight and that her clothes do not fit, that she's worried that she won't be able to get a job because of the bad economy, and that she doesn't know what to say about the gap in her employment history. 'What am I going to say I did for two years — that I was hospitalised and under psychiatric care and doing nothing,' she exclaims. On the other hand, she also says she'd like to have some money and that she feels useless staying home, especially when her sister pressures her to go to work.

Group members jump in to offer advice. Doris says maybe Sara is not ready to go back to work yet. Robert advises her to go on a diet. John tells her not to listen to her sister. Chris and Lisa suggest she 'go for it' and go on an interview. Frank tells her to lie on her application and say she was working in her sister's office. Sara rejects all these suggestions. 'I couldn't lie on my application. I just couldn't do that', she says. 'And if I went on an interview and didn't get the job, I couldn't handle it. I'd be sick for weeks.' Finally she says in frustration, 'I don't want to talk about this any more. Let's talk about something else.' The group then moves on to discuss difficulties Frank is having with his girlfriend.

Readiness to work, pressure from relatives, feeling of inadequacy, fear of failure, how to explain having been hospitalised — all the issues that Sara raises are applicable to other members of this group. Yet the focus is maintained solely on Sara. The group is active. In fact, six members explicitly offer advice. But the problems that are mentioned, even though they are highly relevant to all in the group and are ones with which many group members have had experience, seem not to touch the others as they try to help Sara. This is casework in a group, even with everyone participating actively.

What would make this groupwork is the 'demand' that group members apply the issue or problem of one member to themselves and their experiences and situations. What distinguishes groupwork from casework in a group is an emphasis on the commonalities of problems and situations and the concomitant commonality of feelings to which they give rise. In groupwork, each issue that is raised, even when that issue at first glance seems to have no relevance to others in the group, does have applicability for all. The worker who practices real groupwork draws out that applicability and elicits the commonalities and asks members to examine personally the issues of others. Thus, s/he helps group members to view and to use the issues raised by one member as an opportunity for all.

A seven step progression.

To practice groupwork when one member brings up an individual issue in the group, the worker needs to maintain groupwork's traditional dual and simultaneous focus on the total group and on each individual group member (Newstetter, 1935). To turn an individual's issue into an opportunity for all in the group, a seven-step progression can be identified that draws on the problem-solving approach described by John Dewey (1910):

1. An individual member raises a problem/issue/situation with which s/he is concerned.
2. The problem is clearly identified by the individual and the group.
3. The problem is explored. As it is explored, additional

information may be gathered from the individual about the situation. Group members need to really listen to what the individual is saying. They may ask questions about the problem and about the feelings of the individual. As they listen and question and come to understand the problem through the eyes of the individual who has raised it, they develop empathy and communicate that along with their understanding, concern, caring, and support.

4. The worker asks group members to recount situations they have experienced and dilemmas they have faced that are relevant to the problem that has been raised by the individual.
5. Possible 'solutions' to the individual's problem are identified, drawing on the experiences of other group members that have been recounted in the group.
6. The worker and group members help the individual decide on a course of action or solution that s/he wants to try. The individual is helped by the group to plan how s/he will actually implement that solution.
7. The worker asks all in the group what they have taken out of the discussion that has transpired.

At future meetings, follow-up with the individual about the problem and how things ar going is certainly a recommended eighth step in the progression.

If groupwork rather than casework in a group is to be practiced, particular attention needs to be paid to the timing of the third step in this progression - exploration of the individual's problem. Enough time must be spent in exploring the individual's problem to allow other group members to understand and develop empathy for the individual member and his/her situation. Only if they understand the problem that is being raised will they be able to recount relevant experiences and dilemmas of their own. Too much time spent in exploration with the individual, on the other hand, can contribute to his/her sense of being on a 'hot seat' and of being 'grilled' by the other group members.

In casework in a group, the third step in the progression is frequently rushed and the fourth step, recounting by group members of relevant experiences, is often omitted altogether, as group members rush to offer advice prematurely.

Jim is a member of a group on coping skills in a day programme for the mentally ill. Jim is a lonely and reclusive 29-year-old man who has trouble making friends. He has been diagnosed as paranoid schizophrenic. Jim lives in his own apartment. He frequently annoys the group by talking of masturbation and walking around with his pants unzipped, by making inane comments that interrupt the group, and by pretending to fall asleep and lying across three chairs during the meeting.

At the group's tenth meeting, Jim asks a question of the worker:

> I want to know what you think, Debbie. Hypothetically speaking, suppose you had a friend and you don't have any other friends, but this friend every time he comes over he smokes pot or does a couple of lines of coke in your living room. I mean he is a good listener and is your only friend and you don't do drugs or anything, what would you do?

Before the worker could even respond, group members quickly jumped in to offer advice. Jerry immediately said he'd just tell the guy to get out of his house with the drugs. Allen said drugs are dangerous and this guy's no good. Pam said she wouldn't want anyone doing drugs in her house. Ron said that the guy must not be a very good friend. Will said a friend wouldn't take advantage of you or get you in trouble. Finally, Jim said defensively, 'You know, I don't really care if he does drugs in my house.' He seemed dissatisfied with the discussion that had taken place. Others in the group seemed frustrated as well. As the meeting ended, Pam asked Jim, 'Why did you waste our time if there is no problem?'

In this example, the group participated actively by offering advice to Jim. But obviously, the seven-step progression identified here was not followed. The problem was certainly neither identified clearly nor explored. The members' 'solutions' were offered to Jim in a seemingly belligerent fashion without empathy of understanding. Their own experiences, relevant to Jim's situation, went untapped. The result was that Jim and the group emerged feeling highly dissatisfied.

The worker with this group felt equally dissatisfied and resolved to raise the issue again. When Jim did not show up at the next meeting she was forced to wait for two weeks.

At this meeting, the worker asked the group if they remembered the meeting where Jim spoke of his friend who did drugs at his house. Everyone did remember it. She acknowledged that the discussion had been frustrating for everyone. The group agreed. She asked the group's permission to discuss the issue again in the hope that the group could be helpful to Jim and engage in a discussion that would be more satisfying for everyone. The group agreed.

Jim recounted the situation. This time, though, the worker's questions and comments helped Jim be more specific. When she observed that this issue seemed important to him, Jim responded by telling the group:

> I don't have any other friends and having this one friend is very important to me. This guy I've known all my life. We went to high school together. This guy is a college graduate with a good job. He has his own apartment. This guy is somebody.

The group began to understand and empathise. The tone of their questions and comments changed from a belligerent to a supportive one. Jim's responses, in turn, became less defensive and more honest. He was now better able to hear the group. Even his physical posture changed as he sat upright and faced the group. Allen asked Jim if he was worried about the police. 'Yes, I am', Jim responded, 'But I don't want to end the friendship. I don't want to get caught either with my friend doing drugs'. Pam asked Jim if he ever talked to his friend about being caught when he does drugs at this house. 'I told him it bothered me', Jim said. 'He stopped for a while, but then he started doing it again.'

The worker then asked the group if they could remember situations they'd experienced that were related to that with which Jim was struggling now. Ron told of a time a year ago when he told a friend who wanted him to use cocaine that he would not do it. Others told of other situations — times they'd tried to convince friends or relatives to do something, times others tried to convince them to do something, friends they'd valued and lost, people who'd got them into trouble. All in the group listened attentively to one another until the time for the group was up.

At the next group meeting, the group returned to Jim's particular situation and helped him develop a plan to talk with his friend about his concerns. Drawing on their own experiences, some gave Jim suggestions of what he might say, of actual words he might use. The group even engaged in some role play, with Jim playing his friend and various members playing Jim.

Strengths and mutual aid.

Groupwork is a method of working with people that is affirming of their strengths and of their ability to contribute to others. In fact, the very act of forming a group is a statement that embodies the belief that people have strengths and can help one another. The process of mutual aid, unique to groupwork practice, takes place when members draw upon their own experiences and deepfelt needs to help their fellow members. They, in turn, will relive and relearn through their own offers of help and they will be the stronger for it. Brown (1991) states this well:

> For members to be able to share their ideas and feelings with others is a means of strengthening the giver and the receiver. The collaborative problem solving that goes on during this mutual aid can nurture group members, enhance decision making, and build more cohesiveness within the group.

Breton (1989) emphasises the healing and liberating powers of mutual aid and points out that recognition of the process by which members influence and help one another provides a power that contributes a sine qua non of effective work with groups. It is such mutual aid, she states, that leads to strength and actions and change at the social, economic, and political levels.

The quality of the mutual aid process that occurs in a group is what differentiates groupwork from casework in a group. In fact, Middleman and Wood (1990) identify the worker's focus on helping members to become a system of mutual aid, and his/her understanding, valuing, and respecting the group process as a powerful change dynamic, as criteria essential to groupwork.

The worker's role is to set in motion a process of mutual aid in the group. To set such a process in motion is not easy. The possibility of mutual aid exists in groups, but that does not mean it will flower. Shulman (1979) notes:

> Creating a mutual aid group is a difficult process with members having to overcome many of their stereotypes about people in general, groups, and helping. They will need all the help they can get from the group worker (p.173).

The worker who sets in motion the process of mutual aid takes into account the entire group as an entity rather than just one individual at a time. S/he appreciates that the group is composed of many separate and unique parts, each contributing to a whole that is multi-faceted (Brandler and Roman, 1991). S/he also appreciates that help does not come from the worker alone, but rather from the interaction with other group members as well as with the worker. 'The group is a principal means for the problem-solving and goal achievement, *supplemented* (emphasis mine) by the social worker's direct influence on members' (Northen, 1976. p.117).

William Schwartz, in his simple but profound definition of a group, specified the importance of the interdependence of the members to one another and developed this as a major dynamic for growth and change. A client group, he said, is 'a collection of people who need each other in order to work on certain common tasks in an agency that is hospitable to those tasks' (Schwartz and Zalba, 1971, p.7). The ability of group members to gain from each other, to consider, to understand, to appreciate, and to build on each other's experiences, situations, problems, dilemmas, points of view, strengths and weaknesses - these differentiate groupwork from casework in a group. Such ability, put into motion and enhanced by the worker, is the unique power of groupwork.

Note

This article, which is based on a paper given at the Second European Groupwork Symposium in London, July 1992, will also appear in the *Journal of Social Work with Groups*, 15(4).

References.

Birnbaum, M. (1990) *Group Work, The Spotted Owl: an Endangered Species in Social Work Education*. Paper delivered at the Twelfth Annual Symposium on Social Work with Groups, Miami, Florida, October.

Brandler, S. and Roman, C.P. (1991) *Group Work: Skills and Strategies for Effective Interventions.* Binghamton, NY: Haworth Press.

Breton, M. (1989) *Learning From Social Group Work Traditions.* Proceedings, Eleventh Annual Symposium on Social Work With Groups. Montreal, Canada.

Brown, L.N. (1991) *Groups For Growth and Change*. New York: Longman Publishing Group.

Dewey, John. (1910) *How We Think*. Boston: Heath.

Falck, H.S. (1988) *Social Work: The Membership Perspective*. New Your: Springer Publishing Company.

Hamilton, G. (1940) *Theory and Practice of Social Case Work*. New York: Columbia University Press.

Hartford, M. (1978) 'Groups in human services: some facts and fancies', *Social Work with Groups*, 1(1), 1978.

Konopka, G. (1990) 'Past/present issues in group work with the emotionally disabled: Part II, thirty-five years of group work in psychiatric settings', *Social Work with Groups*, 13(1).

Middleman, R.R. (1990) *Group Work and the Heimlich Maneuver: 'Unchoking Social Work Education.* Plenary address delivered at the Twelfth Annual Symposium on Social Work with Groups, Miami, Florida, October.

Middleman, R.R. (1978) 'Returning group process to group work', *Social Work with Groups*, 1(1).

Middleman, R.R. and Wood, G. (1990) *Skills for Direct Practice in Social Work*.

New York: Columbia University Press.

Newstetter, W.I. (1935) 'What is social group work?', *Proceedings of the National Conference of Social Work,* 1935. pp.291-299.

Northen, H. (1976) 'Psychosocial practice in small groups' in Robert Roberts and Helen Northen (eds.) *Theories of Social Work with Groups*. New York: Columbia University Press.

Roberts, R. and Northen, H. (eds.) (1976) *Theories of Social Work with Groups*. New York: Columbia University Press.

Schwartz, W. and Zalba, S. (1971) *The Practice of Group Work*. New York: Columbia University Press.

Shulman, L. (1979) *The Skills of Helping Individuals and Groups*. Itasca, Ill.: Peacock,.

Sundel, M., Glasser, P., Sarri, R. and Vintner, R. (eds.) (1985) *Individual Change Through Small Groups*. Second edition. New York: The Free Press.

Tropp, E. (1978) 'Whatever happened to group work?', *Social Work with Groups*, 1(1).

Turner, F.J. (ed.) (1974) *Social Work Treatment: Interlocking Theoretical Approaches*. New York: The Free Press.

Woods, M.E. and Hollis, F. (1990) *Casework: A Psychosocial Therapy*. Fourth edition. New York: McGraw-Hill Publishing Company.

WHY GROUPWORK IS NOT PUT INTO PRACTICE:

REFLECTIONS ON THE SOCIAL WORK SCENE IN DENMARK

ULLA HABERMANN

This article looks at the reasons why social groupwork is rarely used by Danish social workers. Several considerations are proposed to explain the situation. Groupwork is left out of the students' curriculi. Working with groups is still considered to be untraditional, only to be used for special purposes. Professionals do not feel that they have mastered this way of working, and furthermore they often have poor working conditions and large caseloads which militates against the use of groupwork. And last but not least, the growth of self help groups have to some extend confused the issue. The auhtor's conclusion is that it is important to stress the differences between groupwork and self help groups, and that self help groups cannot substitute for professional groupwork.

The first thought that went through my mind, when I was honored by receiving the invitation to present a paper at the Second European Groupwork Symposium, was a question: - why is groupwork not used by Danish social workers?

The first thought that went through my mind, when I was honoured by receiving the invitation to present a paper at the Second European Groupwork Symposium, was a question: - why is groupwork not used by Danish social workers?

This is a provocative question, which raises others - none of them are particularly easy to answer. This paper therefore, will raise a considerable number of questions, and some reflections on, or attempts to analyse, the situation, but will not provide many clear-cut answers. The paper does not present a specific study, but is simply based on observations of the practice scene and on readings of recent relevant research.

First of all - to make sure you know what I mean when referring to *groupwork*, let me give a short definition:

> By social groupwork I mean those professionally conducted groups, which meet regularly over a certain period of time to discuss common problems and/or undertake common activities.

Groupwork Vol. 6(1), 1993, pp.17-29

The members are selected and the aims of the group are set by the professional worker.

(In this definition social groupwork does not include 'therapy' but can still be 'therapeutic' - although I know that the boundaries are not always very well-defined or obvious).

When I was asked to present this paper , the request was that I should talk about 'the groupwork I know and that I believe in'.

The fact is that I know the theories very well (as I have been teaching and giving consultations for many years) - and I even believe that groupwork as a method in social work is a gift from heaven, because it gives the participants (the clients as well as the professional workers) so many opportunities of sharing experiences, which do not (often) exist in individual or family casework. It is not that I value one method as being better than the others, but simply that in my opinion the methods are all interdependent.

Groups consist of individuals - communities consist of families and groups. You cannot work with the local community without recognising that it is important to work with individuals and families, and vice versa you cannot work with individuals without seeing them as part of a family, a group or as a citizen in the local community. It works rather like a Chinese box:

The problem is, that I do not very often see this approach put into practice in social work. Usually professionals seem to work with only one or two methods - in spite of their theoretical view of social work - and more often than not the social groupwork method is left out. This, of course, is mostly true in statutory settings, but also in those voluntary organisations which employ professional staff.

In order to elaborate further on my first query: Why is groupwork **not** being put into practice? I will have to look closely at the following questions:

1. Is groupwork left out of students' curricula?
2. Is groupwork totally absent from the scene of the Danish professional Social Services?
3. Why do professionals hesitate to use social groupwork?
4. What is the situation in the voluntary organisations?
5. Do self-help groups muddle up the scene?
6. Is there a belief that social groupwork has outlived itself, and is it being substituted for by self-help groups?
7. Is there a correlation between the 'explosion' of self-help groups, and the 'stagnation' in the use of social groupwork in professional settings?

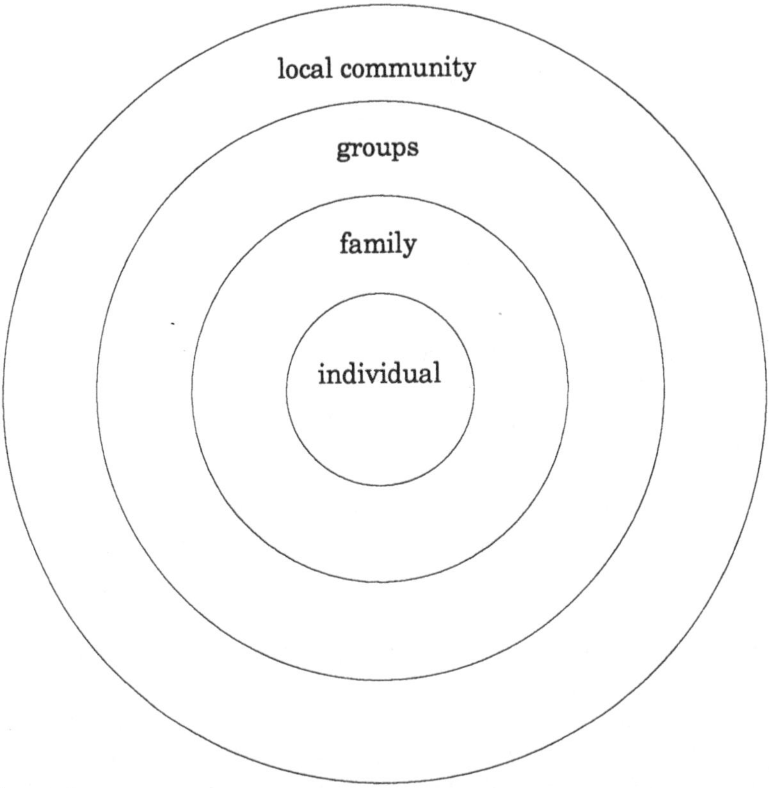

Figure 1

8. Can social groupwork be substituted for by self-help groups?
9. Is there a tendency to individualise and privatise social problems in society?

Is groupwork left out of the students' curricula?

As a former lecturer on social work methods I found myself putting this rather zealous question to the schools of social work, and the answer was not very encouraging. There is in fact very little time allowed - if any at all - for teaching groupwork, and the optimal learning process is never achieved, because the aim is solely an introduction of the method.

In 1975 a new reform of social legislation was introduced in Denmark. The reform was built on the strong belief that the Welfare State was able to solve all the problems of its citizens and that the problems could be best solved locally by the local authorities. The social workers were put in charge of both social benefits and social services, and it forced the workers into a role of controlling budgets, paying out money and only having time for short contacts with their clients.

This of course is not an ideal setting for groupwork, because the clients might feel compelled to take part in a group in order to get their allowances. Furthermore it meant that a change in the curricula of the schools of social work had to be made to meet the requirements of the statutory social services.

This was an attempt to secure jobs for social workers by agreeing to the demands of the employer, which in Denmark is traditionally the local authority. The employers' demands were for individual casework and work with families, not for 'exotic' methods like groupwork or community work. Attempting to rectify this attitude, the schools offer post-graduate courses to professionals, who are specially interested in methods not taught in the three and a half years of basic training. It is possible to state, therefore that because the method of social groupwork is practically unknown to many professionals, it is not of course being put into practice.

However, the issue is not as simple as that. More questions need to be asked.

Is groupwork totally absent from the scene of the Danish professional social services?

The answer to that is- I am glad to say - not too disheartening. Groupwork does exist, in hospitals, in community work projects, in voluntary organisations, in local health services, in groups for crisis and bereavement. But only in special projects, for special target groups, and on special occasions.

One could argue that groupwork is designed for special aims, but in this context *special projects* means projects which are conducted outside the 'normal' work situation and financed by grants - often from the state in order to stimulate the local authorities to work more non-traditionally. *Special target groups* are typically one-parent families, extremely isolated people, young unemployed and immigrant-women. *Special occasions* are often created by crisis situations, where action must be taken - and even the politicians are willing to take risks.

However, these special conditions are not the optimal climate in which one could develop a relatively unknown (and for professional workers a rather frightening) method, because the need for positive results is so urgent that there is no leeway for making mistakes and learning from them.

Social groupwork was on the curricula as early as the 1960s, but it is still considered 'non-traditional'. As stated in a recent research report on innovative projects only published a few weeks ago: ' One of the more untraditional methods used is social groupwork. Only in a few of the projects is this method taken into consideration.' (Jeppesen et al. 1992)

Why do professionals hesitate to use social groupwork?

In spite of evidence and practice experiences that show the need for groupwork, why the hesitation? This question can only be answered by qualitative guesses - or by asking other questions.

Could it be, that professionals are afraid of losing control?

That certainly is more likely to happen in a group than with an individual or a family, especially if you do not feel you have had sufficient training, or think that you have to know all the answers.

It is an interesting reflection that professionals, though highly articulate on the subject of self-determination, still in practice often are reluctant to give people responsibility for their own lives.

Could it be, that professionals are afraid of difficult emotional problems? (like the social workers in the hospital, who argued that male patients with cancer in the testicles could not bear to talk about sexual problems - and indeed when the group was set up, it was the social workers who blushed).

Could it be, that professionals do not really want to set their clients loose, freeing them from the humiliating dependency and the endless role of being the receiver, whilst the professional worker is in the fortunate position of always being the one who gives?

(A Russian woman put this situation into words when she commented on the experience of receiving food aid sent to St Petersburg. She said: ' When we only receive all the time, we become like young birds with open beaks - and we lose our humanity').

Or could it be that the working-conditions for professional workers are not suitable for setting up groups?

This sounds like an easy excuse - but in fact it is not. Very often there is *no room* for groups - especially activity groups - there are *no facilities* for making coffee (which for Danes is absolutely essential to meeting in groups), and there are *no working hours* set aside for such a project, which means that the workers have to do it in their free time. And - as you very well know - groupwork needs hours of preparation, and does not only consist of the time spent with the group.

The poor working conditions, the stress and excessive caseloads, and the symptoms of burn-out make it very difficult for professionals in the statutory services to set up groups.

That is a fact to be acknowledged, even if - in the long run - you do not accept it.

What is the situation in the voluntary organisations?

Voluntary organisations seem better suited for groupwork, because they often work with special target groups (one of the conditions for groupwork), because they are not bound by legal obligations, and because they are able to give the staff flexibility to work in untraditional ways. However, their staff are often professionals with no training in groupwork, and apart from self-help groups there is very little evidence that groupwork is more frequently used in voluntary organisations than in hospitals or by the local authorities.

Furthermore as social groupwork (by my definition) is a professional activity, you do not of course find this method widely used in organisations which work mostly with volunteers.

Do self-help groups muddle up the scene?

In Denmark self-help groups are now developing almost the character of a movement. This seems to reflect the recognition, that the welfare state after all is not able to meet the increasing social and health problems which are not solely economic problems, but rather problems of human relationships and social networks.

Self-help groups have become quite 'fashionable', a network of self-help initiatives have developed throughout the country, and a national self-help support centre was set up three years ago financed by a grant from the Ministry of Social Affairs. In Denmark there are now 60 - 70 local support initiatives helping people to set up self-help groups, and these local support centres each have 5 to 50 groups running.

An empirical study , which was carried out in 1991 on the basis of a representative section of the Danish population, showed that about one in seven Danes had at some time or another been in a situation in which they themselves considered they had a need for a self-help group, and one in five knew someone, who had participated in a group. The study anticipated that at the time of the interview between 0.5 and 1.1 per cent of the population were participating actively in a self-help group. Mostly people participate in connection with grief, family problems, serious illnesses and acute crises situations. (Mehlbye and Christoffersen, 1992).

Self-help groups are not only found in connection with the self-help support centres, but are also set up in hospitals and in voluntary organisations. It is estimated that at least 1350 self-help groups exist at the moment , 650 of them in hospital wards and in voluntary organisations. (Adamsen and Hertz, 1992). It is important to stress that self-help groups - in spite of many similarities - are not identical to social groupwork.

Before proceeding further, I offer a definition:

Self-help groups are small, voluntary groups of peers, who organise in order to achieve some declared aim. Such groups are often established in a defined and limited geographical area. Members are motivated by the common need to prevent or solve a particular problem, often related to social or health issues which are not adequately covered by the official services.

The differences between self-help groups and social groupwork (and therapeutic groups) can be seen in Figure 2.

Figure 2

Social groupwork

- professionally conducted
- meet regularly
- restricted period of time
- members selected/professional aims
- therapeutic
- common problems

Self-help groups

- peer groups
- not always regular meetings
- unrestricted time
- members own idea/set own aims
- non-therapeutic
- common problems

Note - both meet on grounds of 'common problems'

Self-help groups are initiated and led by the members themselves, whereas social groupwork requires aims and leadership set by professionals. Self-help groups are normally set up around a specific problem which the members choose to discuss, and professionally led groups are often set up on the basis of the client's whole life situation.

The key words for self-help are reciprocity, non-professional, anti-bureaucratic and the fact that the members themselves are in charge of the group. The key words of social groupwork are 'solving social problems' and at times 'empowerment'. Some people even go so far as to say that for a true self-help group no professionals can be involved in setting up and/or conducting the group`s work, but most projects allow professionals a role as support-persons. This strict definition of self-help groups, means that groups initiated or set up by local authority employees are not strictly speaking, self-help groups.

How then do we define all the groups set up by the local health and social services (often under professional leadership), who call themselves self-help groups, and who certainly use many of the self-help principles? Some researchers choose to leave the definition to the groups themselves, and others - in order to protect the idea of the self-help group members being in charge - attempt to draw an iron curtain between the two. A rather pragmatic solution to this could be to acknowledge the existence of different kinds of groups for different purposes, but to insist on a clear description of the way the group is organised and how it functions in order for people to choose the right kind of group and in order for the professionals to be aware of what they are involved with.

Is there a belief that social groupwork has outlived itself and is being substituted for by self-help groups?

Has social groupwork become old fashioned in a time when the values of 'charity' are being replaced by those of self-help?

As mentioned above, it is first of all essential that professionals are aware of what they are doing, in what context and for what reason. Social work can be seen as helping the poor (a humanitarian view), as keeping people silent (a Marxist view) and as empowering people (a Paulo Freire-an view). Often social workers adopt the last view without much reflection on how this can be done.

Professionals, when they start working with volunteers, bring with them their professional attitudes and methods of work, and in this way they have a significant impact on the work of the voluntary organisations. But professionals seldom carry the values and attitudes of volunteer work back into the statutory settings - simply because the bureaucratic systems are too inflexible to receive such inputs. This professionalisation of volunteer values is looked upon with some resentment, and I fully agree that this form of 'colonisation' is not of any benefit either to the statutory or to the voluntary sector. The value base of these two worlds have different roots and serve different purposes. If you forget that, you will go wrong.

But indeed in one field of professional activity - namely social groupwork - there certainly seems to be an influence going in the opposite direction: from the volunteers to the professionals.

Therefore it is mainly a matter of clarification, (rather than sourly pointing out) to accept that professionals are stealing the good ideas from self-help groupwork in order to keep up with the times!

Is there a correlation between the 'explosion' of self-help groups and the 'stagnation' in the use of social groupwork in professional settings ?

There is no doubt that professional groupwork is developing a value base inspired by the ideas of self-help and the ideologies of citizen participation. Many professionals are attracted by the way self-help groups work, and volunteer as support persons for the local self-help initiatives, or attempt to set up their 'own' self-help groups. They do this in order to develop their own methods and to get away from bureaucratic settings. On the other hand they seem to forget that the strength of working with small groups always has been the inter-relationships between the group members and the group process. This is not a new 'invention' made by self-help groups. Therefore, in order not to place the discussion in a deadlock, a distinction between two kinds of groups (the professional and the non-professional) no longer is sufficient, when you want to describe what happens in the practice field.

The Figure opposite shows three basic models of working with groups. The reader is kindly asked to use their own imagination in order to visualise the multitude of immediate layers which might occur in practice.

This diagram aims to demonstrate how the three basic forms of groupwork exist simultaneously, and that all three are needed, because they supplement each other and give us a multitude of possibilities, which are essential in social work. The art is to choose the right model at the right time, which is easier said than practised.

The diagram also pictures the 'dream' of many professionals of their groups being able to continue as self-help groups and develop a kind of social network for their members. This is in fact often the pronounced aim of self-directed groups, but the workers often forget that if the dream is to come true, the involvement of the professional must reduce over time as the group becomes able to take on the responsibility for the maintenance of the group. (Ward and Mullender, 1991). This gradual abrogation of control is often seen as an ideal way to encourage the group's independence. But as Heap

Figure 3

GROUPWORK

Classical Social Groupwork	Self-Directed Groupwork	Self-Help Groups
	Setting up the group	
THE WORKER:		**THE MEMBERS:**
takes the initiative	initiator	take initiative (at times suggested from outside)
sets up aims selects members makes decisions	sets boundaries assists and supports facilitates	decides aims and how to work
	Professional Roles	
dominant role decides/controls	active role involved	gives service and support
	Purpose of group	
intervention solving problems	co-operation empowering	consultation self-help
	The Target Groups	
abusers psychiatric patients homeless serious illness (the outcasts)	single parents young unemployed isolated people immigrants (the isolated)	difficult life situations acute crisis & bereavement carers/parents serious illness/disabled person (the vulnerable)

(1988) points out, in a social groupwork context the worker should perhaps continue as the 'central person' throughout the group`s life, at least where certain modelling functions and emotional issues are concerned. Otherwise the group might be confused and disappointed because the worker withdraws from the group.

Thirdly the diagram also shows three different target groups. (Building on recent research on innovative projects in Denmark, Jeppesen, Just et al. 1992)

1. The ' outcasts' - so called heavy groups (such as alcoholics, drug abusers, psychiatric patients). This group of people needs a highly professional and often therapeutic treatment.
2. The 'isolated' (unemployed, single parents, immigrants), who need empowerment to set their own aims and purposes of life, but who cannot (as yet) set up and direct their own groups. The work set up for these groups are often activity groups.
3. The 'vulnerable' (people in difficult life situations , crisis and bereavement, connected with serious illnesses as patients, carers and parents), who needs preventive care, somewhere to turn to in emergency cases and a helping hand to get on with life.

The latter of the three, the 'vulnerable' is the most obvious target group to benefit from self-help.

And now the next question, which has been converted into a statement. Because for me there is no doubt that: *social groupwork cannot be substituted for by self-help groups.*

The reasons for this are:

1. Self-help groups are not- in spite of their great value and excellent achievements - the answer to everything. They do not meet with the needs of many of the traditional target groups in social work.
2. Self-help groups bear in them inevitable tensions because the members themselves are in charge, but they may also need to obtain support from professionals. This is a most delicate balance - and even the most aware self-help initiatives find this difficult to get right.
3. The groups often have internal problems because their values are democratic and they are eager to let everyone be equal. This sometimes means that the groups tend to shrink away from open conflicts in order to maintain a smooth surface (Diemer and Stenbak, 1992).

4. It is often seen that people participating in self-help groups need other kinds of professional help. The key to the benefits they get from self-help groups , which lies in the concept of experiential knowledge used in a reciprocal way, is unique to self-help groups. But it is not always enough.
5. Some people are not interested in participating in self-help groups, and should never be forced to see such groups as their only option. Self-help groups must be seen as an opportunity for people to make their own choices as to whether they wish to participate.

My final question is: *Is there a tendency to individualise and privatise social problems in society?* In Denmark ten years of conservative government has certainly contributed to this way of thinking, and the ethos of 'deserving and non-deserving poor' is creeping back. Furthermore the liberal ideology clearly fits the values of self-help, and there is an immense political enthusiasm for the self-help movement.

Different forms of collaboration between the local authorities and the self-help initiatives have emerged. The public social services urge their clients to contact the self-help groups, and the idea spreads into the public services, where professionals set up (so called) self-help groups for their own clients. The local authorities hope that self-help groups can fill a gap in the public system, and can save professional resources.

The recent studies on self-help groups in Denmark show that participants in self-help groups often benefited from taking part in the group, but also that this benefit is special (i.e. cannot be obtained elsewhere). This indicates that self-help groups are a complement and not a substitute for traditional social work. On the other hand, self-help groups have a preventive potential, which in the long run might save public resources.

And finally - self-help does not mean 'look after yourself only'. It must not develop into an individualisation of people's need for help. The Self-help groups cannot simply be left to themselves, neither professionally nor politically. However they also have to resist the temptation of becoming too integrated into the public systems. One of the secrets of their success is that they have not gone public.

Paper presented to the Second European Groupwork Symposium in London, July 9-10. 1992.

References

Adamsen, L. and Hertz, E. (1992) *Selvhjælpsgrupper indenfor SUM-programmet og tilgrænsede områder*. Copenhagen: Akademisk Forlag

Adamsen, L. et al. (1992) *Selvhjælpsgrupper for mennesker med livstruende sygdomme*. Copenhagen: Akademiske Forlag.

Diemer, A. and Stenbak, E. (1992) *Selvhjælpsgrupper. Om seks projekter i danske lokalområder*. Copenhagen: Akademisk Forlag.

Habermann, U. (1990) 'Self-help groups: a minefield for professionals', '*Groupwork*, 3 (3).

Heap, K. (1988) 'The worker and the group process: a dilemma revisited', *Groupwork*, 1(1).

Jeppesen, Just, K. et al. (1992) *UdstRdte og sårbare*. Copenhagen: Socialforskningsinstitutet.

Mehlbye, J. and Christoffersen, M.N. (1992) Selvhjælpsgrupper - omfang, karakter og erfatinger i nationalt og inernationalt perspektiv. Copenhagen: AKF.

Ward, D. and Mullender, A. (1991) ' Facilitation in self-directed groupwork', *Groupwork*,4 (2).

AWAY WITH THE EXPERTS?

SELF-HELP GROUPWORK IN GERMANY

JURGEN MATZAT

Statistics on the scale of self-help groups, illustrated here in the German context, indicate that they are now a quantitatively significant factor in health and social care systems and services. Definitions for the not very precise term 'self-help group' are given, and a typology with three broad categories is suggested 'anonymous type' (e.g. AA); larger 'self-help organisations' (acting nationwide as a kind of patients/members' trade-union with similarities to other non-governmental organisations,; and self-help groups' in the narrower sense, focusing mainly on direct interpersonal encounter in small relatively stable groups. Significant effects of self-help groupings are listed, and possible therapeutic mechanisms are discussed.

The latter part of the paper considers the kinds of consultation and support which professional helpers can offer self-help groups, making their knowledge and skills available whilst respecting group autonomy and self-determination.

I find myself in a paradoxical situation; addressing an audience of distinguished professional groupworkers and speaking about a form of groupwork which takes place without them, and which will and should take place without them. I am going to speak about largely uncharted territory which many of you may never have explored. Some may think, if they do it without us, why should we be concerned with their affairs?

I think we should. Speaking from a German perspective, self-help groups have developed into a relevant phenomenon in our health and social welfare system (Matzat, 1987). Estimates suggest there are about 50,000 self-help groups in what was previously the Federal Republic of Germany. (I should add that self-help groups could hardly develop in the former East Germany. They were, to put it mildly, not welcome, as the state's ideology insisted that all social problems were already solved, or were about to be solved in the near future by state agencies. We speak of a 'guardian state', but `East Germany', like other states of the former Eastern Block, is catching

Groupwork Vol. 6(1), 1993, pp.30-42

up rapidly. That would be another exciting topic to address, but I shall not digress further.)

A more precise calculation of the incidence of self-help groups in certain defined catchment areas was made during the four year period, 1987-1991. Seventeen demonstration projects all over West Germany were funded by our federal government: the researchers found that in urban areas there was one self-help group to every one thousand inhabitants, and in rural areas about half as many. I imagine these results are not too different from the situation in England. I am not so sure about other parts of the United Kingdom, as our two countries are the most 'advanced' in Europe (speaking in terms of the self-help movement!) (Humble and Unell, 1989). Of course, all such estimates and calculations suffer from two big sources of error: how to find, and how to define, self-help groups. Many of them bloom in places which are hard to find, and sometimes it is hard to distinguish them from other forms of groupwork. I will return to these topics later.

First, let me give you two more indicators of their ubiquity. In Germany there is an umbrella organisation called *Bundesarbeitsgemeinschaft Hilfe für Behinderte* (Federal Association for Help for Disabled People) which currently has fifty six organisations. Here people suffering from chronic illnesses and disabilities band together. Give me the name of any chronic illness, and I can give you the name of a relevant self-help organisation. The largest of them is the *Deutsche Rheuma-Liga* (German League against Rheumatism) with 130,000 members.

There is one more indicator of the growing relevance of, and interest in, the spread of self-help groups in Germany: in more than 220 cities or districts there are self-help supporters, be it full-time workers in so called 'clearing houses' (to use a rather American term) or 'contact and consultation centres' (the most widely used German expression) (Humble and Unell, 1989, Chaps 7-12 on 'Local support for self-help'). Self-help groups are also sustained by all kinds of health and social welfare agencies on a part-time basis. These self-help centres differ greatly in number and qualifications of staff; in funding; in emphasis and orientation; in catchment area and degree of integration in larger institutions. But they all offer basic information and support to self-help groups and - especially important - to interested individuals. They have a range of functions: they explain the general concept of self-help groups and offer a means of access to established groups; they help new groups to get started; they supervise groups in trouble if requested; they collaborate with other professional services; they are in contact with politicians and administrators; and they serve as a public relations agent for the self-help movement. Self-help clearinghouses of this type exist in England also. The prototype and perhaps still the best example is Judy Wilson's 'Self-Help Team' in Nottingham[1]. A directory of self-help support centres is compiled in Britain by the Self-Help Centre in London[2], and the 1989 version listed addresses in about 60 cities.

My main topic is the role played by self-help groups, and I have not yet defined what I mean by this term - a completely unacceptable position for an academic! To make it easy for myself- and at the same time to recognise the British contribution - I quote the following definition:

> Self-help groups are defined as groups of people who feel they have a common problem (typically concerning a medical, social or behavioural condition) and have joined together to try to do something about it (Richardson and Goodman, 1983, p.2).

This definition is short and concise, an example of British pragmatism. Another more detailed, and some may say more normative, definition was worked out by the German Association of Self-Help Supporters (*Deutsche Arbeitsgemeinschaft Selbsthilfegruppen e.V.*)

> Self-help groups are voluntary, mostly loose associations of people, whose activities are directed towards common coping with illnesses, psychological or social problems, by which they - either themselves personally or as relatives - are affected. They don't want to make a (commercial) profit. Their goal is a change in their personal life situation and often influence on their social and political environment. In regular, often weekly, groupwork they stress authenticity, equality, a common language, and mutual aid. In doing so the group is a means to counteract outer (social) as well as inner (psychological) isolation. The goals of self-help groups focus on their members, and not on outsiders; in that respect they differ from other forms of citizen's initiative. Self-help groups are not led by professional helpers; some consult experts now and again on particular questions however.

I was a member of the commission who worked out this definition as part of a comprehensive brochure containing basic information and guidelines for self-help groups and self-help support, and I remember well how many hours we spent discussing it until a consensus was found. Our personal and professional attitudes, education, experiences, goals, preferences, and focuses of interest differed very much. The colourful reality of the self-help scene differs even more. To bring a minimal structure into this unclear field, permitting at least a rough categorisation, I suggest distinguishing between three basic types of self-help groupings.

Anonymous type

Its most prominent example, the AA (Alcoholics Anonymous), is the prototype to which all other Anonymous groups refer. There is EA (Emotions Anonymous), NA (Narcotics Anonymous), PA (Parents Anonymous) and many more. In the United States, a list of Anonymous type self-help groups has more than 70 items. The latest examples in Germany, more popular in women's magazines than in reality, are 'Shopping Anonymous' and 'Love-addicted Anonymous'. These may seem rather odd, if not absurd. But what they demonstrate is the growing attraction of the general concept of `addiction' (an illness, not the person's own fault) to explain all kinds of behaviour disorders, and what the anonymous-concept promises is an adequate method to fight addiction.

AA was founded in 1935 in Akron, Ohio, and was the birth of a movement. In Germany, AA did not arrive until 1953 when it came in the kitbag of American soldiers occupying Germany after World War II. Their groups, just like all self-help groups of the anonymous type, are 'open', which means: people can join the group and leave it whenever they want to, the only requirement being a desire to recover. Thus there is no formalised membership, and consequently no membership fee; no formal status of the group (unlike a registered club, association, society or charity); and no board or committee (only a chair-person for one meeting at a time). But there is the 'programme', '12 steps' and '12 traditions'. These texts, representing the developed experiences of people with alcohol-related problems and of self-helpers, offer guidelines for daily life as well as for groupwork, and are to be regarded as a kind of 'therapist's equivalent' in anonymous groups. Which expert would ever have predicted that these people, supposedly weak-willed and heavily dependent on alcohol, would be able to perform successful groupwork without experts? And what a lesson they have taught us!

In anonymous groups, participants hold a series of monologues rather than dialogues or discussions. 'No questions, no good advice, talk about yourself', they say. Here we find a close similarity to the confession rituals of Christian communities with their well-known cathartic effects. They also respect explicitly a spiritual dimension on the road to recovery, the 'surrender' and hand over to a 'higher power' (as they personally understand it). This, again, is a very clear reversion to Christian thinking, and psychologically speaking, to a 'super-ego approach'. This skeleton of a clear and strong programme has obviously proved worthwhile for millions of people with alcohol-related problems to compensate for a lack of personal ego-strength. Equally certainly, this style does not suit everyone.

Self-help groupings

These are called self-help organisations in Germany. They are represented best by the large patients' associations mentioned previously, for example the League against Rheumatism. They appeared in several waves historically: people left disabled after two World Wars, parents of children with learning disabilities in the Sixties, people suffering from chronic illnesses in the late 1970s. Usually they have a very formal structure and status, similar to the non-state and non-profit social welfare organisations which play a predominant role in Germany's social system. They function nationwide, at federal state level, and sometimes they have local groups. They stress 'outer self-help' by representing the interests of their members, and also others suffering from the same problem. In this way they act as a kind of 'patients' trades union'. They offer legal advice; they publish regular journals; and they collect money to stimulate and support research, and to employ professional staff, especially at their national headquarters. Members sign an agreement and pay a fee. These organisations seek public funding, and some are remarkably successful.

Only a small minority of the members of these self-help organisations are really active and deserve to be called 'self-helpers'. They very often carry a tremendous workload, and they sacrifice limitless time, money and energy. If we had the right to label their behaviour, we might call them over-involved, acting out a 'helper syndrome', (precisely as many of us do). We concede that they benefit from the positive effects of the 'helper therapy principle' (Riessmann, 1965) that we professional helpers benefit from every day - help somebody, and you will benefit most - but in the context of a collective self-help process in a group it may seem rather counterproductive. Self-helpers have only very few chances to (self) control their behaviour by supervision or similar mechanisms. As 'helper' and 'helpee' are dialectic complementary roles, the 'over-involved' members in self-help groupings contribute to some degree to the widespread passivity found among the majority of their co-members. Of course, this fact does not prevent them from complaining about the others' passivity! In summary, it can be said that self-help organisations tend to be used (or misused?) like any other agency in the care system. Their members, and even more so other sufferers, behave simply as consumers.

Self-help groups in a narrower sense, often referred to as 'discussion groups' or 'psychosocial self-help groups'

Their setting reminds us of that of professional groupwork, at least in the field of psychotherapy (Matzat, 1989-90). The group is 'closed' (or 'slow open'); membership is clearly defined by self-declaration and mutual agreement (a kind of 'contract-equivalent'), and by regular reliable participation and attendance, but not by subscription and fees. A limited number of people (perhaps 6-12) meet regularly (usually once a week) over a considerable period of time in a neutral room (i.e. not in somebody's home). They have an open discussion on very personal matters, their feelings and emotions, their hopes and anxieties, their conflicts and their symptoms. They focus on their personal history, their relations between themselves and with significant others outside the group. They talk about their families of origin and their actual families, about their partners, friends, and colleagues. They try to be as frank and open as possible and to clarify their points of view. Although it was a bit overdone when Nathan Hurvitz (1974) characterised their work as 'psychotherapy without psychotherapists', it is clear that psychological and emotional aspects certainly enjoy special attention, if not actually given priority.

How can this work? This is the sceptical question asked by all the experts who went to schools and universities, spent years in training and collecting professional experience, and who paid for all kinds of courses, further training, and supervision. Can lay people do everything themselves? Are we experts about to clear our desks, leave the offices, and join the queues at the job centre?

Well, I can offer some comfort: our situation is not quite that bad! (Although I must admit there are some pretty worrying findings from comparative studies on the effectiveness of professional and lay helpers. But we shall not pursue this here.)

First, let us have a closer look at what effects we can observe in self-help groups, then let us try to understand why and how these are created, and finally let us find out what are the remaining jobs for professionals to do.

It is not easy to speak about the demonstrated effects of self-help groups for two reasons: first, because of the tremendous variety of approaches, 'methods', and goals. (Who, for example, could tell you about the effects of groupwork or psychotherapy in general?): secondly, because of the lack of research and experience. Self-help groups do not fit very well into research 'designs', they resist 'interventions', there are no 'matched control groups' etc. And who should feel a need for evaluation, as there is so little or no money in self-help? Fortunately, we are not entirely without data; we do know quite a bit about outcomes, particularly through the observations of experienced self-help groups' consultants.

The first, very banal but overwhelming, proof is simply their existence and growth in number. Why should people build them up, keep them going, join them, invest their energy in them if it is not because they feel the benefits! There is no other obligation, no commercial profit, no pressure from outside. The participation itself must be rewarding enough. The results of investigations (by interviews, questionnaires, and psychological tests) can be summarised in an abbreviated way as follows:

1. a reduction in depression;
2. a boost in self-esteem and personal growth;
3. more personal contacts (within the group and outside);
4. more skills in getting through conflicts;
5. the seriousness of one's own situation is seen in relative terms;
6. a reduction in feelings of isolation (including proneness to suicide);
7. less tendency to somatisation (with use of drugs and hospital treatment as consequences);
8. not less overall, but a more selective use of the care system (the well informed patient).

(Daum, 1986; Trojan, 1986)

How do self-help groups achieve these effects? This is hard to answer, as we are not witness to their processes, and if we question them about it, they usually do not have the terminology and the concepts to answer in our terms. So we have to rely essentially on our interpretations and theoretical reconstructions. The mechanisms involved include the following:

1. 'Modelling' is certainly one of great importance. This is probably true for all human learning processes and, in self-help groups, it is almost the aim and object of one's participation. How do other people survive the loss of a child? What exercise helps

best against your arthritic pain? What tricks help you to go to a cinema in spite of claustrophobia? How could you stay sober over so many years? The essence of this modelling is: 'Show me how you helped yourself, so that I can imitate your behaviour as far as it suits me'.

2. The 'helper therapy principle' has been mentioned before. It refers to the fact that a helper usually feels good, self-assured, and competent. The Christian ethic, deeply rooted in many of our minds, teaches us: 'It is more blessed to give than to receive'. The helper is regarded and regards himself or herself as a morally good person; if the helpee is one too, that throws the role differentiation into question. This effect is particularly to be observed among the 'founders', 'leaders', 'chairpersons', or 'speakers' of self-help groups. In these cases, the helper function is more or less rigidly fixed to a formalised role. It is amazing to see how people cling to these positions over many years despite all the burden and distress connected with it. They grumble about it in private, but never complain in public. Some groups run hospital or home visit services. Here also the helper's role is well established. The helping process goes one way only, no mutual aid in sight. The self-stabilising effect on the other hand is obvious. The essence of this process is: 'please let me help you, so that I can prove to myself how good my situation is (compared to yours) and how well my coping mechanisms work.'

3. The direct empathy or 'identification resonance' (v.d. Avort and Harberden, 1983) by fellow sufferers is a fundamental characteristic. In self-help groups you do not have to explain much (especially if the group is homogeneous). The others know what you are talking about. They have similar symptoms, pain, fears, side-effects of drugs etc. You also feel less ashamed of your disabilities and their consequences. Compassion and understanding is more or less guaranteed.

   Doctors and other experts may know how to treat an illness, but what do they know about living with it and with the consequences of the treatments? The sense of this is: 'You, my group colleagues, are the only people in my world who really understand me, better than professional helpers, better than friends, even better than my family.'

4. 'De-stigmatisation'. Many problems which self-help groups face are connected with open or hidden forms of stigmatisation. Examples of this include: groups of homosexuals, AIDS

sufferers, substance abusers and people from ethnic minorities. It is also true, perhaps to a milder degree, of many forms of illnesses and disabilities. People feel excluded from social life and they withdraw into themselves.

(I remember seeing a poster showing a person in a wheelchair at the top of some stairs leading down to a sign saying 'public convenience'. The caption says: 'For me, it is neither public nor convenient'.)

Stigmatised people often prefer isolation to confrontation. Sometimes whole families are affected by this process. Their home is no longer their castle, it is their prison. In self-help groups 'normality' is stood on its head: inside the group it is normal to suffer from this specific problem! Without the problem, no admittance. If you cannot say the password: 'I am an alcoholic', the world of an AA meeting remains locked for you. If you have the ticket, that is if you are a fellow sufferer, you may join the group and suddenly you are no longer part of a minority, you do not have to hide, you are no longer different. No, now you are part of the mainstream. What a relief!

5. The 'combination of potentials'. Our training as professionals is quite biased towards diagnosing and analysing symptoms, illnesses, disabilities, limitations etc. We often focus on the negative, the `deviation', the minus. And as if it were the most natural thing in the world, we start from the assumption that it is our knowledge, our methods, our techniques, our tools which will cure or help, if cure or help is possible. We learn and think much less about potential in our clients, about what they can still do, even with their limited capacities. Especially: what can they do together and for each other?

   People with different physical disabilities or impairments do not call the ambulance, they help each other. And they can do so because the nature of their disabilities are not the same. Their remaining faculties differ enough to complement one another. That is exactly what self-help groups do - of course spontaneously, not in a systematic or reflective way. They combine the strength, the experience, the knowledge, the talents, and the will power of their members. This combination, not only the aggregate, of qualities may be regarded as a kind of 'therapist equivalent' in self-help groups of this type.

6. Furthermore, all our esteemed professional tools in human science, all forms of counselling, psychotherapy, and groupwork, have not fallen onto this blue planet from another star. Most

> therapies are nothing more than a systematic and elaborated application of certain elements of 'natural' helping behaviour. Parents use it, healers use it, priests and teachers use it, and so called 'natural helpers' use it. And the findings of psychology and social science do not remain in the quarantine of laboratories and university libraries any more. At least some of this knowledge infiltrates certain groups in our population. I do not know if what I say is specific to Germany, or if I display a professional bias as a psychologist working in a university clinic for psychosomatic medicine and psychotherapy, when I point out that many people have already undergone different forms of psychotherapy, have been to encounter groups or similar workshops, have gained prior experience of groupwork in universities, churches, or hospitals. And we should not forget that the mass media, magazines and TV deal with medical, psychological, and social problems with increasing frequency. In Germany, any Freudian slip of Chancellor Kohl during a press conference is repeated ten times an evening in each and every news programme. There must be a sizeable part of our nation who understand.

Other convincing examples of psychological knowledge finding its way into attitudes and behaviour patterns of everyday life are the way children are brought up, the changes in gender roles, and educational styles in kindergartens and schools. To return to self-help groups and their 'methods' and 'techniques': there we find rudimentary forms of interpretation, confrontation, reinforcement, feedback, focusing, verbalisation of emotions, correcting emotional experiences, analysis of transference, holding function etc. Of course, the group members would not use this terminology, they may not even know all these words, and no doubt it is only a rather primitive form of psychological techniques we are talking about. But - and I feel this is tremendously important - they are opening themselves up to a new perspective on life, on the world, and on themselves, a view through psychological glasses. I do not wish to glorify this, and I do not overestimate the degree and the speed of this development, but it goes in a direction which has my full support. This is perhaps the most important reason why I have been involved with self-help groups for so many years.

Finally, if self-help works so wonderfully well and without professional involvement, what is left for us to do, for groupworkers and other experts in the care system? I think there is a lot. First of all, in our agencies we have an excellent opportunity to disseminate among our clients the idea of collective self-help as an alternative or as a supplement to professional services. This includes a cognitive aspect, the simple information about the existence of self-help groups, their basic structures and ways of working, and possible access to them. But we should not forget the other side of the coin, the emotional aspect. We should not only encourage our clients, but we should be ready to discuss their ambivalence, their hopes and fears. A prime aim of the counselling process is to help someone find his or her own decision which they then have to translate into action and accept responsibility for. If we perform this counselling in our most professional way, it is quite legitimate and does not detract from self-help principles. Secondly, we can help new groups get started. This means as necessary: bring potential members together, offer an adequate room, play the role of a presenter during an initial session, focus some questions concerning group processes which will most probably occur in future; for example, basic general rules for group discussions like the ten commandments of 'theme-centred interaction' (after Ruth Cohen) etc. These services performed by a professional do not necessarily harm the self-help ideology. On the first evening a self-help group does not yet exist! It is a gathering of individuals trying to find out if they want to become a self-help group. (I call it the 'zero session'.) If they say yes, they will meet again next week for their first session as a self-help group, this time without a professional worker.

Thirdly, we only suggest some advice, knowing - and saying - this is from an expert's perspective, and self-help groups may choose to function in a different way. If they make use of it we will most probably never hear about it again. This can be compared to an assistant at a birth who will never see what blossoms out of this tiny crying something. This can be a most uncomfortable perspective for a 'proper' groupworker who is used to following through the magical development of her clients, to enjoying it, and to attributing quite a bit of the progress to her own efforts and abilities!

Only a few of us can add more authentic, more valid advice to self-help groups: that is those of us who are or were members of one ourselves, or who have collaborated over a long period of time with self-help groups, learnt from that experience, and can now transfer it to new groups.

The fourth resource which we can offer is consultation or supervision for existing groups. Again we act as professionals with all our knowledge and experience. But we have to admit how modest our experience still is in this relatively new field of groupwork, and we have to respect those group members who will possibly persist with different views. They are the ones who decide what is useful and what is not. Remember how junior colleagues are supervised: their clients are not removed from them and taken over by the supervisor. Full responsibility is left with the colleague. We need to behave in a similar way with those self-help groups with which we co-operate. Put it this way: we do not consult them, we consult WITH them!

Such consultation sessions should be clearly differentiated from ordinary group meetings. They are not a group meeting with a group leader, even if the group unconsciously tries to manipulate the professional into this position. The great danger is that we may be seduced by the invitation. We like to hear: 'Oh, this evening with you was so much more productive than our usual group meetings. Couldn't you come again next time?' And next time, and next time - because it was so nice: thus unwittingly reverting to the traditional professional groupwork model. There is nothing wrong with it, we are all practising it. But we should clarify both to our clients and to ourselves what is going on, and define it accurately. Thus, our technique in consulting WITH self-help groups requires a high degree of restraint, clear limits and roles, modesty in our contribution, and a stress on searching and reinforcing the creativity and successes of the group and its own potential to solve problems.

A good reaction to a request for help from a self-help group would be: 'Well, I'm not sure how a self-help group should act best, but in professional groupwork we would probably do this and that, for this and that reason.' An even better reaction is: 'Well, I'm not sure if the following is a good idea for your group, but I have heard from other self-help groups they tried this and that when they were in a similar situation.' Perhaps the ideal reaction is: 'Well, I'm not sure if I have any good advice for you. Anyway, I put my professional knowledge at your disposal. But the best thing I could do for you might be to help you establish contact with one or more other self-help groups, so that you can exchange your experiences and consult between yourselves on a mutual basis. If you ask me to do so I am quite prepared to facilitate the discussion.'

One last thing we can do is to make the idea of groups widely known; to become a spokesperson and an advocate for them.

Sympathetic experts have always been important promoters of self-help groups. They act as a sort of linchpin between the self-help system and the professional care system. They establish co-operation, they settle misunderstandings, and they reduce prejudices. We can inform our colleagues about the value of self-help groupwork and try to persuade those who have doubts. Hence this paper.

Notes

1. The Self-Help Team, 20 Pelham Road, Sherwood Rise, Nottingham NG5 1AP. Tel: 0602-691212.
2. The Self-Help Centre, Regent's Wharf, 8 All Saints' Street, London N1 9RW. Tel: 071-713-6161.

References

Avort, A.v.d. and Harberden, P. (1983) 'On identification resonance' in Hatch and Kickbusch (eds.) *Self-Help and Health in Europe*. Copenhagen: WHO.

Daum, K.-W. (1984) *Selbsthilfegruppen. Eine empirische Untersuchung von Gesprächs-Selbsthilfegruppen*. Rehburg-Loccum: Psychiatrie-Verlag.

Humble, S. and Unell, J. (eds.) (1989) *Self-Help in Health and Social Welfare: England and West Germany*. London: Routledge.

Hurvitz, N. (1974) 'Peer self-help psychotherapy groups: psychotherapy without psychotherapists' in Roman and Trice (eds.) *The Sociology of Psychotherapy*. New York: Jason Aronson.

Matzat, J. (1987) 'Self-help groups in West Germany: developments of the last decade', *Acta Psychiatr. Scand.*, Suppl. 337, 76, pp.42-51.

Matzat, J. (1989-90) 'Self-help groups as basic care in psychotherapy and social work', *Groupwork*, 2(3), pp.248-256.

Richardson, A. and Goodman, M. (1983) *Self-Help and Social Care: Mutual Aid Organisations in Practice.* London: Policy Studies Institute

Riessman, F. (1965) 'The helper therapy principle', *Social Work*, 10(2), pp.27-32.

Trojan, A. (ed.) (1986) *Wissen ist Macht. Eigenständig durch Selbstihilfe in Gruppen.* Frankfurt: Fischer.

Groupwork with Siblings of Children with Special Needs: A Pilot Study

Georgina Ferraro and Julie Tucker

This is an account of groupwork undertaken with 5-7 year old siblings of children with special needs. The group was run by two social workers in a voluntary agency setting. This was a pilot study to try and evaluate the effectiveness of a groupwork approach as a preventative tool in work with siblings. Research has indicated that siblings may be vulnerable to teasing, bullying and be at risk of developing psychological difficulties. Adult siblings have advocated the use of groupwork at an early age as a preventive measure. We expected the group to focus on issues related to being a sibling of a child with special needs. However, in this particular group, it was found that the primary function was to give group members time and attention which made them feel special.

Background

In 1988, Badger et al. provided an overview of the literature relating to siblings of children with special needs. They identified a number of interrelated areas of potential vulnerability, e.g. that siblings are more likely to experience restricted social activities, to be the victims of teasing and bullying, and to be at risk of developing psychological difficulties and problem behaviour. These children are also likely to be ill-informed about their sibling's disability, and to experience feelings of guilt and resentment. They are unlikely to disclose their feelings to others, particularly to parents, for fear of burdening them further, thus rarely giving their feelings a chance of expression. Siblings are also unlikely to have the opportunity to talk to other children in their situation.

Hart and Walters' (1979) research into the needs of siblings identified their need for opportunities to share their experiences with others in a similar position through groupwork projects.

The KIDS Family Centre, Camden, is a voluntary agency offering a range of services to families of children with disabilities, including a specialist social work service run by two Family Project workers who set up and ran this particular piece of groupwork. Historically, the KIDS Centres have always recognised the particular needs of siblings, and included them in their services.

The Camden Centre had, for some time, provided informal provision specifically for siblings, e.g. daytrips and outings. Through this contact, the extent of the needs of siblings became apparent, as did the fact that such informal contact fell short of their needs. Therefore, the Family Project workers decided it was time to evaluate the worth of a more formal and structured groupwork programme. At around the same time, the need for siblings work was further highlighted by a group of adult siblings attached to KIDS, who met to share feelings and experiences with each other - their overwhelming conclusion was that many of the needs that they still had as adults could have been met by a siblings group when they were children. They reiterated the difficulty they had experienced as children in expressing their feelings and needs within the family context. The final impetus for the project came from a number of KIDS parent users who were all experiencing similar concerns about their 'other' children, and wanting some help. The cost and time effectiveness of a groupwork programme, as opposed to an individual one, was obvious. Both of the Family Project workers are qualified Social Workers who have previous experience of running activity based groups for children. One worker is also a sibling with the personal experience which that inevitably brings.

Referrals and membership

Referrals in the pilot study were taken from families using the KIDS services. Whilst there was clearly a need right across the age range, we decided to target the 5 - 7 age group because we were keen to use the group as a preventative measure, and this was the youngest age-group we felt able to work with.

The criteria for referral did not require a child to have presenting problems, but merely to be a sibling in that age range, and for both parent and child to agree to the referral.

We received twelve referrals in total, out of which we composed a group of eight members, mixed in ethnic background but all female. We very much would have preferred to run a mixed gender group, but due to a very small number of male referrals, this was not possible.

Aims of the group

The aims and objectives of the group, for the benefit of parents, were described as follows:

1. To give the children some time and space for themselves.

2. To provide fun activities including physical games, artwork, drama, outings, and a general positive experience.
3. To provide a safe environment where feelings about their brother/sister can be expressed as and when they arise. Also, any questions about disability can be asked, or worries they may have can be shared.

Essentially, the aim was to run an activity-based, closed group for a specified number of weekly sessions. This was not a therapy-based group, but we hoped that by fulfilling Aims 1 and 2, we would create the potential for a safe enough environment to enable the 'same-boat' principle to operate for group members in terms of identifying with each other's feelings. We hoped that having painful/angry feelings heard and acknowledged by the group would, in itself, be therapeutic.

We were able to find a consultant experienced in groupwork, special needs and issues of race. The consultant played an important part in planning the group and looking at the group's process and dynamics. She played a central role in the group's 'review', which was after the tenth session, and assessed how far the group had achieved its original aims. The consultant also helped us look at issues of race, disability and individual needs, as well as helping us evaluate the impact of the group on the agency, us as workers and our workload. In conjunction with our consultant, we decided to run the group for 13 weekly sessions. This frequency and duration was selected for various reasons. Firstly, for a group of children of this age, a less frequent group might have seemed to have had little continuity, and previous experiences of less structured siblings work had highlighted the difficulty of forming a highly bonded group.

We chose 13 sessions on the basis of our previous experience of short-term groupwork with young children. Our experience has indicated 13 sessions to be the optimum number for getting the most out of a group's dynamics without running the risk of fostering dependency. However, we had made an allowance to extend the sessions if necessary. In fact, 13 proved to be exactly the right number of sessions for this piece of work. The group was run on our own premises, once a week after school and included tea. Transport was provided, as we saw this as a vital component of good attendance.

Before the start of the group, we devised a method of recording for both individual progress and group process. The group was recorded immediately after each session. Before the group began, we visited each child and family, during which the rule of group confidentiality was explained and a questionnaire was used to identify any concerns or areas parents would like us to focus on. Each weekly session was planned beforehand on the basis of what had occurred in the previous week; the group's wishes; and areas on which we had previously agreed to focus.

Method

We started the work with an open mind about where it would lead, and very much wanted to use the children as a yardstick to gauge what to address, when and how. However, we did think it was important to provide a basic structure each week, particularly for children of this age group. We wanted the sessions, overall, to be fun and enjoyable.

At the onset of the group, we quickly established ground rules in conjunction with group members, and introduced the basic structure as follows: some warm-up games (soon chosen by the group); tea with the sharing of good news/bad news; a main activity followed by a final game, and ending with using the 'face dice'.

The making and sharing of tea served as an important group cohesion exercise, as the children planned and prepared the food, and provided a nurturing element in the group.

We used various games and activities that were designed to facilitate group member contact and trust building and sharing. Many of the activities we chose helped to boost individual confidence and self-esteem, e.g. 'Spin the bottle' (whomever it lands next to you must pay a compliment to). At the conclusion of the group, the workers made leavers certificates for each child which described their individual strengths and contributions to the group. During all activities, however, the workers tried to remain aware of the need to build self-esteem.

The central activity for each session was usually planned around a particular theme, e.g. one session's activity was a family drawing. We chose this to see how they saw themselves in relation to the rest of the family, and how they chose to represent their disabled sibling.

This session was quite early on and gave us a basis from which to work. The activity demonstrated quite significantly the group members' very different levels of understanding and/or acceptance of their siblings' disability. Another activity we chose was body drawings, to look at self body image and to look at the issue of difference.

Group members were always encouraged to discuss whatever they wanted to bring to the group. This was facilitated by the use of a weekly ritual at teatime of turn-taking the sharing of 'good news' and 'bad news'. In fact, this was the main forum used by group members to talk about their families, siblings, and disclosing other intimate information. The role for the workers was to hear and acknowledge children's individual feelings, but we also used it to encourage other group members to share similar feelings, if they had them. The workers would also try to enable the group members to think about the effect of family events on themselves, e.g. if a sibling was ill, we tried to encourage the child to express how they were feeling about this - e.g. were they feeling worried, angry, sad? Initially, we found that group members found it difficult to identify their own range of feelings - as research has indicated, siblings often have to subjugate their own feelings. This led us to choose some central activities that would encourage some identification of feelings, e.g. games which involved miming/acting out feelings and then moving on to talking about things that made them happy or sad.

We also closed each session with another ritual, using facial dice, i.e. dice which have a range of six facial expressions on them - happy, sad, surprised, angry, etc. Group members take turns to throw the dice and use the facial expressions to talk about their feelings about what has happened in the group. Initially, all group members found it difficult to express any negative feelings, but as time went on members learnt to use this very appropriately and were able to express angry and sad feelings about group events.

The workers adopted a co-leadership model of working, and took turns in leading or facilitating all the group activities. As always, some members identified much more strongly with one worker or the other, but we tried very hard to counteract this by strict rules of turn-taking.

Issues raised

The group very quickly became cohesive and developed its own identity. Commitment to the group was amply demonstrated by the high level of attendance: out of 13 sessions, one child missed one session. Members soon established ownership of the group and introduced their own rituals, for example games and fantasies which would be repeated each week. They often overrode our sessional plans and devised their own. However, the good news/bad news and the facial dice remained included, as these appeared to be important rituals to members.

Whilst the group members used the good news/bad news ritual to share information about siblings, home life and worries, the group overall shared a general reluctance to pursue issues of disability in relation to being a sibling. Groupworkers' attempts to bring disability into the forum by any other method, e.g. even warm-up mime games designed to facilitate discussion about feelings - leading up to a role play about disability, were thwarted very early on by the group. The group achieved this by refusing point blank to participate in our planned activity and suggesting their own alternative which was much more about having fun. As the workers, we felt compelled to respect the group's wishes, and made a decision to avoid direct reference to 'disability' and being a sibling. Instead, we tried to look at some of the 'disability issues' in another form, for example via the concept of difference. This was an obvious choice, as the group interestingly proved to be very preoccupied with difference, particularly physical difference.

There was a lot of comparison of appearances amongst group members which, in turn, raised a number of race issues, as the group was ethnically mixed. However, the main focus was upon the minibus driver - a black woman with dyslexia whose appearance was masculine and, therefore, confusing to group members. The group victimised her quite vindictively on the basis of her sexuality, her colour, and her difficulty in remembering the route. We spent a considerable amount of time trying to deal with this in the group - however, we found the most effective means was encouraging and supporting the driver to deal with remarks made directly. We also planned some activities to look at difference, such as body images, and found that a number of group members were disappointed with their appearance. We wondered how connected this preoccupation was to the issue of disability - did it provide a safer, that is, more removed means of addressing the same issues?

As workers, we actually found it very difficult to gauge the appropriate level regarding disability, because group members demonstrated very different levels of understanding about their siblings' disability. We found this to be dependent on how their parents dealt with the issue of their child's disability, for example Katie believed that her sibling did not walk because he was a baby - in fact, he was a three year old with spina bifida. At the other extreme, Susan was able to describe what her autistic brother's world is like in a very informed and insightful way.

Evaluation

In a parental evaluation questionnaire administered shortly after the group had ended, all the parents said that the group was helpful, not just for the children but that there were spinoffs for other family members. About 60 per cent of parents reported some changes in their child's behaviour. Half way through the group, a number of parents had become particularly concerned about 'acting out' regressive and angry behaviour. Our interpretation was that group members were beginning to recognise their own needs and letting them be known. Parents clearly found this disconcerting despite wanting the group to be addressing their child's needs. However, towards the end of the group, the most ongoing change parents noted was the increase in their child's confidence and assertiveness. Most parents reported that their child had a better awareness of disability outside the family as opposed to an increased understanding of their own sibling's particular disability. This was no surprise to us, as the group members had rarely focused on their own sibling's disability in the sessions. Three out of seven parents felt that there had been an improvement in the sibling relationship. Any feedback given to the parents by the child about the group had been positive.

As workers, we felt the group had fulfilled all of its original aims although it was clear that group members were reluctant to use the group to address disability and the experience of being a sibling specifically. It is difficult to establish why this is the case. It is possible that this age group was merely too young. However, another group of the same age may have used the time very differently. It may be that when we were trying to raise these issues, group members thought that we were going to talk, yet again, about their sibling as opposed to them, i.e. they were unable or too young to separate their siblings' disability and the impact of this upon themselves. Perhaps if the group had continued, eventually these children may have become more receptive to work specifically around disability and issues of being a sibling. However, it may be that what we have to learn from this group is that siblings of this age want fun and time for themselves, and that addressing disability is the agenda of the workers and the children's parents. This obviously needs testing out by further groupwork with this age group. We are often reminded in disability literature that children are individuals first and siblings second - this could have been a very important element in the group. The children wanted to be themselves with a separate identity, and did not want the focus to be on the sibling in group time. Perhaps an older age group would be more able to use a group to examine the impact of a sibling's disability on themselves, and be less fearful of 'yet again' the sibling getting the limelight.

What was very evident, however, was that the group was extremely important and special to the group members. Having the time and attention especially devoted to them not only made them feel special but this, in turn, appeared to enable these children to be more assertive about their own needs at home. Parents confirmed that having a group for siblings only, had been very important in itself because the focus of attention is so often on the disabled sibling.

Both workers and parents observed that the existence of the group forced parents to focus their attention on the needs of their 'other' children - it may well be that this was the most vital function of the group. The existence of the group also led parents to assess their own needs, and a number concluded that what they needed was a parents' group with similar aims and activities. The KIDS Centre currently has three successful parent groups running. This pilot study has clearly identified the need for work with siblings and a format was developed that proved to be successful. Our ultimate aim is to develop an ongoing groupwork programme for siblings of all ages. In order to do this, we need to be properly resourced and funded and the KIDS Central Office is currently working hard on future funding for a part-time groupworker. We think this is an essential move forward because of the time-consuming nature of running groups properly. Certainly, in our case, the group took up much of our working time - placing a great strain on the rest of our workload. However, the rewards outweighed the extra stress - we both found the group a very exciting and challenging experience - an important element in long-term support with families of children with special needs where change can be very slow.

Reference

Adams-Greenly, M., Shiminski-Maher T., McGowan, N. and Meyers, P.A. (1986) 'A Group Program For Helping Siblings of Children With Cancer', *Journal of Psycho-Social Oncology,* 4 (4), Winter.

Badger, A. (1988) 'The brothers and sisters group: a group for siblings of children with physical disabilities', *Groupwork*, 1(3), pp.262-268.

Breslaun, N. and Prabucki, K. (1987) 'Siblings of Disabled Children', *Arch. General Psychiatry,* 44, December.

Flynn, A. and Meakin, M. (1989) ' Support for Siblings', *British Journal of Education,* 16(1), March, pp.15-17.

Hart, D. and Wallers, J. (1979) *Brothers & Sisters of Mentally Handicapped Children.* Thomas Coram Research Unit, University of London, Institute of Education, 41 Brunswick Square, London WC1N 1AZ

Oaklander, V. (1969) *Windows To Our Children* . The Centre for Gestalt Development Inc., PO Box 990, Highland, NY 12528.

Skrtic, T.M., Summers, J.A., Brotherson, M J. and Turnbull, A.P. (1984) 'Severely handicapped children and their brothers and sisters' in Blacher, J., (ed.) *Severely Handicapped Children and Their Families*. London: Academic Press.

Neutralisation of Group Control in Youth Gangs

T. Wing Lo

Effective group control in a delinquent gang compels its members to conform to its socially unacceptable group norms. It also helps maintain group equilibrium, reduce group conflict, and lead to a high cohesiveness among the gang members. The solidarity eventually incites more delinquent behaviour. This article examines deviant group norms and group control mechanisms in delinquent gangs in Hong Kong. It argues that outreach social workers have to neutralise group control in order to release non-conformists from the pressures exerted upon them by other delinquent members.

Group norms and group control

Group norms are shared ideas of correct behaviour which give direction to the group members about what should and should not be done under specified circumstances. As a kind of rule or standard, they define the range of behaviour that is tolerated and accepted within the group. They also introduce a certain degree of regularity and predictability into the group's functioning and suggest that certain rewards will be invoked for conformity and punishments for deviation. As Mills (1984) summarises precisely, group norms are the organised ideas of what members should do and feel, about how these should be regulated, and about what sanctions should be applied when behaviour deviates from the norms.

On the other hand, group control is 'the social interactional patterns by which the behaviour of group members is influenced, restrained, or directed.... They provide pressures toward conformity' (Northen, 1988, p.34). When a member deviates markedly from a group norm, other members put pressure on him or her to conform. S/he is sanctioned first by group pressure to change and, if this fails, by being ignored (Homans, 1961; Mills, 1984). Sampson and Brandon (1964) differentiate two kinds of non-conformist: the opinion and role deviants. The former receives more communication, especially hostility and questions. Other members try to understand his/her position and exert pressure to change his/her opinion. In contrast, as the role deviant's differences are seen as more pervasive, s/he is not the target of communication or hostility, but rather is simply ignored.

In both cases, however, the group exercises some degree of social control to force the deviant to comply with the group's expectations.

If a member can live up to a group's standards, s/he wins the approval of others and experiences a sense of satisfaction. If s/he cannot, feelings of failure develop. At this point, the member has four options: to conform, to change the norm, to remain a deviant, and to leave the group (Hartford, 1971). The final choice is based on two vital factors. Firstly, if the group is of great significance to him or her, then norms are likely to be accepted and conformity is assured; were this not so, that member would leave the group. Secondly, and most importantly, the existence of effective group control can also influence the decision. If group control is weak, s/he is likely to remain a deviant. Only strong group control would induce conformity.

Moreover, group control goes with group cohesiveness in the following cycle:

1. the more cohesive the group, the more effective the control;
2. the more effective the control, the more members' compliance to group norms;
3. the more members' compliance to group norms, the more cohesive the group.

Because of this, group control is a variable that social workers can manoeuvre to achieve group conformity. Sanctions imposed by a group may mean the withdrawal of approval, refusal to satisfy desire for status, changes in the kind of rewards for services, changes of group ranking, or even isolation (Clark, 1972). Usually, group control can create a force towards conformity with two purposes: to maintain and promote acceptable behaviour, opinions, and attitudes in the group, and to modify or change those regarded as unacceptable (Douglas, 1979).

In social groupwork, social workers understand that without some degree of conformity, group cohesiveness would not develop, and thus the group could not function to its optimum level. In order to reduce group conflict and to maintain a group equilibrium, we use group control to gain compliance from a deviant member. The most common strategy is to use group pressure to force him or her to conform if their thinking and behaviour violates the established group norms. Sometimes, we induce new and socially acceptable norms to a group by mobilising all the members in the controlling process (for example, see Case 1). Nevertheless, a universal application of this method is limited by the uniqueness of groups.

Thus, social workers have to take account of differences in group structure and subculture before using group control. In some circumstances, such as in the case of delinquent gangs, this method must be used carefully; or else the intended effect is not achieved. Case 1 illustrates many of the points made.

Case 1

Jenny, a 14-year-old girl, often hung around with her delinquent peers living in the same housing block. Once, she ran away from home and stayed with her peers for a few days. Her parents looked around for her, scolded her friends and pestered them. When the outreach social worker (street gang worker) found out about this, he tried to involve all the gang members to exercise control over her misconduct. By doing this, he hoped to establish a positive group norm: 'running away from home is wrong'. He met them on the housing block and succeeded in mobilising them to persuade her to return home. Everything went all right until trouble occurred after ten minutes. As Jenny refused, the gang leader tried to force her with a stick but mistakenly hit the head of a follower, Peter. The leader wanted revenge, but Jenny immediately ran away with some girls. He asked the boys to fetch her back for punishment. Later, a 'Big Sister' (Jenny's protector) passed by and heard about the incident. She asked the leader to give way, but failed. However, they compromised and she asked Jenny to come and let Peter hit her with the stick. In the end, she complied with the order. Throughout the process, the outreach social worker did not intervene. But in the later stage he stopped the boys punishing her further and counselled Jenny on her vulnerable situation.

This case highlights many interesting points that are worth discussion. Obviously, a scapegoating process was going on at the crisis moment. The gang leader tried to cover up his fault by displacing his anger onto Jenny, thus freeing himself from the guilty feeling caused by hitting the wrong person. Peter also transferred his hostility from the leader to her. And there was a 'healer', the Big Sister, who rescued the scapegoat from the 'persecutor' (Balgopal and Vassil, 1983; Garvin, 1987; MacLennan and Felsenfeld, 1968; Northen, 1988). With regard to group control, two points can be highlighted here. Firstly, the intention and technique of the social worker in creating a positive group norm - running away is wrong- by involving the gang members in the problem-solving process is constructive, as they are more inclined to observe the norms if they have participated in the decision making (Konopka, 1983). Secondly, and most importantly, the social worker's misunderstanding of group control after the hitting incident turned a treatment condition into a disaster. His original purpose of using group control (urging) to establish a positive norm (running away is wrong) ended up in allowing group control (violence) to reinforce deviant group norms (truce talk, an eye for an eye, and obeying gang leaders). Thus, the case shows that the role of outreach social workers is crucial. If we misinterpret the gang dynamics, in particular the relations between group norms and group control, we create more problems than solutions.

Group norms of delinquent gangs in Hong Kong

In their daily interaction, gang members develop common practices, common evaluations, and shared tastes in addition to those which brought them together. According to Napier and Gershenfeld (1981), there are four kinds of norms, namely: formal norms, explicitly stated norms, non-explicit informal norms, and unconscious norms. Douglas (1979) also contends that norms can either be formalised as codes or be transmitted by precept, approval, disapproval, and imitation. In Hong Kong, delinquent gangs are associated with Chinese triad societies, and thus their norms are mainly transmitted from triad rules and codes. Although the norms are not formally prescribed on paper, they are often talked about by the gang members. I observed the following codes during my working with street gangs:

1. don't 'cal dai' (don't join other gangs);
2. don't be 'yee ng tsai' (no squealing);
3. don't 'po wong' (do not report anything to the police);
4. obey triad leaders;
5. 'bong tall' (help gang members in fighting);
6. 'chow kei' (give financial help to gang members in times of trouble;
7. don't 'ngau dai' (don't be scared in committing crimes);
8. no cheating on gang members;
9. don't 'tuk pui chek' (do not speak ill of gang members behind their backs or spread disadvantageous information about them).

The above norms of delinquent gangs reflect the essence of sworn brotherhood of Chinese triad society. Some of the norms, e.g. no cheating and remaining loyal, can be regarded as normal if they belong to legitimate social groups. However, as triad societies are criminal rackets which use youth gangsters to work for them in illegal operations, the norms serve as means to control their behaviour in the course of committing crimes. In this respect, these norms should be regarded as socially undesirable.

Very often, a gang member understands that there are norms with which to conform for acceptance in the group. But this by no means implies that norms are identical with typical behaviour among the gang members. Rather, they only embody conceptions of ideal behaviour for a good member. Usually, the more cohesive a group, the higher the normative integration (Heap, 1977), and the more likely the members are to conform to its codes. However, many delinquent gangs in Hong Kong are not highly cohesive (Lo, 1984), and thus the members' non-conformity to these socially unacceptable norms is not an uncommon phenomenon. This gives room for the outreach social workers to manoeuvre the situation in daily encounters with street gangs. We have to continue to undermine their solidarity so that they are not cohesive enough to commit crimes. One way of achieving this end is to neutralise the effect of group control, thereby freeing non-conformists from any immediate pressure to follow the group norms.

Group control in delinquent gangs in Hong Kong

Every group has its own control mechanisms, and delinquent gangs are no exception. In fact, many of their control mechanisms are unique to their own structures and subculture. Thrasher (1963) has identified these as rapport, applause, ostracism, humiliation, and violence. Sherif and Sherif (1964) also found group control in the form of urging, hazing, insulting, cold-shouldering, chastisement and exclusion. During my frontline practice, I observed the following group control mechanisms. I have reconstructed them into a continuum, as shown in Figure 1.

In Figure 1, several kinds of control mechanisms are identified. The first one at the positive end is rapport. As the gang members are usually brought up in the same neighbourhood, some of them have developed strong emotional ties to other members. These emotional ties often suffice to motivate an individual to follow the deviant behaviour of peers. Applause and hero-worship function as control mechanisms because human beings have the desire for status and recognition. For example, a boy who goes first into a fight will be praised by his friends, and this 'honour' will reinforce similar behaviour in the future. Moreover, some gang members admire him as a hero, and he is an example to those who want the same status. Another mechanism, togetherness or group spirit, is a feeling of power conferred by the mere force of numbers. This feeling often

Figure 1
Continuum of group control mechanisms

Negative control

Individual pressure	Violence Humiliation Ridicule
Group pressure	Expulsion Ostracism Urging Togetherness
Individual pressure	Hero-worship Applause Rapport

Positive control

distorts an individual's moral perspective so that a gang member, who is normally hesitant of fighting on his own, immediately joins his mates when trouble occurs[1].

Urging is a concentration of communication towards the non-conformist by other gang members. The frequency of such interaction would be high for some time. Should the interaction fail to bring him into conformity, the amount of communication directed towards him markedly declines. At this point, a form of ostracism or cold-shouldering is used. He may be set apart so that no one talks or listens to him, or be dropped from activities of the group. This confers upon him a sense of isolation in which he feels outgrouped. Furthermore, a member can be punished by being expelled from the group. Although expulsion is an unusual phenomenon in delinquent gangs associated with triad societies, it does happen in those gangs that are not so cohesive. Fringe members and newcomers are more likely to be expelled than the core members, if they do not conform to group norms.

To some gang members, being scorned is a more painful experience than being expelled. Ridicule, a means of making fun of a non-conformist, varies from simply laughing at him, teasing him, and mocking him, to hazing him with sarcastic demands. When the degree of ridicule is high, it becomes a kind of humiliation. Gang members label those who fail to live up to the group's expectations. For instance, as insults, they use the label 'Yee Ng Tsai' for squealers, and 'Ngau Dai' for those who 'chicken out' in gang fights. Their purpose is to embarrass them and let them lose face in public. Lastly, the threat of physical punishment is also common in delinquent gangs, especially when the incident in question is related to the violation of some important norms, such as squealing and spreading rumours or disadvantageous information about another gang member.

The ten mechanisms mentioned above can be regarded as the contingent reactions of the gang to a member's non-conformity. The reactions range from different forms of positive control to negative control, or a combination of both types. Positive control, such as rapport, applause, hero-worship, urging, and togetherness, are equivalent to rewards. These enable a gang member to secure a more satisfactory self-image, self-esteem, and social approval. Negative control mechanisms, such as ridicule, violence, ostracism, humiliation, and expulsion, are forms of punishment. Punishment may entail rejection, disapproval, and the denial of gratification, all of which have the tendency to lower the non-conformist's sense of well being. As shown in Figure 1, the closer a mechanism to either end, the greater the positive or negative element.

Moreover, group control is hardly effective without sufficient pressure, which can be exerted on two levels: individual and group. The mechanisms placed in the middle range of the continuum are those which must be exercised by most of the gang members in order to have a significant effect. A boy will not feel isolated or pestered if he is avoided or urged by only one of his peers. He will feel loss, however, if the whole group is against him. Nevertheless, the control mechanisms towards the two ends of the continuum may be effectively utilised by individual members to make another member conform. For example, threats of physical violence by the gang leader, humiliation by a peer, and emotional ties or positive identification with another member can greatly influence an individual's behaviour. In these circumstances, no group pressure, but individual pressure, is used to force him to conform. In understanding group control, therefore, we should pay attention to various types of control mechanism and simultaneously consider both individual and group pressures as well as positive and negative elements during the process of group control.

Negative effects of group control in delinquent gangs

Effective group control exerts pressure on gang members to act according to group norms. The crux of the argument is that the norms of delinquent gangs are socially unacceptable. When group control is effective, gang members are compelled to observe norms which eventually lead to more delinquent behaviour. Some negative consequences of group control, such as isolation and rejection, are unbearable for the non-conformist. As a result, not only is he compelled to follow a group norm on the occasion in question, but he will not dare to violate it again in the future. Thus, the anticipation of sanctions as well as sanctions actually carried out can influence gang members. As Cartwright and Zander contend:

> ...the greater is a member's subjective probability that punishments will result from nonconformity, the more likely is he to try to avoid the appearance of deviating (1968, p.145).

Moreover, although group norms are the product of social interaction in a gang, once established they become the norms of individual members and influence their attitudes and behaviour even when they are outside the group. When they face the same situation alone, they perceive the situation in terms of the norms of the gang (Northen, 1988). For example, a boy who identifies with the norm of using violence to solve a problem will apply it within his work setting. One of the necessary conditions for internalisation of group norms is effective group control, which reinforces behaviour through rewards and punishments.

Furthermore, effective group control helps maintain the equilibrium in a gang by defining the normative standard and the scope of tolerable behaviour. Dentler and Erikson assert that deviance in a group provides 'an important boundary-maintaining function' and gives the group structure 'a visible shape' (1970, p.173). To deal with the non-conformist by means of group control, the gang is able to reaffirm its essential cohesion and indicate what it is and what it can do. Homans also contends that punishment used in group control has some of the 'effects of ritual' so that 'the offender is chastised and the norm vindicated' (1962, pp.308-9). On the one hand, it punishes and brings the deviant back towards conformity, and on the other, it reawakens all gang members to the importance of conformity to the norms, thus keeping the norms alive in their minds. Mills (1984) even argues that the exercise of group control is more than equilibrating. Rather than simply restoring a previous state, it increases group solidarity.

Techniques of neutralisation

Successful group control in a delinquent gang reinforces conformity with socially unacceptable group norms. This not only enhances its cohesiveness but also leads to more delinquency. Outreach social workers can prevent this kind of reinforcement by neutralising the group control mechanisms. When we notice that the mechanisms exist in daily interaction, we intervene in the 'here and now' to ease the pressures that the gang exerts onto non-conformists. This allows them to have more freedom for resistance and self-determination, and eventually discourages them from observing group norms. There are three ways in which our influence can be utilised successfully. We can exert a new pressure on the group by direct squashing and confrontation; or change the direction of existing pressure by means of creation and diversion; or reduce its magnitude by the methods of protection, reducing interaction, clarification, and universalisation. These techniques will be discussed in the following paragraphs (with illustrations from Case 1 in parentheses).

Direct squashing

When the crisis situation generated by a group control mechanism becomes confused and out of control, we use our authority to stop its continuance. (For example, the worker might tell the whole group: 'Stop beating Jenny, or else I'll go away and forget you all.') This approach is not recommended in daily practice unless a very good rapport with the gang members has been developed, or the outreach social worker has taken over the gang leadership. If there is good rapport, the 'request' produces a counter-pressure, 'obeying or losing the worker', upon the members, and forces them to reconsider their deviant act.

Confrontation

We challenge the gang members to recognise their destructive behaviour, to deal with differences between the accusations and the facts, and to face the consequences of their actions which they deny (Balgopal and Vassil, 1983). (Thus the worker might say to the leader: 'It's you, not Jenny, who hit Peter. Why did you scapegoat her? Why don't you have the courage to recognise your fault?') This forces a member to consider his/her actions and helps that person to face their own self-created realities. In order to prevent the solidification of defensive tactics, confrontation should be carried out as soon as possible after the crisis situation. For the best effect, we should bring together all the major participants (i.e. the leader, Jenny, and Peter) so that different viewpoints can be elicited (Douglas, 1976). If we can control the crisis incident, other members can be allowed to watch the confrontation so as to break down their identification with the delinquent gang leader. As with direct squashing, we should only employ this technique when we have a good rapport with the gang, so as not to jeopardise our working relationship.

Creation

We deliberately create some new issues which might not actually exist but, because they are of greater concern to the gang members, can elicit immediate responses from them. (For instance, the worker might say: 'When I came here, I saw a team of policemen approaching from the other side of the estate. If we don't disperse now, we'll be in big trouble.') This would draw their attention away from the non-conformist, stop such control mechanisms as togetherness, ridicule, and urging, and help relieve the non-conformist of immediate group pressures.

Diversion

We change the group activities to ones that are welcomed by the gang, or that the non-conformist is better at than other members. (Immediately after the hitting incident, the worker might say: 'Let's go and play a game of football.') Moreover, we can pick another target to be a scapegoat, perhaps the leader himself, to divert the tensions and negative attention that other members have focused on the non-conformist (Brown, 1986). (e.g. The worker might scorn the leader in front of other members for hitting Peter by mistake.) However, if we are to diffuse the leader's anger, we have to encourage him to express it elsewhere (MacLennan and Felsenfeld, 1968). (Thus the worker might comfort the leader: 'I understand you're angry with Jenny. But don't be angry with this young woman. Let's go for a drink/a game of billiards.')

Reducing interaction

Group activities are re-organised in a more structured way, or carried out in subgroups, in order to minimise contagion and group pressure (Brown, 1986). (The worker might separate the group into two football teams to compete against each other for a prize.) This is extremely useful when a non-conformist has to defend himself against the pressures of other members. When the interaction between members is reduced, it inhibits the development of group pressure in the 'here and now', and frees the non-conformist from being urged, pestered or blamed by the group.

Clarification

Often gang members do not mean to humiliate or scorn another member. But due to behavioural contagion (Lippitt et al., 1968), they spontaneously imitate the behaviour of the one who initiates the action, especially when they feel a sense of 'togetherness' (e.g. when one started to fetch Jenny back for punishment, the others followed). Thus, we have to keep communication channels open and messages clear between the group and the non-conformist. We focus on the underlying key issues and help the group to sort out confusion and conflicting feelings that should not have existed (Balgopal and

Vassil, 1983). (The worker might clarify: 'We're here to help Jenny to go home, right. Why are you trying to beat her up? We know she didn't mean to hurt Peter. It was only an accident.') When the members understand what exactly happened, they reduce the pressures on the non-conformist.

Protection

We intervene verbally to restrain attackers from exerting pressures on the non-conformist (Brown, 1986), especially during urging, ridicule, and humiliation. Let us look at Case 2:

Case 2

After a delinquent gang lost a football match, the leader wanted revenge and urged John, the strongest boy in the gang, to go with him. He understood that if John took the lead, everyone would join them. However, John had never been very keen on gang fights. When he hesitated, the leader scorned him, 'are you scared to fight with a broken bottle?' John was motivated by the humiliation. He wanted to go and fight.

In case 2, John was forced by an effective group control mechanism, humiliation, to join the fight. His tension was so high that he wanted to release the tension by meeting the group's demand. This is a typical example of how group control reinforces delinquent group norms. If the worker had not neutralised the control mechanism, John would certainly have gone with them. The worker immediately intervened. He confronted the leader, 'breaking a bottle is no 'rep', but losing the match is 'Yu' (i.e. losing face); why don't you all go home to do some more practice instead of fooling around and causing trouble here?'

In this example, not only did the worker protect John from humiliation, he also re-directed the control mechanism, and thus the pressure, back to the trouble-maker. Moreover, we need to be sensitive to group rejection, especially during ostracism, and counteract it by showing our concern for the non-conformist (Konopka, 1983), perhaps by talking more to him or even taking him out for a meal or to a film.

Universalisation

We generalise the non-conformist's behaviour to the gang as a whole by stating that the problem is not unique to him but is common to the whole group (Balgopal and Vassil, 1983). This not only relieves his feelings of failure and isolation, but also urges other gang members to reconsider their own values and standards. In Case 2, for example, the worker can remark: 'Aren't you guys afraid of getting hurt in fighting? It's silly to act tough as everyone is scared of being hurt.' The worker can continue to give examples of whoever in the gang had failed to join in past fights. By making them feel guilty of their past behaviour, the pressures which they exert upon the non-conformist are minimised.

The above eight techniques are useful in counteracting the pressures that a gang or any of its members exerts on a non-conformist. If applied at appropriate times, they can be a welcome source of relief to him. They also mark the social worker's concern for him in times of trouble. Nevertheless, there are limitations in dealing with some positive control mechanisms, such as rapport and applause. This is to be expected as both identitive and utilitarian (i.e. reward) powers tend to generate more commitment on the part of gang members than coercive power (Etzioni, 1965). Thus, it is likely that their resistance to deviant group norms is low, and it is more difficult to neutralise positive mechanisms than negative mechanisms. In these circumstances, the worker can only employ direct squashing or confrontation to control or challenge those members who, though unwilling to join in delinquent acts, follow the others because of emotional ties or hero-worship. Moreover, intensive individual guidance should be provided to strengthen their ego and enhance their problem-solving capabilities.

Conclusion

Effective group control in delinquent youth gangs compels the members to follow the socially unacceptable group norms and helps maintain group equilibrium, thus creating more delinquency. One of the tasks of the outreach social worker is to neutralise group control which either positively or negatively forces the non-conformist to conform through individual or group pressure. Usually, the more negative the group control, the less difficult the worker's intervention. We can employ a variety of techniques to counteract the pressures at the group level so as to relieve the tensions and anxiety of the members concerned. In contrast, the more positive the group control, the more difficult our intervention. In this respect, direct squashing, confrontation and individual guidance can be employed to restore and strengthen the youngsters' problem-solving capacities. If group control can be neutralised, delinquent group norms will seldom be observed by the gang members. As a result, heterogeneity of values arises in the gang and, eventually, undermines group cohesiveness and prevents the repeated occurrence of mutually reinforced delinquent behaviour.

Note

1. As most gang members are male, the use of the male pronoun is used in the rest of the paper, except when explicit reference is being made to females).

References

Balgopal, P.R., and Vassil, T.V. (1983) *Groups in Social Work : An Ecological Perspective*. NY: Macmillan.
Brown, A. (1986) *Groupwork*. Hants: Gower.
Cartwright, D. and Zander, A. (eds.) (1968) *Group Dynamics*. London: Tavistock.
Clark, R.E. (1972) *Reference Group Theory and Delinquency*. NY: Behavioral Publications.
Dentler, R.A. and Erikson, K.T. (1970) 'The functions of deviance in groups' in Mills, T.M. (ed.) *Readings on the Sociology of Small Groups*. Englewood Cliffs, NJ: Prentice-Hall, pp.167-174.
Douglas, T. (1976) *Groupwork Practice*. London: Tavistock.
Douglas, T. (1979) *Group Processes in Social Work*. London: John Wiley & Sons.
Etzioni, A. (1965) 'Organisational control structure' in March J. G. (ed.) *Handbook of Organisations*. Chicago: Rand McNaily, pp.650-677.
Garvin, C.D. (1987) *Contemporary Group Work*. Englewood Cliffs, N.J.: Prentice-Hall.
Hartford, M.E. (1971) *Groups in Social Work*. N.Y.: Columbia University Press.
Heap, K. (1977) *Group Theory for Social Workers*. London: Pergamon Press.
Homans, G.C. (1961) *Social Behavior: Its Elementary Forms*. NY: Harcourt, Brace & World.
Homans, G.C. (1962) *The Human Group*. London: Routledge & Kegan Paul.
Konopka, G. (1983) *Social Group Work: A Helping Process*. Englewood Cliffs, NJ: Prentice-Hall.
Lippitt, R., Polansky, N., Redl, F. and Rosen, S. (1968) 'The dynamics of power', in Cartwright, D. and Zander, A. (eds.) *Group Dynamics*. London: Tavistock, pp.236-250.
Lo, T.W. (1984) *Gang Dynamics*. Hong Kong: Caritas.
MacLennan, B.W. and Felsenfeld, N. (1968) *Group Counselling and Psychotherapy with Adolescents*. NY: Columbia University Press.
Mills, T.M. (1984) *The Sociology of Small Groups*. Englewood Cliffs, NJ: Prentice-Hall.
Napier, R.N. and Gershenfeld, M.K. (1981) *Groups: Theory And Experience*. Boston: Houghton-Mifflin.
Northen, H. (1988) *Social Work with Groups*. NY: Columbia University Press.
Sampson, E. and Brandon, A. (1964) 'The Effects of Role and Opinion Deviation on Small Group Behaviour', *Sociometry*, 27, pp.261-281.
Sherif, M. and Sherif, C.W. (1964) *Reference Groups*. NY: Harper Row.
Thrasher, F.M. (1963) *The Gang*. Chicago: University of Chicago Press.

The large group:

THE HEART OF THE SYSTEM IN GROUP CARE

Adrian Ward

This paper explores anxieties amongst group care workers about the use of the large group as a forum for discussion and therapy. It is argued that these fears, although common, are self-perpetuating and anti-task, and that they may originate in an attempt to deny the reality of living together in groups. By contrast, working with the large group in the form of a daily community meeting of all staff and users, although difficult to establish and demanding to sustain, can become the central reference-point of daily living and indeed of all therapeutic work in group care settings - 'the heart of the system'. The aims of this paper are firstly to identify the nature of the difficulty, secondly to analyse the practical and therapeutic functions of the community meeting in group care settings, and thirdly to discuss the implications of these findings for the training of group care workers. The paper argues for establishing a more optimistic and positive self-fulfilling prophecy, so that workers can create opportunities for the creative and beneficial use of large groups - and in particular, so that the practice of the community meeting can become more widely-established in group care.

The central fact about group care is that it involves groups of people - staff and users - living and working together. They all belong to one large group, whether or not that group becomes formalised into an identified meeting, and whether or not they identify strongly with that group. They all therefore affect each other for better or worse, and while some of these effects are very obvious for all to see, others are much more difficult to detect, although potentially just as powerful. I should like to be able to say that this central fact about group care is 'undeniable', but experience suggests that in many places it *is* denied, in that group care workers do not engage - or are not encouraged to engage - sufficiently or appropriately in working with the large group. The consequence of this denial is that much of the potential benefit of the group care situation risks being lost or wasted. There may be many reasons for such denial and avoidance, but I would propose that one important reason is a widespread

Groupwork Vol. 6(1), 1993, pp.64-77

anxiety among staff (but often also projected onto users) about being in and working in large groups. This anxiety will not, of course, be the *sole* cause of the relative absence of large groupwork in most group care settings, and many workers will turn first to other more familiar frameworks simply because they have been more fully researched and developed, as in the case of the theory and practice of small groupwork and individual counselling. Nevertheless the anxiety about large groups is powerful and widespread, and worthy of exploration. My aim in this paper is to explore this anxiety, and to outline some of the practical and therapeutic functions of the large group in these settings.

The large group and its attendant anxieties

Why are people so anxious about working with large groups? In some ways this is an especially surprising phenomenon in group care, where one might expect the workers to be confident and positive about groupwork, but many group care workers do seem to lack the confidence to work with the whole group of staff and users. This anxiety is sometimes so great that it seems to lead into a self-fulfilling prophecy, whereby workers anticipate difficulty with large groups, and their anxiety then brings that very difficulty into the group.

In the literature on groupwork in group care, many authors reveal considerable unease with using the large group. For example, an otherwise-positive paper by Brown (1990) which provides a useful framework for analysing 'The group mosaic in residential and day centre settings', nevertheless offers a bleak view of working with large groups. Brown describes community meetings thus:

> They are sometimes fairly disastrous, and can be destructive, the reason for this being that large groups (say of more than 20 persons) can be very frightening places (Brown, 1990, p.277)

While such statements undoubtedly reflect many people's views, they may have the unfortunate effect of perpetuating the myth of the destructive large group - although in this case it should be said in their defence that Brown and Clough do offer elsewhere (1989) several useful ideas on how to make large groups more manageable. My argument in the present paper is that anxiety about working with the large group has several components, which may interact with and compound each other, but which need to be identified if they are to be overcome. I shall suggest two of these components at this stage, while others will emerge later in the discussion.

The first of these components derives from the fact that not all such anxieties relate solely to *large* groups: while it may be true that some people, both staff and users, do find the thought of being in a large group frightening, it is also true that many people find membership of *any* size of group threatening. Nitsun (1991) argues that there are strong 'anti-group' feelings in many people (both professionals and others), and suggests that people may feel uncomfortable with the very idea of joining a group for a variety of reasons:

> I believe that there is a widespread and fundamental resistance to groups, arising partly from the wish for the fantasied, idealised containment of the two-person relationship and the threat that the group poses to this fantasy (Nitsun, 1991)

Although Nitsun is writing about the small group, there are clear parallels with commonly-expressed feelings about the large group, and it may be that such 'anti-group' feelings simply become stronger, the larger the group in question.

Secondly, fear of the large group in particular may relate to an intuitive grasp of the power of the phenomenon. Being in a large group *can* be a powerful experience, although this power can be harnessed to beneficial ends, and a successful and well-run large group can actually be a liberating and empowering experience. It may be that many groupworkers and group care workers have not experienced being a member of a successful large group themselves - in fact they may have experienced quite the opposite - and thus they do not carry within them a belief that such a thing is possible. Here the importance of training is obvious, in that it is essential that training for groupwork and group care should do more than merely confirm people in their original prejudices and anxieties, but should actively encourage them to experience, think and learn about the many and various contexts of groupwork, and should give them access to positive models of many different types of group, rather than only the traditional 'small group'. It is not my intention, of course, to argue against people subsequently developing a preference for working with a certain size or type of group, just as they will opt for a certain style of group leadership, but to propose that such choices should be as explicit, well-informed and understood as possible.

I should acknowledge at this point that there is some debate about precisely when a 'small' group becomes 'large' - for example, Hopper and Weyman (1975) point out that for some people a small group consists of no more than 5 - 7 members, whereas for others a group does not become large until there are more than 16 members. For some people a large group seems to mean 'a group just larger than I can cope with', whereas for others a small group is probably 'a group which is so small that I feel claustrophobic'. Perhaps a more useful approach to this issue would be to think in terms of the *proportions and context* of the group rather than merely its size. Thus a group of 14 people which meets as part of a conference for 200 people will probably be experienced by many members as a small group, whereas a group of 14 people who comprise the total group of staff and users of a residential unit is probably experienced by most members as large. Somewhere in the middle comes the concept of the Median Group, a term used by group analysts for groups of 18 - 20 people (de Mare et al., 1990), although here again the boundaries between one size of group and another will to some extent blur according to the subjective experience of the participants. My argument is not that the size of a group is entirely in the eye of the beholder, but that it is more than a matter of mathematics - it is also experiential (see Hopper and Weyman, 1975, for further discussion on group size).

Threats to identity

Returning to the theme of the power of the large-group experience, a central anxiety relates to the feeling that one's very sense of identity is somehow threatened by the group. This anxiety may be experienced in a wide variety of ways, from those who fear complete annihilation to those whose defence is to hope to slip through the whole experience unnoticed. It may be helpful here to think in terms of the contrasting frameworks of association which we may draw upon for our anxieties about 'small groups' as against 'large groups'. Whereas we may tend to frame our small-group anxieties in terms of family-relationships, with parental transference-figures and rivalry with siblings to the fore, our large-group anxieties may relate more to the broader and in some senses deeper questions of our relationship with society (even 'humanity') as a whole. Thus membership of a large group may elicit fear of utter isolation into anonymity because 'nobody has even noticed my existence', or anxiety about the destructive power which cliques and factions may be able to assume in the absence of protective leadership and/or containing consensus; equally, we may fear being subsumed into a featureless and perhaps institutionalised *Lumpenproletariat* which will draw us along into its collective will, quite against our own individual choice.

Another way of thinking about such anxieties might be to attempt to visualise them: thus if we think of the large group as a slowly turning roundabout which we need to jump aboard before it gathers too much speed, the anxieties might be visualised in terms of the fear of being left behind altogether, or of stumbling as we try to climb aboard, or perhaps of not being able to climb down again once we are aboard. Once we do join the turning circle, the fear may relate to being spun off into oblivion by centrifugal forces, or to being drawn ever closer into the centre against our will. These images are offered not in order to construct any elaborate theory-base upon them, but as a way of encouraging practitioners to realise the nature and source of their own anxieties about large-group membership. The exploration in training exercises of visualisations such as these can certainly facilitate shared learning about the anxieties. For a more considered theoretical account of some of these processes, Pierre Turquet's (1975) paper on 'Threats to identity in the large group' is strongly recommended, while van der Linden offers an interesting application of Winnicott's concepts in addressing the question 'How does the large group change the individual?' (van der Linden, 1988); for more extensive discussions of large-group dynamics see Kreeger (1975), Whiteley and Gordon (1979), and de Mare et al. (1990).

Large-group phenomena in group care settings

If anxiety is so common and so strong, why should we even attempt to work with large groups in the group care setting? My argument is that in group care there will always be large-group phenomena operating, whether or not we are conscious of them, and whether or not we are actively trying to understand and exploit them. For example, both staff and users will have feelings about joining, belonging to and leaving the total group of the place, and some of these feelings will relate to the anxieties just described. If this much is true, then such feelings may be influencing the success or otherwise of the team in achieving the task of the unit. It is therefore the responsibility of team members, both individually and collectively, to identify the ways in which such factors may be operating, and to try to influence them so that by and large they will operate towards, rather than against, task-achievement. In particular, it can be argued that the task of the unit will be less likely to be undermined by large-group anxieties if these anxieties are understood and addressed.

I would suggest that there are at least three ways in which large-group phenomena are experienced in any group care setting (Figure 1). There is firstly the actual living-group which is enacted continuously in the daily life of the unit, comprising all the myriad combinations of people and their interactions, the network of multiple relationships between users, between staff, and between users and staff. In this sense, the large group represents the context within which all other modes of work in the group care setting are 'embedded' (Douglas, 1986). Secondly, there is the 'group' which each person carries around in their head - the sense in which the whole place including the people in it assumes a psychic reality to which each person relates. Feelings about this 'internal community' (Hinshelwood, 1987) will influence and be influenced by real events in the place as well as by the conscious and unconscious experience of the individual. Thirdly, perhaps the most direct and focused way in which the large group may be experienced is in the planned gathering of the membership of the unit into a large group meeting, usually known as the community meeting or house meeting.

Figure 1
Ways in which large-group phenomena are experienced in group care settings

1. The actual 'living-group' enacted in the daily life of the unit.
2. The 'internal community' - the image of the group and its members, and the feelings about these, which each person carries in his/her head.
3. The community meeting or 'house meeting'.

While the focus of this paper will be largely upon the third of these categories, the planned use of the community meeting, it is in effect the first two which provide the context and the rationale for community meetings. It is primarily *because* everyone living and working in group care belongs to an on-going large group that a forum is needed in which this aspect of their experience can be focused and clarified. Within the living-group, as well as within each person's 'internal community', are enacted and debated many of the main underlying themes of group care work, such as the dynamics of power (and especially of decision-making) between individuals and groups, the intangible qualities of 'morale' and 'atmosphere', and the sense of purposefulness or futility in daily existence. If powerful phenomena such as these are left to develop unacknowledged, or are only discussed in splinter-groups or dyads, the risks for the enterprise are considerable. Where this happens, the implicit ethos of collective and mutual responsibility which often underpins the work of group care settings risks being undermined and even subverted, as there is then no true forum for collectivity and mutuality. For those who wish to pursue this theme further, Hinshelwood (1987) applies the insights of Kleinian psychoanalysis to a detailed examination of the interplay in the therapeutic community setting between the individuals, their respective 'internal communities' and the actual living-group, especially as experienced in the community meeting.

The community meeting

Having suggested various sources and expressions of the anxiety about large groups, and having identified three ways in which large group phenomena are experienced in group care settings, we shall now explore the third of these ways in more detail, by considering the planned use of community meetings. By the term 'community meeting' I refer to the regular meeting, for a variety of functions, of the total group of staff and users in a group care setting. The literature on such meetings relates mostly to the therapeutic community, and especially the therapeutic community for adults with mental health problems (see Trauer, 1987, for a full literature review). However, the community meeting need not be restricted to such settings; indeed, a case can be mounted for the use of community meetings in many other group care settings - family centres, probation work (see Cook, 1988), and residential settings for various groups (e.g. with young adolescents, Worthington, 1990). I have described elsewhere (Ward, 1984), the introduction of community meetings in residential work with young children.

Since many community-based group care units are now very small units, even 'family-sized', it is important to be clear that working with the 'large group' applies even in these settings. For the purposes of this discussion, the 'large group' refers to the total living-group of a group care setting or of a unit within such a setting, whether that is a group of 8 or a group of 48. What is important is that the total living-group of users and staff should meet together on a planned and regular basis, in recognition of the fact that they live and work together.

Now, bearing in mind the discomforts, fears and resistances mentioned above in relation to large groups, it is evident at once that for such a meeting to be successful, certain conditions must be established. In particular, all of the participants will need to be clear and in broad agreement about the specific functions and possibilities of the meeting - otherwise, as with any other method of work, people will be left uncertain and may become anxious, filling in the absence of declared and agreed functions with assumed functions of their own invention, such as the persecution of the powerless. Here, then, is a third component in the anxiety about large groups: anxiety raised by confusion and uncertainty about the specific functions and possibilities of the group. If we are to address this anxiety it is therefore important to be clear about the range of possible functions of the community meeting.

The functions of the community meeting

Within this range of functions, I propose below (Figure 2) a number which seem important in creating an argument for the greater use of this method. This first list covers the practical and social-emotional functions of the community meeting, and it will be evident to the reader that, if the meeting does fulfil these functions, it is likely to become a central focus of all the work of the community - the place to which and from which all important business is taken.

Figure 2
Some practical functions of the 'community meeting'

1. Planning the events of the day/week together, so that everyone knows what is happening and why.
2. Reviewing what has happened during the past day/week and why: learning from experience.
3. Discussing the 'rules of the house': whose rules they are, how they are enforced and why.
4. Discussing the routines of the house: users and workers evaluate and change their daily living experience.
5. Problem-solving: for users to bring conflicts, unsolved losses, confusions, etc. for resolution within the security of the group.
6. Handling general feedback between users and staff, e.g. on behaviour and its effects.
7. Working at understanding, predicting and dealing with the feelings involved in living together in a group, e.g. the comings and goings of users and staff; inconsistencies thrown up by shift-work; plus feelings related to issues of power, prejudice and dependency.
8. Handling crises, e.g. emergency admissions, sudden departures, major disturbances.
9. 'Assembly': getting everyone together, acknowledging the fact of living together and having to get on with one another.
10. Working with the 'whole person', encouraging people to give as well as take, enable as well as disrupt, etc, and enabling all members to perceive each other as whole people as well as having roles such as staff-member and user.

In addition, however, there are other functions which the community meeting can play in the life of a group care unit, and especially in a unit which has therapeutic aims. Some of these other functions are suggested by Melvyn Rose thus:

> The subject matter of community meetings always was complex. Trying to make sense of relationships, trying to describe feelings, and trying to describe their origins required the youngsters to develop new ways of thinking as well as speaking (Rose, 1990, p.130)

The community meeting offers the users the opportunity for developing such new ways of thinking by performing a number of therapeutic functions, for example:

Figure 3
Some therapeutic functions of the 'community meeting'

1. Providing a central focus and reference point for 'The work of the day' (Kennedy, 1989), i.e. enabling maximum learning to be derived from the handling of significant issues arising in the everyday life of the group.
2. Offering a collective sense of 'containment' for troubled individuals and groups, in the sense in which this term is used by Bion (1962) and others: the bearing of anxiety, and the ability to think about and recognise mental pain.
3. Providing a place for the large group to struggle with achieving its potential for mutual help and healing, and with comprehending its own group-identity or 'group ego' (Worthington, 1990, 101).
4. Providing a place in which unconscious phenomena such as the 'reflection process'[1] may be understood and resolved, as a means towards achieving the sense of containment and thus the healing potential described above (see note 1, p.77).
5. Providing a forum in which issues of personal and social power within the group may be safely raised and learned-from, rather than being re-enacted in destructive ways, e.g. racist comments, bullying.

([1] see note 1, p.77)

Some may argue that it is artificial to separate the practical from the therapeutic functions of the community meeting in this way. In some communities, on the other hand, clear distinctions are drawn between therapy-meetings and business-meetings, while some communities evolve different functions for e.g. 'morning meetings' and 'evening meetings' (see Gilman et al., 1987). My own view is that, however these patterns and distinctions develop during the evolution of any given community, unless the practical functions are being achieved, there is no chance of achieving the therapeutic functions. In other words, the meeting has to succeed at an immediate and practical level if everyone is to feel it is worth investing in. In some places, indeed, the practical functions will suffice. Where people have been unsuccessful in attempting to implement a system of community meetings, I would suspect that they may have been trying to be 'therapeutic' before they were being genuinely useful: this is how group-members become alienated, frightened and angry. It has been said that 'An institution can be run at a management level without therapy, but therapy cannot exist without management' (Butlin, 1975). Fear of the large group seems to me very close in some respects to the fear evoked by the fantasy of therapy without management - a fear of being swallowed up by the ocean, of being overpowered.

Indeed, the issue of personal and social power provides a useful illustration of the overlap between the practical and the therapeutic functions of the community meeting. It is the situation of many of those using group care services that they may have felt powerless at various levels, whether in terms of personal relationships, or in terms of their experience of racism or other powerful prejudiced actions; in some cases such powerlessness may have been further aggravated by the whole operation of the welfare system (Ward, 1993). If group care services are to address and remedy such powerlessness, they need to be informed by an ethos of empowerment, and they must offer structures in which people can rediscover and exercise their personal and social power. The community meeting offers one such structure, in which people can not only deal with current practical and emotional issues, but can also reflect together upon and learn from earlier experiences. The responsibility of the workers in such a system will be to provide appropriate support to enable people to make full use of structures such as the community meeting.

Training

Finally, to return to training. The risk in presenting a paper such as this is that, by identifying the range of anxieties associated with the topic, I may have set in motion a further version of the self-fulfilling prophecy that 'large groups are frightening places'. This is certainly not my intention, and I hope that the paper can serve instead to help people enter into a more confident and positive prophecy - that 'large groups are manageable and creative'. I would suggest that the most effective place for such a message to be promoted is on training-courses. If group care workers are going to be more confident, knowledgeable and skilled in leading and understanding the large group, they will have to learn by experience. Training courses will therefore need to include practical as well as theoretical work on large group phenomena. In particular, I want to point out the relevance for training of the phenomenon of the reflection process as described above.

The concept of the reflection process suggests that the various patterns of interaction between staff, residents and others will also be re-created in training - and indeed that this is a necessary phenomenon through which issues arising in the work can be 'processed' into useful learning. In order to facilitate this process, the curriculum design of training courses must incorporate a range of working methods which will adequately reflect the modes of practice in the settings from which course-members are drawn. (I am following here the principle that the mode of training should match the mode of practice [Ward, 1990]). In the case of group care, where the mode of practice usually includes elements of both individual and groupwork as well as informal 'working alongside' in 'groupings' (Brown and Clough, 1989), training methods will therefore include elements of individual work and consultation, small groupwork, informal 'working alongside', and in particular, large groupwork.

The Postgraduate Diploma/MA in Therapeutic Child Care at the University of Reading has been designed to operationalise this principle. In particular, each day in college for the students on this part-time course starts and finishes with a joint meeting of staff and students. These meetings serve several purposes, each of which has some parallels with the use of meetings in the therapeutic community (which is the work-setting of many members of the course). The opening meeting is intended to enable students to 'tune in' again to working in college and with the other group members, to share information and feelings about their last week's work, and to anticipate the process and content of the day's work. The closing meeting is intended to bring the day's work together and finish it appropriately, and to encourage analysis of and reflection upon the whole day's work.

These meetings are used for discussing feelings as well as facts, and just like a community meeting, they need to be firmly managed in respect of time-boundaries and other boundaries. In terms of the reflection process, the process of these meetings is probably influenced at least as much by the members' unconscious reflection of what is happening to them in their place of work as they are by their conscious analysis of the information which they bring. My hypothesis is that this process of reflection, and the learning which grows from it, is facilitated by the fact that the style and structure of these meetings bears considerable similarity to the way in which the community meeting operates in the therapeutic communities.

There is also an experiential group (led by an external facilitator) which runs throughout this course, and which has direct parallels with the staff sensitivity and consultation groups in many therapeutic communities. The aim of this group is to enable students to reflect upon their personal experience in relation to their work, their training and each other, and to enable them to deal with individual and inter-personal problems arising within the group and to learn from these. This group thus not only enables students to work on 'here and now' issues related to the group and to individual personal concerns, but it also allows for further reflection on issues related to working in the large group both in the communities themselves and on the course.

Thus students gain the experience of being in and working in a large group, and have further opportunities to reflect on this experience in other groups, as well as learning about the theory of large-groupwork through seminars etc. The aim of this approach to training is to encourage students to feel more skilled and confident in working with the large group, and thereby to spread the message that the power of the large group can be harnessed as both a practical and a therapeutic tool. While the example offered here relates to a specialised post-qualifying course, there is also a need for qualifying social work courses to address large groupwork. This will be the subject of a separate paper, and I would be glad to correspond with others who may share this concern. Suffice it to say here that a range of methods exists, including the adaptation of staff-student meetings and the flexible use of existing structures of seminars etc to provide experiential learning. Similarly, although this paper has been concerned with the whole spectrum of group care, most of the examples have been drawn from residential child care: the reason for this bias lies in my own commitment to this particular area and my concern to improve practice in this field. Nevertheless, the arguments made here apply equally to other settings: for example, Mullender (1990) has a useful discussion of the 'resident's forum' in residential settings for elderly people. If the use of large groups is to become more widespread in group care practice, such examples will probably need to be collected together and disseminated more widely for trainers and practitioners.

Conclusion

I began this paper with the question, 'Why are people so anxious about working with large groups?', and in the course of the paper I have suggested several answers, most of them relating to fear of the unknown:

Figure 4.
Sources of anxiety about working with the large group in group care settings

1. Fear based upon a resistance to groups in general.
2. Fear related to an intuitive but misinterpreted grasp of the power of the large group, especially in terms of perceived threats to identity.
3. Fear and anxiety generated by not understanding unconscious phenomena such as the reflection process.
4. Anxiety raised by confusion and uncertainty about the specific functions and possibilities of the large group.
5. Fear evoked by the fantasy of therapy without management.

Since there is so much fear of that which is not known or not understood, I am proposing that the answer lies principally in training, and particularly in creating the opportunities on training courses for people to gain positive experience of being in, and working in, large groups.

An shortened version of this paper was published as 'The large group: the heart of the system in residential care' in van der Ploeg, J.D., van den Bergh, P.M., Klomp, M., Knorth, E.J. and Smit, M. (eds.) (1992) Vulnerable Youth in Residential Care. *Leuven-Apeldoorn, Holland: Garant.*

Note

1.The reflection process refers to the phenomenon whereby the behaviour or emotions of one individual or group may unconsciously reflect or 'mirror' those of another (see Mattinson, 1970). Thus the dynamics of inter-user relationships or of user-to-staff interactions may be recreated within the staff team (and vice versa). For example, in one residential unit for adolescents, a sudden increase in sexual acting-out among the residents caused confusion and concern among the staff team, until discussion between the staff team and their consultant revealed that a secret sexual relationship which had developed recently between two key staff-members had been causing confusion and jealousy within the team (much of it unconscious), and that the young people had been excited and provoked by this atmosphere. Once this connection was established and understood within the team, the atmosphere in the unit began to return to normal. Similarly, current events or moods in *external* social or political groupings may have considerable impact upon the internal social climate of the unit. The reflection process is a familiar phenomenon in general terms to many group care workers, and in its various manifestations it often helps to explain events and moods in a group which are otherwise difficult to understand, yet it is often difficult to detect in practice, and even more problematic to explain and to learn from. The community meeting, by making such phenomena available for public scrutiny in the large group, may help to make these phenomena manifest, understood, and thus available to be harnessed for their therapeutic potential. The fear and anxiety which is generated by the absence of understanding can thus be allayed, and the community meeting can play a significant role in creating the required understanding.

References

Bion, W.R. (1962) *Learning From Experience*. London: Heinemann.

Brown, A. (1990) 'Groupwork with a difference: the group 'mosaic' in residential and day care settings', *Groupwork,* 3(3), pp.269-285.

Brown, A. and Clough, R. (ed.) (1989) *Groups and Groupings. Life and Work in Day and Residential Settings.* London & New York: Tavistock / Routledge.

Butlin, E. (1975) 'Institutionalisation, management structure and therapy in residential work with emotionally disturbed children', *British Journal of Social Work,* 5(3), pp.283-295.

Cook, R. (1988) 'A non-residential therapeutic community used as an alternative to custody', *International Journal of Therapeutic Communities*, 9(1), pp.55-64.

de Mare, P., Piper, R. and Thompson, S. (1990) *Koinonia: From Hate Through Dialogue to Culture in the Larger Group.* London: Karnac Books.

Douglas, T. (1986) *Group Living. The Application of Group Dynamics in Residential Settings.* London: Tavistock.

Gilman, H.E., Russakoff, L.M., and Kibel, H. (1987) 'A bipartite model for community meetings: the separation of roles', *International Journal of Therapeutic Communities*, 8(2), pp.131-140.

Hinshelwood, R.D. (1987) *What Happens in Groups. Psychoanalysis, the Individual and the Community.* London: Free Association Books.

Hopper, E. and Weyman, A. (1975) 'A sociological view of large groups' in Kreeger, L. (ed.) *The Large Group. Dynamics and Therapy*. London: Karnac Books.

Kennedy, R. (1987) 'The work of the day' in Kennedy, R., Heymans, A. and Tischler, L. (eds.)*The Family as In-Patient. Families and Adolescents at the Cassell Hospital*. London: Free Association Books.

Kreeger, L. (ed.) (1975) *The Large Group. Dynamics and Therapy*. London: Karnac Books.

Mattinson, J. (1975) *The Reflection Process in Casework Supervision*. London: Institute of Marital Studies.

Mullender, A. (1990) 'Groupwork in residential settings for elderly people', *Groupwork,* 3(3), pp.286-301.

Nitsun, M. (1991) 'The anti-group: destructive forces in the group and their therapeutic potential', *Group Analysis,* 24(1), pp.7 - 20.

Rose, M. (1990) *Healing Hurt Minds.* London: Routledge.

Trauer, T. (1987) 'Community meeting research', *International Journal of Therapeutic Communities*, 8(2), pp.141-154.

Turquet, P. (1975) 'Threats to identity in the large group', in Kreeger, L. (ed.) *The Large Group. Dynamics and Therapy*. London: Karnac Books.

van der Linden, P. (1988) 'How does the large group change the individual?, *International Journal of Therapeutic Communities,* 9(1), pp.31-39.

Ward, A. (1984) 'All you can do is bring your own self', *Community Care,* 17 May.

Ward, A. (1990) *The Reflection Process in the Supervision and Training of Group Care Workers.* Unpublished paper given at International Special Education Congress, University of Wales, Cardiff, 1990.

Ward, A. (1993) *Working in Group Care*. Birmingham: Venture Press.

Whiteley, J.S. and Gordon, J. (1979) *Group Approaches in Psychiatry.* London, Routledge & Kegan Paul.

Worthington, A. (1990) 'The function of the community meeting in a therapeutic community for pre- and young adolescents', *International Journal of Therapeutic Communities,* 11(2), pp.95-102.

Reviews

Feminist Groupwork
SANDRA BUTLER AND CLAIRE WINTRAM
Sage Publications, 1991, price £10.95 (pbk) ISBN 0 8039 82100

I eagerly approached the task of reviewing this book because I was interested to see how it offered a specifically feminist approach to groupwork which might form an identifiable model or methodology of groupwork practice. Secondly, since it was written by social workers I hoped it would have relevance and significance to groupworkers working in the statutory sector, particularly for women probation officers, social workers and youth workers. I was however disappointed by the book from both aspects. It is written in a heavy style which is long on polemical statements of feminism and rather brief on description of groupwork approaches.

It is clearly written from a deeply committed feminist perspective. The authors state that 'it is possible to use groupwork methodology as a springboard for conscientisation'. Such is the central thesis of the book and its feminism is well researched and articulated. Its groupwork methodology however is less clear. The authors describe how for example: 'Flipping between the overly political and the overly personal and therapeutic adds links to the chain of understanding about the self in its political context'. This is clearly a very difficult thing to attempt, in that links between theory and practice in social work and particularly social groupwork are never simple. The latter quote also gives some indication of the heaviness of the text which even when describing the experience of the practice of groupwork with the women lacks vitality and freshness. Some of the writing is, it has to be said, pretentious. Statements such as, for example, 'Liberal minded practitioners may have hearts of gold but so do hard-boiled eggs' do make the reader's task a hard one.

The authors conclude they have: 'Above everything else...begun the process of locating working class women's groups within a context of women's action and achievements'. That is a worthy aim which is confidently stated. To do this they claim to 'have encapsulated the interplay between feminism, women's identity and the practice theories of groupwork'. There is a constant interplay of feminist ideas and a range of groupwork methods drawn from a range of approaches. The authors describe for example (p.20) how the book is written. It is:

> ...a hybrid of concepts and models drawn from a whole range of sources. Each component is critically examined from a feminist baseline, if found wanting it is discarded, but if potential exists it will be adapted for the purpose of feminism.

Thus the groupwork methodologies described in the book are used in the service of feminist principles.

Questions remain for me however about the extent to which the ideology of feminism and the methodology of groupwork are reconcilable by a synthesis which can be defined as feminist groupwork in the way the authors suggest. They do explore some of the tensions particularly for professional women workers in the latter chapters and this is important but there are clearly some continuous major dilemmas which the quotes from the women themselves in the groups reveal.

The authors describe what they did in the group sessions in some short and varied examples of women's actions and statements from the group and some descriptions of the groupworker's use of structured experiences. For me these were frustratingly brief and as such they tended to beg questions which the authors did not address. The fascinating conflict for example between two group members who see their own and other women's responses to rape in very different ways and hurt each other in the group by their opposing beliefs and values is outlined by the authors. The resolution of their critical encounter in the group is quickly passed over by the authors who insist on overlaying this issue by generalised statements about the need for 'effective communication using conflict to lead to understanding'.

The book is well referenced and scholarly in its feminism. From a groupworker's perspective there is significantly less material, however, and many well-known groupwork texts are absent. This left me with an unease that groupwork approaches were of considerably less significance to the writers than the feminist ideology which was at the heart of their work. The book clearly will be of considerable interest to readers who want to explore in detail a feminist analysis pursued through consideration of women's internal and external lives. I suspect it will be of less interest to groupworkers particularly those who struggle with the pragmatics of working with women in statutory agencies.

Sue Ross, Assistant Director of Social Work, Borders Regional Council

Editors' note

Reviewers' opinions are independent of the editors, however readers will be interested to know that Sandra Butler and Claire Wintram won the 1992 Distinguished Author Award, presented by the American Association of Human Psychologists, for this book's contribution to women's studies. In view of this, the editors would welcome comment and further discussion from readers.

Group Counselling with Juvenile Delinquents
MATTHEW FERRARA
Sage Publications, 1992, price £12.75 (pbk) ISBN 8039 3885 3

This publication is essentially a handbook. It is designed to guide practitioners through a group counselling programme for juvenile delinquents. Set in a particular world view concerning the delinquent, its application seems likely to be in residential or secure facilities. It may offer ideas for community-based work with young people in trouble but the control the programme is intended to exert would have to be mediated through the other influences at work in community provision. It is an American publication and as such maybe this limits its applicability in Britain given the differential experience of serious delinquency in the USA as distinct from this country.

The approach of the book is heralded in the sub-title 'the limit and lead' approach. The goal is presented as deceptively simple and described thus: 'eliminate negative delinquent behaviour and replace it with positive, appropriate behaviour. To attain this goal, negative behaviour must be confronted and eliminated and positive behaviour must be taught and reinforced.' A twin-track approach to treatment is then set out in detail based around a normative framework for juvenile delinquency. The author treats as unproblematic how to define the delinquent and assumes there is a commonly understood distinction between the delinquent and the non-delinquent. This assertion ensures that the counsellor able to accept the normative framework can pursue their mission safe in the knowledge of the moral worth of the correctional enterprise.

The two strategies in this treatment approach have complementary aims. The first is to establish and maintain a safe and stable environment within which the second strategy of behavioural change can be attempted. The first aim is to be achieved by using the techniques of guided group interaction whereby the group counsellor engages in interventions which either seek to limit negative behaviour and/or offer leadership and guidance towards more positive group interactions. There are many useful ideas here for facilitating group engagement. This sets the parameters within which group maintenance is achieved and sustained and enables or, at least, creates the conditions whereby behavioural change can begin.

The second element, cognitive behavioural therapy, is then introduced and a strategy for action and an array of techniques are described in detail. We are becoming more familiar in this country with the work of Robert Ross and many of the ideas in this book come from the same school of thought. Offering a hope that 'something works' rather than the 'nothing works' conclusions of earlier treatment interventions it purports to offer successful ways of inducing behaviour change in young people.

The rest of the book offers detailed prescriptions concerning: the techniques to be used; a detailed training programme for prospective group counsellors; a training programme for young people to understand and use the techniques; and a schedule for ensuring administrative support. It is written in an accessible style, with good attention to detail and replete with examples of worksheets, modules, experiential exercises and training schedules. If you can live with the normative framework then provided you run a well-resourced centre with committed staff who can fully implement the programme, this is the blueprint you have been looking for.

I felt somewhat uneasy, however, with the value system which underpins the approach and which seems to exclude considerations which are vital to successful group interventions with young people. Although not explicitly stated, the target group for these interventions may be the very serious and committed delinquent probably only seen in this country in Youth Treatment Centres and occasionally in secure accommodation. Delinquency is defined by Ferrara on a continuum from mild to severe but within a very broad rubric - 'if a youth violates the rights of others in an attempt to meet a need, then this youth has committed a delinquent act.'

Absent from either this definition or more generally in the text is any recognition of the wider structure of society and those factors which impinge upon young people. Such factors act in a differential and unjust way and produce some considerable distortion in who becomes defined as delinquent. Even if the population he refers to is the most severely delinquent it will inhibit successful outcomes if class, race and gender perspectives are ignored. It is not simply a technical exercise no matter how well thought out the strategies. This would imply clarity over who is defined as delinquent and a high degree of choice available to young people in committing so-called delinquent acts.

There is a lamentable absence of any discussion of class, race and gender issues throughout the text. This is almost as if behaviours are totally universal and not mediated through the differential experiences of black and white men and women, and gay men and lesbian perspectives, both for the young people themselves and for the staff. This is for me a crucial omission. In this light the approach seems highly controlling and of necessity undervalues the experience of those going through the programme.

In conclusion it would not be necessary to reject the book in its entirety for its value base. I found many of the techniques interesting and thoroughly worked out in the way they attempted to offer a consistent and constructive environment for group counselling with young people. With this caveat (and maybe without if you are a Ross convert!) it is worth using as source book for ideas.

Paul Senior, Senior Lecturer in Social Work, Sheffield Hallam University and a Senior Probation Officer (Training), South Yorkshire Probation Service

A Structural Analysis of Small Groups
SUSAN LONG
Routledge, price £35.00 (hb) £12.99 (pbk) ISBN 0 415 06501 1 (hbk)

At one time or another all writers and practitioners concerned with small groups have struggled to define what exactly they perceive to be the separate entity which we call a 'group'. What is it that differentiates a so-called 'formed' group from a random aggregate of individuals? Why have terms like 'group mind' and 'group identity' emerged to explain a phenomenon which would logically appear to have no existence separate from that of the individuals who comprise it? It is axiomatic that if a number of individuals meet together over a long enough period of time that there will arise a perception on their part and likewise in any observers of their behaviour, that an entity which is understood by all to be a group, has arisen, an entity which did not exist prior to the coming together of the individuals involved.

Another problem which has concerned group theorists for an equally long period of time has been the attempt to define what exactly is the contribution that individuals make which is so fundamental to the creation and development of this entity a 'group'? This has been variously described as commitment, energy, resources etc., and that each individual who stays within the compass of a group is rewarded in various ways for making this contribution. Of these, perhaps resources defines in the simplest pragmatic form what group members are able to contribute. But what all are agreed upon is that whatever that contribution may be it is only a part and often a small part, of the time, presence and resources potential of the individual member. The fact that there is a traffic from within that small part of the individual's experience which resides within the group boundary to the world outside and from that larger experience into the confines of the group is wholly acknowledged; that within the group itself all individual members confine and constrain their contributions and protect various areas of themselves either from exposure or use is also well known. But where in all this are the tools of language to enable us to describe what actually happens between individuals within the confines of the group and over a period of time? We believe such happenings are sufficiently tangible and observable to warrant our describing them as a new existence which has come into being. Does the concept of the development of trust, itself such an ambiguous, tenuous and shape-shifting term, cover the genesis of a group entity? I hardly think so.

Susan Long has set herself the task of constructing some possible answers to these problems. However when considering her main sources of her ideas and in attempting to develop a vocabulary to describe the structures she wishes to emphasise she used the obfuscating language of psychoanalysis to a far greater extent than her main thesis would require. It has always been my contention that a true understanding of even the most complex ideas should require no use of bastardised concoctions from classical languages for their explanation and expression.

Long's main sources are in fact two, psychoanalysis and systems theory: the principal proponents are Freud, Bion, Lacan and Mahler. Fundamentally she draws a close comparison between the processes of integration in the early stages of group development and the early developmental period in the maturation of a child.

After the first five chapters which present her sources at length, Long in chapter six offers her research methodology. This exposition is fascinating and should be read by anyone anticipating setting up some form of measurement of group process and group outcome. She starts from the concept that systems are 'defined from within and explained from without', and proceeds to discuss all the problems inherent in measuring a system which is conscious of and observing itself. There is some good discussion of ideas derived from linguistics which indicate that for instance a sentence is never clearly understood until it is complete and even then that understanding is constrained by antecedents and anticipation. So Long states that groups are systems in which 'subjects constantly interact with the results of their own observations and define the systems within which they are embedded.'

The study of actual groups presented in later chapters is concerned to describe and clarify them in terms of those structures which organise the early integration of groups and to identify the structural organisation of early integrative processes. The methodology used for this purpose consists of qualitative and quantitative analyses of recorded textual data of each group.

There is a degree of assumption that this form of analysis of the record of a group is actually concerned to locate and describe entities and processes which exist, and rather less than I like that these analyses are interpretive and owe as much if not more to the theoretical constructs which form the bases of the instruments of analysis than they do 'real' processes operating within the group. But it is axiomatic that the language available to us for this kind of task is markedly inadequate and as a result we usually only succeed in over-simplifying, rigidifying and coarsening something which is infinitely variable and fluid. The concept of structure itself in this research is a good example.

Part II is devoted to an analysis of the first session only of three separate groups the members of which have the basic task of studying their own group processes and each having the services of a consultant and an observer. The close comparison with child development is heavily stressed and charts displaying this comparison can be found on pages 133-4.

Part III continues the study of group three from the previous section recorded over fourteen sessions of one and a half hours each. Here the method is to select three major episodes of prime importance in the structural development of the group and to analyse those episodes both at a surface level and symbolic level in relation to the growing identity of the group particularly in terms of power, leadership and authority.

This is a very interesting book clearly set out, logically pursued but unbalanced in that to devote the first five chapters to a discussion of sources serves no good purpose as they are only of use as descriptive terms and are not essential to an understanding of the early integrative processes of a group at either a surface or a symbolic level. Such a lavish allocation of space to sources also serves to diminish the content devoted to the application of the methodology derived from them to analyse the integrative and episodic nature of the development of group structure. Nevertheless, for anyone seriously concerned with the development of ideas about the identity of 'groupness', the transindividual processes suggested here are a bonus.

Tom Douglas, Fellow of the University of Keele

The Inner World Outside: Object Relations Theory andPsychodrama
PAUL HOLMES
London, Tavistock/Routledge, 1992, price £12.99 (pbk)
ISBN: 0 415 05551 2

Warm puzzlement may summarise my reactions to this book. My warm response began with the design of the cover: evoking self and object in an aesthetically engaging way; such a refreshing start. I continued to feel engaged as I followed the author's account of his work with one member of a group, George, throughout his book. During this 'personal journey' the author refers to himself in the third person as 'Paul', yet remains so warmly personal. For example, on page 97, having described a mistake he has made, the author goes on to explain it as the result of his countertransference. He does so not by showing George's neurosis, as others have done, but by openly sharing with his readers his own past hurts, and how George activated them.

Countertransference has been explained by many, but have they conveyed it so well? Direct commonsensical explorations of rather complex psychoanalytic concepts appear in this book more than once. At some points they are simplified without being made simplistic, at others independent contributions are made which help clarify known concepts. Altogether, I ended convinced of the author's genuine therapeutic ability; and that is a very precious gift which is difficult to convey.

Straight away the book begins with an extract of the session chosen for demonstration. Then a personal introduction follows, but the overall plan of the book has to be discovered through reading: a bit of a puzzle at first. Yet, I soon realised that excerpts from the same session would follow. Each excerpt is a springboard leading to explanations of various topics: assessment, repetition and transference, the inner objects world, relationships and roles and so on. Chapter 6, 'The inner world and the drama of psychotherapy', seems to reflect the authors intention to bring out, in action, unconscious conflicts of each group member. The need to enact unconscious conflicts is explained by their history; stretching back to early childhood. The author assumes that since these conflicts occurred so early 'when early object relationships surface in adult life they first do so through non-verbal feelings and actions' (p.84). Psychodrama is a 'transitional space' within which the conflicts can now be resolved. The author is trying to enrich psychodrama with ideas from psychoanalysis, object relations theory, self-psychology, and even parts of systems theory.

His journey is most interesting, but it ends with an unexpected surprise. The declared intention is to provide 'a unified account' of psychodrama and object relations theory. Yet the book ends without a single object relation demonstrated in practice. Not that the author's practice does not call for object relations; for example, in page 15 George cries over a toy soldier. Now: what a beautiful opportunity to expand on George's associations. What sort of toy was this? What part of George's feelings about his father had to be repressed and then symbolised as a toy? How did the therapist help George re-own that split part? Instead, the practice episodes are of encounters between George and various other people: father, mother, his boss, or his wife. These encounters are vital and helpful. Yet, no object relations theory lacks objects in practice. I have spent some time wondering about this gap between theory and practice. It is of course, for the author to explain it. My guess is that the problem lies in the choice of particular frameworks. Indeed, the connections among the supporting theories chosen by the author have interested others too. However, each of these theories is really a cluster of frameworks by now. Therefore, the choice of any particular framework within each theory does have conceptual, ethical, and practice implications. The author rightly points out to Moreno's belief in liberating people from fixed roles and enhancing their spontaneity (pp.36-38, 94-96). Moreno's belief in 'tele', our inborn connectedness with one another, could have been clarified too. If it was, Melanie Klein would not have featured so centrally. It seems helpful to remember that for Klein, the baby was capable only of satisfying its own biological needs. She believed that appreciating relationships was learned only later in life.

This is exactly where Fairbairn disagreed. Fairbairn saw the baby being born as a 'dynamic unity'; capable of and seeking relatedness with others. Moreno's 'tele' seems far closer to Fairbairn's understanding than to Klein's framework but hardly more than lip service is offered to the difference between them (p.66). Equally, why bring in so much of Kernberg? Essentially, Kernberg promoted a model which implied the adaptation of individuals to society. Instead, the Fairbairn-Guntrip axis could have been extended, as

Bacal and Newman (1990) did, towards the self-psychology of Kohut. Kohut's framework of self-actualisation would have enabled the author to be consistent with Moreno's search for individual creativity.

Groupworkers may be puzzled too. As noted before, the use of psychodrama is justified as a way of enabling members to regress to pre-verbal stages of their development; when they were still unable to talk. But, following Bion, members who refuse to take part in psychodrama are considered to have regressed. So, we end up with the puzzling implication that refusing to regress was evidence of regression (p. 180). Historically important as he undoubtedly was, Bion's model seems to lead to such contradictions. In practice, grappling with them can unnecessarily confuse many group members. Why not stay with Foulkes (in spite of his own failure to understand the value of psychodrama), or even move on to understand fully the systems approach (Durkin, 1981)?

Some of the very interesting conceptual explorations (see for example p.70) could have been offered more simply and clearly, and my final regret cannot be denied. I do not admire politically correct linguistics for its own sake. But more was implied on the very first page of this book. I was dismayed to see women group members described by their appearance while the men were noted for their achievements (p.1). I would have preferred descriptions of men and women by what they do: their work (at the home, in the office, the factory), their hobbies, the non-verbal cues they offer, and so on.

These reservations notwithstanding, groupworkers who look for a direct and genuine account of psychodramatic practice will be inspired by those warm, sensitive, and humanistic parts of the text. Those looking for the full application of object relations to psychodrama will have to wait a little longer.

Oded Manor, Senior Lecturer in Social work, Middlesex University

References

Bacal, H.A. and Newman, K.M. (1990) *Theories of Object Relations:Bridges to Self Psychology*. New York: Columbia University Press.

Durkin, J.E. (ed.) (1981) *Living Groups: Group Psychotherapy and General System Theory*. New York: Brunner/Mazel Pub.

Focus on Psychodrama
PETER FELIX KELLERMAN
Jessica Kingsley Publishers,price £16.95 (pbk) ISBN 1 85302 127 X

This is a good, basic book on psychodrama which guides the reader through the history, context, principles and practice of psychodrama. The book is a further development of the authors own experience of psychodrama research which was first addressed in a PhD thesis, based on interviews with hundreds of psychodrama participants. The authors aim is an attempt to:

> ...present a systematic analysis of the essential therapeutic ingredients in psychodrama. By delineating the variables at work in this method and by proposing more uniform definitions to some central psychodramatic concepts, I hope to improve the general standard of practice and research and to reduce some of the confusion which surrounds the theory of psychodramatic technique (p.13).

Kellerman reminds us that Moreno himself had a varying set of definitions for psychodrama which include a theology with religious postulations, a dramatic art form with aesthetic ideals, a political system with social values, a science with research ambitions, a method of psychotherapy with curative goals and a philosophy of life; however he suggests that psychodrama should be defined as a 'specific method of psychotherapy, a treatment approach to psychological problems' (p.18).

Kellerman proceeds to provide definitions of the key psychodramatic concepts and processes and a summary of where, when and how it should be applied. The body of the book describes psychodramatic theory, who is the psychodramatist, and various psychodramatic properties, such as catharsis, action-insight, tele, and acting out. I am particularly interested in the direct way that the author tackles the question of 'charismatic leadership': he points out the dangers of power and control and the unhelpfulness of 'basic assumption dependency groups', but adds:

> ...whether we like it or not, whether we try to induce it or prevent it, at one time or another individuals and groups have the need to submit in shared admiration of their therapist (p.61).

He suggests that the 'cultish aspects' (Gohen, 1971) delayed psychodrama's entry into mainstream psychiatry. However it needs to be stated emphatically that all therapies can be guilty of pandering to the narcissistic leader or the cult movement in a way that is unhelpful to the consumer.

Chapter 14 called 'Processing' talks us through the necessary processes after the psychodrama has taken place, which he likens to 'live supervision' in family therapy; we need more on this and also the question of psychodramatic supervision of practice as an on-going process needs to be fully addressed.

What I like about this book is that Kellerman is prepared to look at the critiques of psychodrama and suggest real strategies for tightening practice. He devotes a section to leadership guidelines in Chapter 4 and then an extended appendix which has 100 questions for the leader to ask themselves after sessions, called 'The Psychodrama Director Processing Checklist'; this could also be adapted to the practice of other therapies especially arts therapies.

More could have been made in Chapter 9, entitled 'As-If', of the many variations of this concept, especially as it applied to play therapy with children, the actors training and of course dramatherapy itself. The sections on 'role' I found needed more fleshing out as there is an extended contemporary body of research available.

Nevertheless, this is a book for psychodramatists and other psychotherapists alike. Its format is clear and unpretentious, and it makes sense of many 'drifting ideas' that have been around in the action-orientated therapies field. It will be a helpful book for arts therapists generally and for dramatherapists in particular, as they too face issues around definition and practice.

Sue Jennings, Consultant Dramatherapist and Senior Fertility Counsellor, The London Hospital Medical College

GROUPWORK

Volume 6 Number 2 1993

Guest Editor: Lynne Muir

SUBSCRIPTION, ADVERTISING AND BUSINESS ENQUIRIES
Should be addressed to the publishers, WHITING & BIRCH LTD, PO Box 872, Forest Hill, London SE23 3HL. TEL: 081-244-2421 (Int'l +4481 244-2421). FAX: 081-244-2448 (Int'l. +4481-244-2448)

SUBSCRIPTION RATES
British Isles £32.00, North America US$65, Elsewhere £37.50
Special reduced rates apply as follows:
Individuals to private address: £16.00 British Isles, North America, US$35 Elsewhere £20.00. Special reductions available for members of AASWG and Groupwork Exchange Network.
Groupwork is published three times a year.

PAYMENT
Should accompany order. Cheque or banker's draft (made payable to WHITING & BIRCH LTD) may be in any convertible currency to the relevant amount. Direct transfer can be made to our Girobank account (no. 5440564). The following credit cards are also accepted: Access/Mastercard, Visa, Diners Club, American Express. Quote card number, expiry date and give cardholder's name and address if different from delivery address.

GROUPWORK is cited in: *Applied Social Sciences Index & Abstracts, Sociological Abstracts, Bibliographie Zeitscriftenliteratur aus allen Gebieten des Wissens, Social Care Update, Social Work Research & Abstracts, Special Educational Needs Abstracts*. and *Studies on Women Abstracts.*

PUBLISHED BY WHITING & BIRCH LTD, LONDON. ISSN 0951-824X
Printed by Bourne Press, Bournemouth.

EDITORIAL

The planning and organising of an edition of GROUPWORK takes up to a year before it comes to fruition, and this one is no exception. What is unusual is for an edition with five specialist articles on bereavement to follow close on the publication of the Irish collection (volume 5, number 3, 1992) which, not surprisingly, had a number of papers on loss and bereavement. Consequently this issue can be seen as a continuation of a theme as it also includes two further articles from Ireland.

Four of the papers focus on loss within the family. Sheila Finlayson and Dawn Rowe describe working with a family of black children who had been separated on the death of their parents. They poignantly show the pain the children experience and how 'happy families' is not always a viable alternative. Estelle Hopmeyer and Annette Werk from Canada presented some of their paper at the 1992 Groupwork Symposium in Atlanta. Evaluation of groups in any systematic way is a developing practice. This comparative study of four bereavement groups which looks at reasons for joining a group, what was gained from the group and issues that need time in the group is a welcome addition to the evaluation literature. Some of the gender differences in hopes and expectations which they identify are reinforced in the paper on the Asian mothers group. Cruse is a nationally recognised bereavement support network but its work with groups is not as well known. Joyce Rimmer describes the system of family circles which has been developed to offer groupwork help.

It is interesting to note the type of group used in post-traumatic stress debriefing as described by Frank Parkinson. The structure is quite different to many social work groups in that the time span of the group life is short, the rules are fairly rigid and the objectives are very specific.

The final two articles included in this edition are from Ireland and deal with different kinds of loss. Brian McCarthy and Bernadette Duffy demonstrate that an institution, while taking away many privileges, can also provide an arena for the personal growth of its residents. They capture the flavour of group meetings in a residential setting with the inclusion of quotations and an honest recording of the process. The theme of loss is again reflected in the article by Elisabeth Cormack who says that the person with a learning difficulty often experiences the loss of attachment to a parent who, in their turn, experience the loss of an idealised, intelligent child. This group for sexual offenders with a learning difficulty explores some of these issues of loss and makes a strong case for groupwork with this client group.

The variety of groups covered in this edition range from the traditional social work time-limited , task specific group to the more open-ended, on-going support group. It illustrates the range of possibilities open to the practitioner. Reading these articles in preparation for this edition has once again highlighted for me the enthusiasm and commitment to good practice that is shown in these writings. I am particularly grateful to John Hodge for his suggestions and perceptive comments on the first five papers included in this edition.

Lynne Muir, Guest Editor

Working with a Family Group of Bereaved Children

Sheila Finlayson

Children's understanding of loss and its consequences change as they grow older. They continue to need opportunities for talking about their feelings to someone who accepts them and ensures that they do not feel alone. When a parent dies, children may also lose home, school and friendships. This article discusses children's needs following loss and describes a family whose experiences highlight the vulnerability of some bereaved children. Groupwork offered a way of providing a safe setting in which their intense need to have their feelings heard and respected could be met. The young people were given an opportunity of enhancing their understanding of themselves and one another and of establishing ways of communicating and relating which it is hoped will contribute towards their maintaining family ties although they live in different places. The groupworkers, in turn, extended their knowledge of the young people's perception of themselves and their life experiences.

A group for a family

Michelle, aged nine, gave concern to her family and school because of behavioural problems which included stealing from home and school and aggressiveness in the playground. Her mother had died three years previously, and her father when she was three. She was the youngest of four children, all of whom lived with their maternal aunt. Their parents, Rose and Sam, both born in Jamaica, had lived in the UK since childhood. The four children were born about a year apart - Amy, Sandra, Leon and Michelle. Shortly after Michelle was born, Rose had a mastectomy. When the children were aged seven, six, five and three, their father was killed in a car crash. Leon had been living with his maternal grandparents in Jamaica for a year and remained there. Amy was sent from London to her paternal grandparents in Birmingham where she remained for a year. Sandra was devastated by the separation from a sister to whom she was very close.

Rose's cancer recurred and she knew she had a limited time to

Groupwork Vol. 6(2), 1993, pp.93-106

live. When Michelle was five, Rose took her to Jamaica to bring Leon home. By this time he was seven and had lived with his grandparents for three years. The family lived together until Rose's death a year later when the children were aged ten, nine, eight and six. Their grandmother came to the U.K. for the funeral and while she was in London, her husband was killed in Jamaica. The children left London to live with their mother's sister Mary who had three children of her own.

All of the children had felt loved and valued by their mother. They had revelled in her joy of living, her refusal to allow her illness to defeat her, her humour, her pleasure in being with them. In their aunt's household, their smiling faces concealed the acute loneliness of grief that appeared not to be shared. While struggling to live through the shock of their mother's death and accept its reality, they had to adapt to the different life style of their aunt's household and settle into a new school. Their aunt, in turn, was facing the loss of her favourite sister. There is a belief that bereavement draws a family together, that sharing grief facilitates close and caring relationships. Living through the process of intense emotional pain, guilt, anxiety, anger and depression is not, however, generally contributory to family harmony. At a time when children need the security of consistency and the reassurance of tender understanding, they may experience adults who are withdrawn, irritable and unpredictable in their responses (McFarlane, 1987). Michelle was referred to the Child Advisory Social Work Service for counselling by the Social Services Department a year after her mother's death She was typical of many children who have experienced a series of losses and for whom help is sought when their behaviour gives cause for concern in school and at home. Her responses to her mother's death and its consequences illustrate issues we need to be aware of in helping children and young people who have experienced the loss of important relationships, whether by death or separation.

Michelle had little contact with her previous life. She did, however, daydream about it constantly, was unable to sleep and felt overwhelmed with anxieties about her every day life. Later she became convinced that it was her fault her mother had died. There was no basis of truth in this, nor was she unusual in experiencing these beliefs. She was progressing through a normal child's experience of the loss of a significant relationship. She felt anger about her hated present life and her powerlessness to put back the clock or change her situation. She posed the question: 'Why me?'

At school her lack of progress academically and her social isolation worried staff who tried to be understanding and supportive. Frequently children's experiences after bereavement are not ones which acknowledge and validate emotions. They can be a nightmare of incomprehensible feelings which if expressed bring adult criticism. At a time when their self esteem needs to be protected and cherished, children may be victims of adult censure which they have little or no capacity to evaluate (Jewett, 1982). Teasing by other children may also be a problem (Yule, 1992).

Amy was disobedient and began to fail in school; Sandra became Amy's shadow and always tried to please; Leon was rude and defiant and stayed out late; Michelle at nine was considered for special education because of stealing and aggression. She was referred to the Child Advisory Social Work Service for counselling with her aunt's permission. A Social Services social worker provided support for the family on a voluntary basis. Given the opportunity to talk about and cry for her mother and to have her feelings accepted as normal, her behaviour problems disappeared within three months and the proposal of special education was abandoned.

At the point when Michelle's individual counselling was ending, Amy and Leon ran away from the aunt with whom the children had lived for four years. Their aunt said she could no longer care for Michelle and only Sandra remained in the household. Amy, Leon and Michelle went to stay with Jane, Amy's white godmother. Amy went to London five months later in a vain attempt to recapture the life she had lived before her mother's death. Leon and Michelle were content with Jane but the Social Services Department discovered that Jane had a police record which made it impossible to allow the children to remain with her. They were moved first to a children's home and then to members of their father's family with whom they had had little contact since their mother's death. Michelle went to their grandparents and Leon to an aunt. There was no contact with Jane or their aunt Mary.

'No one understands how alone you feel when you haven't got a mother'. Amy, almost 16, returned disillusioned from London and Sandra, aged 14, left her aunt Mary. Both girls went to live with a paternal aunt. Leon had not settled with his aunt and was placed in a children's home from which he ran away to Jane's. When he finally accepted that he could not live with Jane, an offer by a school friends' parents to foster him fell through because like Jane, they had police records. Michelle, as a six year old at the time of her mother's death, did not have the cognitive and emotional development to understand her loss in the same way as an adult. Amy, at fifteen, making the poignant comment about living without a mother, had already reached a developmental stage when she was able to conceptualise what it might have been like if her mother had lived.

An understanding of child development is necessary in helping children to mourn. Sadness is not the only emotion related to grief; children, like adults experience anxiety, guilt and anger. Children under two are unlikely to understand the significance of death. Between the ages of two and five, the understanding of death is still incomplete and children are at risk of believing that the loss was because they were bad. They need to be given the opportunity of talking about this and being reassured that their feelings are normal and that they were not to blame. Anxiety is likely to be the predominating emotion. From five to seven, children understand the finality of death. They may still blame themselves and do not have the cognitive ability to process their thoughts and feelings (Polombo, 1978). Over seven, children will begin to question why they have been deprived of loved ones and anger may predominate. It is not until a child is at least twelve and has developed a capacity for abstract thinking that the full implications of the loss are understood in a similar way to an adult, bringing the possibility of renewed pain.

It follows from this, that while an adult may live through bereavement and to a greater or lesser extent, resolve it, a child will understand and react to loss differently both according to his/her developmental stage at the time of the loss and as he/she reaches further developmental stages. Opportunities will be needed to re-examine the experience and its implications (Fahlberg, 1991). Children need explanations suited to their ability to understand and to have their feelings accepted as normal reactions, not only at the time of a loss but subsequently. All too often these needs are not met and children express their feelings in behaviour unacceptable to adults. Sadness and tears may bring consolation but behaviours such as aggression, failure to concentrate in school and stealing which may reflect guilt, anxiety and anger, are likely to bring condemnation and punishment. Children may be asked to give reasons for apparently irrational behaviour but be unable to offer explanations because they cannot, without help, relate current feelings to past experiences.

Loss is a major issue in people's lives. Not only loss by death but also loss through separation from parents, relatives, countries and cultures of birth and moving between extended family members and in and out of care settings. The consequences of a parental death, especially of a lone parent, may include loss of home, school and familiar environment. In the midst of grief, children are faced with adapting to the lifestyle of another family and the demands of forming new relationships. Individual, family and groupwork are all valuable methods of offering help. Every experience of loss is unique, but confirming the normality of experiences and sharing feelings with others who are perceived as likely to understand and listen can be a way of helping with the emotional reactions and loneliness of grief.

The context

At the time when the group was set up, Amy and Sandra were aged 16 and 15 and were living with a paternal aunt. Leon was thirteen and living in a children's home; Michelle was twelve and living with paternal grandparents. None of the children was happy with his/her placement.

A Social Services social worker had recently taken over responsibility for the family and we discussed the needs of the young people and how to meet them. It was apparent that the series of further moves and losses, as well as having their own implications, might also have laid bare feelings from the past. In addition, the young people were scattered between family members and a children's home and it was believed that the relationships between them needed to be protected and encouraged.

There were, therefore, three objectives in proposing the group. Firstly to enable the young people to speak about and share their feelings about a series of major losses and rejections. Secondly to talk about the family history in order that this would be known about by all the children, and thirdly to confirm and build upon their importance to one another. The objectives were discussed with the young people; the girls were keen to participate but Leon was more cautious because he said his life was already difficult and he feared further pain. Six weekly sessions of one hour were agreed. There was the additional issue that the Social Services worker having recently become involved with the family wished to develop her understanding of them and her relationships with them.

Both the workers are female, one black, the other white. Discussions about the family's plight and how to help had quickly established respect and rapport between the workers which was based on similar values and a common understanding of the professional issues. They also believe that there is a value for children in experiencing good relationships between black and white people. The family were at ease with white people, their mother having had close white friends such as Amy's godmother. The white worker had also counselled Michelle and discussed racism with her. When black issues arose, such as ancestry or racism, the young peoples' views or feelings could be shared by the black worker and validated by both black and white workers. It was believed that the young people felt comfortable with two workers and that since there might be intense individual needs in the group, it was preferable to co-work. A psychodynamic approach was agreed. Sharing feelings of empathy with the young people's pain and sadness that there was no apparent solution to their need for a loving home, strengthened the workers confidence in working together. The black worker saw the young people outside the group as their Social Services social worker. Michelle, for example, spoke of being hit by an uncle and this had to be investigated. Her account was accurate but incurred the anger of her grandparents and she therefore resented the intervention. The issue was raised in the group and provided an opportunity for all the children to hear the social workers' views and to witness conflict being dealt with in a constructive way.

The process

In planning the group, the workers took into consideration that they were running a family and not a strangers group. There were well established patterns of communication and behaviour as well as existing norms, beliefs and values. The workers agreed on a non directive approach, to model listening skills and encourage the young people to put difficult thoughts and feelings into words. It was also thought important to ensure and demonstrate that feelings were accepted and respected and to reflect what was happening in the hope that the young people would learn about the consequences of their interaction. Enhancing their understanding of themselves as individuals and of one another would, it was hoped, enable them to be supportive towards one another.

Since both workers are women, and more than anything the young people wanted a mother, there was the possibility of being drawn into that role. In fact the black worker was asked by Sandra to undertake returning a faulty coat and to write a note protecting her from detentions. She responded by encouraging her to take responsibility for sorting out her difficulties either independently or with the help of the carers. Both workers were acutely aware of the young people's pain and acknowledged to one another feelings of powerlessness to meet the children's needs. It was essential to keep professional boundaries clear at the same time as demonstrating empathy. Since Amy in particular was dominant and critical it was also necessary to resist giving parent messages such as advocating that the older children should be kind to the younger.

Neutrality in the sense that the worker sided with no individual was especially important given the intensity of rivalry and competitiveness which was immediately apparent. There was also the fact that Michelle had received individual counselling and initially made an attempt at establishing a different status for herself in the group. She suggested that the black worker was shown the room where she received counselling and the art work she had done. Giving her a different status in the group could have exacerbated her role as scapegoat as well as diminishing the credibility of the workers with the other young people. Michelle was told that the black worker could be shown the room and her work at a time when the group was not meeting.

In the first session, in order to engage Leon, he was asked about his life in Jamaica. Amy encouraged him to tell a story of stealing sweets which resulted in a beating from his grandmother. The workers asked whether he had been beaten with a hand, a stick or belt. This led to the children describing beatings from various family members, including their mother, who hit them with a 'feather touch' because she could not bear to hurt them. They cried when she was angry but fought back tears when beaten by their father who used a slipper. They also gave a matter of fact account, interspersed with inappropriate laughter, of faeces being smeared on their faces by their oldest cousin. The feelings underlying the jollity were commented on and accepted. Physical abuse seemed to hold little significance, however, in comparison with the emotional abuse of being ignored and not valued. Leon had been made to stand naked except for his underpants by the oldest cousin and the girls described their anguish in being unable to protect him from this humiliation. They told their aunt who refused to intervene.

It was established that the young people had spoken neither to one another nor to anyone else about their distress. During counselling, Michelle had mentioned being scapegoated in the family and this had been raised with her aunt. With hindsight, too little was known of the children's predicament. There are problems for children trapped in difficult family relationships both in terms of their ability to judge whether abusing or critical adults have right on their side and how to seek help without risking further problems. Their aunt Mary had told the Social Services Department that she was able to accept the children's grief and speak about their mother.

This was not the children's perception but there was no-one they trusted to talk to about their thoughts and feelings. Groupwork with the siblings as well as individual counselling at an earlier stage might have protected them from some of their pain and isolation.

In the second session, the suggestion of making a geneogram as a focus of common interest was welcomed. Amy volunteered to write it and began with her mother's family. She sought information about names and spellings from the others but her sisters and brothers attention quickly waned. Sandra began to write her own version which the children pointed out derisively did not include their mother or them. 'Why should it, they're not here any more', she replied. The workers commented that the children were all still here. Sandra shrugged, reflecting isolation and loneliness and the failure of the family to reach out to or be supportive of one another. Amy was protective of the geneogram, supervising its being kept at the end of the session. She clearly valued being linked by family relationships.

Another example of this arose while Leon and Michelle were waiting for their sisters at the third session. Leon wrote a list of the family and their birthdays. He included the workers. Michelle said it wasn't fair that she was the only child with a birthday not in September, giving voice to her feeling of being the 'outsider'. Amy and Sandra were interested in the list when they arrived and spoke about past birthdays.

Rivalry about who had had /was having the worst time was a theme. As part of piecing together family history and involving them all, each member of the group was asked to list his/her moves. Leon was confident his list was longest and Sandra was shouted down for adding holiday visits to hers. When Leon was distressed by moving to a long term children's home, the workers attempted to elicit his sister's support. Michelle's reaction was that he was lucky, she would much prefer to live in a children's home than with her grandparents. Amy and Sandra said nothing and Leon was silent and sad.

Roles were adopted and maintained from the first session. Klein (1972) suggests that group members create structures which feel safe and facilitate communication. Amy, as the eldest, was the accepted leader. The group functioned hierarchically with information being given mainly by Amy and Sandra. The two younger members were rarely, and only by the direct intervention of the workers, allowed to provide information. In the first session, Amy also established the group norm of saying how difficult their lives were. She described attempting suicide at the age of 14 and planning to kill her aunt Mary with poison stolen from school. There was a powerful sense of desperation in her undramatised description of her feelings. Her siblings listened in silence to this new information, only questioning which chemical had been thought to be poisonous. The workers responded by acknowledging how acutely unhappy Amy must have been and commenting that everyone in the group seemed to feel for her.

Sandra was Amy's ally in creating an older/younger split. They functioned as a pair but denied that they were emotionally close. Speaking about their life before their father's death, they said they were very close until Amy was sent to her grandparents, but never re-established that relationship. When Amy moved into independent living accommodation, she made little effort to keep in touch with Sandra. We wondered if the younger children had hopes of Amy filling a mother role. Outside the group she spoke of feeling a responsibility to make a home, especially for Leon. Amy and Sandra were always the instigators of teasing and criticism: their brother and sister reacted angrily or defensively but they rarely initiated negative comments. It was evident that they felt hurt and put down. Their sisters implied that their remarks were made in fun but the workers suggested that the consequences might be hurtful.

Leon was sometimes the clown but at other times angry about the deflection of serious conversation by the use of teasing and jokes. He was also adept at changing the subject when the topic was painful or he felt excluded. While being confident in expressing anger about current events, he had difficulty speaking about past pain. He was asked about the death of his grandfather in Jamaica but allowed his sisters to describe what had happened. The workers said it must have been very difficult for him to lose his grandfather as well as his mother and wondered how he had managed such painful feelings. Leon said simply that 'it was too much', he had not been able to think about it. The workers commented that sometimes there is too much sorrow to be able to manage it all.

Michelle was the scapegoat of the family group and it was necessary to be active in protecting her. She lounged in her chair and joined in the giggles but said little spontaneously. Any contributions were likely to result in a put down by her sisters. Both Leon and Michelle at times stormed out of the room. One of the workers ensured their safety, acknowledged their hurt, stated their importance to the group and requested their return. Given choice, they always came back.

The workers knowledge of the young people as individuals was that they were all articulate and interested in talking about feelings and events. They were thoughtful, wished to be considerate and were generally moderate in their expressions of anger. In the group, feelings of anger, powerlessness, anxiety and sadness were used competitively. They seemed unable to relate to one anothers' feelings, to make supportive or positive comments, but to be overwhelmed by their individual need to be heard. Teasing and giggling were used, Sandra acknowledged, 'so that we don't get too got down by everything' and as a way of sabotaging contributions made by Leon and Michelle. Much of the teasing was about hairstyles and clothing and seemed innocent except that it was evidently an assault on self esteem. The workers commented that laughter and jokes seemed to be a way of hiding pain and Sandra added 'and signs', highlighting the need to be attentive to non verbal language.

Douglas (1976) suggests three reasons for conflict. It may be a way of seeking status, a way of avoiding a task which seems too difficult or group members may find themselves in conflict between the demands of the group and families or peer groups. The function of the behaviour in this group appeared to be related to the first two premises. Amy and Sandra's teasing maintained their dominant position. All of the young people at times used jokes and criticism to change the subject when the discussion became too painful. Sandra, for example, during a discussion about the difficulties of life at their aunt Mary's, described how taking the family dog for a walk was used as an excuse to escape from the house. One day it was forgotten and left behind in the park!

As a way of mitigating the dominance of the older girls, the same questions were at times asked of each group member. One of these questions was, 'Are the people you are living with interested in your thoughts and feelings?' Amy and Sandra both said that they had no idea whether their aunt was interested, but they never spoke to her about thoughts and feelings. Leon declared that no one knew him at the children's home and Michelle said her grandparents would not be interested in what she thought. It was clear that the concept of sharing thoughts and feelings was familiar and desired. When asked about their relationship with their mother, they said that she was always willing to listen and was interested in the events in their lives. The workers commented that all of them felt no one listened to them and perhaps since it was something they all wanted, they could listen to one another.

There were feelings and views which were acknowledged as being held in common. They all regarded the loss of their mother as a catastrophe and given three wishes all wanted her alive as their only wish. All idealised her, they argued fiercely about who was most like her. Since her death, they agreed, they had not felt important to anyone nor had they felt they belonged anywhere. They all sought a family to replicate what they had lost. Amy had, perhaps, some understanding that what she sought did not exist when she said that she had thought both her aunts' households were attractive until she lived in them.

Arguments between adults upset all the young people and they often felt responsible for them even if there were no logical reason to do so. We wondered if this related to the reported violent personality of their father. None of them spoke of regretting his death.

It was important to them all to have been 'special' to their mother. Sandra sadly told how Amy was special because she was the first child born after the miscarriage of twins; Leon was special as the only son and because he was talented at maths; Michelle was their mother's favourite. Sandra felt she had never been special. Within her comment was the pain of having lost the possibility of achieving being special as the relationship was frozen at the time of her mother's death with no possibility of development or change. The workers reflected back her feelings and encouraged her to expand on them. Her expression of pain brought a respectful silence. We noted a difference between the older and younger children in that the older pair were more reflective about the past and the consequences of their mother's death while the younger two were more concerned with their present difficulties and pain.

They all agreed on the importance of being respected and valued. Amy told how her aunt would arrive home from work and not acknowledge her presence. Leon recounted an incident in school when a teacher talked in front of other pupils about his 'private business'. The workers responded to opportunities for enhancing the young people's sense of self worth, for validating their rights to be heard, valued and respected by making supportive comments. Amy and Sandra brought a girl cousin to the third session. They accepted without argument that their cousin could not be included in the group meeting but boasted to her about the drink and biscuits which were provided. This could have been interpreted as seeking to be seen as special but no comment was made since at the time it did not seem appropriate.

Related to feeling not valued was their assertion that no one listened to their views and feelings. This statement was mildly questioned by the black worker and it was grudgingly conceded that she listened 'a bit' because she was responding to Amy's request for independent living. All the young people felt trapped and powerless and at times treated like objects. In the first session, Leon complained that he had not been told about the precise arrangements for the group. His feelings of anger were accepted as reasonable and the suggestion made that it might have reminded him of past experiences when he felt moved about like a parcel. He nodded vigorously. Amy saw independent living as taking control over her life and maybe creating a family of her choice with the addition of a baby.

Michelle was the only member of the family who had received individual counselling. She had described being her mother's favourite child and how she felt this made her loss even more acute. Her relationships with her sisters and brother were portrayed as tenuous and hostile. The group interaction fully supported her view. Michelle's position as favourite had engendered deeply felt resentment and jealousy which was perhaps all the more significant because their mother was dead. There had been and would be no opportunity to topple Michelle from her envied perch. Death left the issue of favourite child forever unresolved. As well as relationship difficulties which make loss more difficult, there is the sorrow for young people that they never really knew their parents because they were too young at the time of death to know them by adult standards.

Amy and Sandra were open about their resentment. The hypothesis was made that their mother may have thought Michelle would be her last baby and that she would not live to see her grow up. Amy conceded that it was not Michelle's fault that she was the favourite, that it wasn't fair of them to hate her for it, but that made no difference to their feelings. Intellectual understanding or insight does not necessarily dispel emotional reactions. The workers asked Michelle if it was helpful for her to hear her sister say that it was not her fault they felt such anger towards her. She shrugged her shoulders.

On some occasions when teased or criticised, Michelle cried. This invariably enraged her sisters. They were asked about their attitude to tears and said crying was 'good, it helped you let things out', but it shouldn't be used to try and get your own way. Michelle's' tears, it seemed, triggered memories of being blamed by their mother for upsetting Michelle or seeing her being given anything she wanted. The comment was made that Amy and Sandra seemed to enjoy putting their brother and sister down. Amy agreed that as a family, they liked getting one another into trouble. Sandra created a feeling of unity in the group by describing the angelic status of their youngest cousin at their aunt Mary's. It was agreed he could do no wrong and enjoyed getting them all into trouble. This led to a discussion about the joy of having 'holds' over one another, it gave them a feeling of power. Amy on this occasion drew Michelle into the group by telling her that she had a 'hold' over Sandra. At other times, the group exposed feelings of raw insecurity, of feeling defended and protected by no-one.

All the young people had great difficulty speaking positively to one another. Amy, for example, had said in Leon's absence that she felt for his situation in the children's home and regarded him as her top priority in making a home. This conversation was recounted to Leon. Initially his response was offhand but a few minutes later he asked Amy if she would spend some time with him at the children's home after the group meeting. She said she was too busy and suggested he visit her. Leon was clearly hurt and advanced upon her grinning but put his scarf, tightly, around her neck. The workers intervened, saying no-one must be physically threatened and commented that maybe Leon was upset because it was important to have visits from your family when you were in a children's home. Leon responded with a loud 'Yes'.

Paying attention to language and its meaning for the young people as well as body language was important. Amy moved into independent living, leaving Sandra at their aunts. Sandra said it was 'boring' without her sister and needed encouragement to describe her feelings as missing Amy. She also described 'chatting', her way of describing group interaction, as 'boring'. When asked to explain what she meant by 'boring' she said 'uncomfortable'. The workers tried to be sensitive when to allow the subject to be changed because it was too painful either for an individual or the group to pursue at that time.

Either directly or disguised by grins and banter, much pain and anger was expressed in the group. The young people gave little impression of liking or valuing one another when they were together, yet there was a strong feeling of connection between them. Outside the group they were supportive of one another; Amy, who constantly scapegoated Michelle lent her her precious trainers. Michelle, when asked whom she would talk to if she had a problem, unhesitatingly said 'Amy'. Leon and Michelle had not previously admitted to being friends, but Leon took his sister to the cinema on her birthday and Michelle began to visit him at his childrens home. All the children wished the group to continue, Leon with the reservations that it must be taken seriously and everyone must attend. Given the choice of an outing, the children were agreed that they wished to go together to visit their mother's grave. The workers were left in no doubt of the young people's importance to one another and that they valued an opportunity to put their thoughts and feelings into words. At the end of the initial agreement, the young people decided that the group would continue to meet fortnightly for an indefinite period.

My one requirement: that you stay with me.
I want to hear you, grumble as you may.
If you were deaf I'd need what you might say
If you were dumb I'd need what you might see.

If you were blind I'd want you in my sight
For you're the sentry posted at my side:
We're hardly half way through our lengthy ride
Remember we're surrounded yet by night.

You're 'let me lick my wounds' is no excuse now.
You're 'anywhere' (not here) is no defence
There'll be relief for you, but no release now.

You know whoever's needed can't go free
And you are needed urgently by me
I speak of me when us would make more sense.

Brecht in Willett, J. and Manheim, R. (1956)

References

Douglas, T. (1976) *Group Work*. Practice. London: Tavistock.

Fahlberg, V. (1991) *A Child's Journey Through Placement*. Indianapolis: Perspectives Press.

Jewett, C. (1982) *Helping Children With Separation And Loss*. London: BAAF.

Klein, A. (1972) *Effective Groupwork*. New York: Association Press.

McFarlane, A. (1987) 'Family functioning and overprotection following a natural disaster', *Psychological Medicine*, 17.

Polombo, J. (1978) *Parent Loss and Childhood Bereavement*. Paper presented at conference on Children and Death, University of Chicago, 17-19 March 17-19, pp.727-738.

Willett, J. and Manheim, R. (1956) *Bertolt Brecht: Plays, Poetry and Prose: Poems Part Three.* London: Methuen.

Yule, W. and Gold, A. (1992) *Wise Before the Event: Coping With Crises In Schools.* Chichester: Wiley.

A comparative study of four family bereavement groups.

Estelle Hopmeyer and Annette Werk

This practice report will discuss the results of a comparative study of four bereavement groups currently meeting in Montreal, Canada. These groups serve four different populations who have experienced the death of a family member. The populations are those bereaved through cancer, suicide, loss of a young child by cancer, and loss of a husband. The treatment discussed in this paper is offered through self-help / support groups, where those who have been bereaved help each other cope with this devastating experience. The goals of the study were: first, to evaluate and subsequently improve the group service offered to these bereaved populations and second to use the comparative data on the structural elements to develop a training manual for professional and peer facilitators.

Bereavement

While bereavement, the state of having suffered a loss, is a natural part of life, it is important for social work professionals to understand how grief affects people. Rando (1988) has very succinctly described the multi-dimensional experiences of grief. She has divided these reactions into three groups: the psychological, the social and the physical. The psychological, or the feelings, thoughts and emotions, can vary in terms of range and intensity and can include the following: anxiety, anger, fear, guilt, relief, sadness, depression, yearning, and search for meaning. The social or behavioural can be experienced as a lack of concentration, lack or energy, an inability to sustain relationships or to nurture. The physical reactions can also vary but might include eating or sleeping disorders, heart palpitations, sickness or mortality including suicide.

The special circumstances of a death can also have an effect on the grief process. A sudden, or unanticipated death, often violent as in the case of suicide, has significant impact. Feelings that the death was preventable is another critical variable. The 'what ifs' and 'if onlys' are often part of the aftermath of a suicide, or the death of a child. When the death occurs out of the natural order as in the case

Groupwork Vol. 6(2), 1993, pp.107-121

of a child's death, it has important significance for the resolution of grief. Social factors and social recognition of the death also need to be considered. There is a stigma attached to a suicide that has created a group of disenfranchised mourners (Doka, 1989). Support systems are not readily available to these populations.

Grief work and groupwork.

Lindeman (1965), Rando (1988), and Worden (1991) have helped us to appreciate the normalcy of grief reactions and the need to do 'grief work'. Parkes (1972) has identified three forms of service that could be beneficial for those suffering from uncomplicated or normal grief: professional counselling, help from a volunteer trained by a professional, and peer support from other bereaved persons.

The treatment discussed in this paper is offered through self help/ support groups, where those who have been bereaved help each other to cope with this devastating experience. During the grieving process, feelings of isolation and alienation frequently develop because the bereaved person feels that others cannot understand his/her loss. Further, existing relationships seem to emphasise this emptiness and loss. For example, married friends painfully remind the widowed of their new status; family gatherings emphasise the absence of the child who is no longer alive. The bereaved often discontinue activities, avoid familiar places and people, and displace their anger onto others, reinforcing their isolation.

Self-help/support groups create a support system for the bereaved. The literature (Gottlieb, 1985, 1988; Schwartz-Borden, 1986; Videka-Sherman and Lieberman, 1985) suggests that these groups can:

1. help develop and strengthen informal support for the bereaved;
2. help participants gain hope, receive new ideas on how to problem solve, receive information regarding other sources of help, improve skills related to social relationships, and become less lonely and isolated;
3. provide a sense of belonging, help develop feelings of fellowship and solidarity.

These benefits can be summarised as commonality, normalisation, solidarity, reciprocity and control.

While studies suggest that participation in self-help groups can facilitate the positive outcome of mourning there has been limited systematic study of the groups themselves. Further, no comparative studies were found which could offer insight into the effectiveness of groups based on their structural elements, i.e. setting or auspice, leadership, membership, programme content or duration. Gottlieb (1988) maintains that to maximise the beneficial aspects of the groups there is an urgent need for comparative studies that systematically vary the structured components.

This research, then, had several purposes. The first was to evaluate and subsequently improve the group service offered to these bereaved populations. The second goal was to use the comparative data on the structural elements to develop a training manual for professional and peer facilitators. Finally, the researchers plan to use the data for theory building with specific application to teaching in two main curriculum areas: social work practice with groups and social work practice with the bereaved.

The study

Members who attended one of the four groups over a period of several years were mailed an adapted version of the social support network questionnaire designed by Dr. Shelley Taylor at UCLA (1990).

The respondents were asked to describe their social network, to identify their reasons for attending the group, to indicate their satisfaction/dissatisfaction with their group experience and to identify their ideal group format. The questionnaire also provided space for comments and an overall evaluation of their experience.

The sample consisted of 102 respondents. The breakdown according to specific group and by gender can be seen in Table 1. The gender issue will be discussed in the section on membership.

Table 1
Demographics

Group	Females	Males	Unstated	Total
Widows	28			28
FSOS	37	5		42
Hope and Cope	15	8	2	25
Parents	5	2		7
Total	**85**	**15**	**2**	**102**

Description of the individual groups

Hope and Cope Bereavement Support Group

A support group based on the self-help model for family members (excluding parents) who have been bereaved by cancer. The group is close-ended after the second session and meets for six to eight sessions by-weekly. Members are pre-screened by a social worker. Leadership is by two peer facilitators assisted by a professional social worker. Educational material is presented regularly.

Bereaved Parents Support Group
A support group based on the self-help model for bereaved parents whose children have died of cancer. The group is closed, meeting every three weeks. Members are pre-screened by the social worker who facilitates the group with the assistance of a peer facilitator.

Family Survivors of Suicide
A self-help group for family members who have lost a relative to suicide. The group is open-ended, meeting twice monthly at the School of Social Work. Notices placed in the local newspaper prompt self-referrals while others may be referred by social agencies or the clergy. Members are not pre-screened. Group management and facilitation is by the members. A professional social worker is consultant to the group and frequently attends meetings by members' request.

Widow to Widow Programme
A support group for newly widowed women. The group is close-ended meeting weekly for eight to ten sessions. Each group is co-led by a widow peer facilitator and a professional. Educational material is presented regularly.

The groups compared

The four bereavement groups differ from each other in terms of setting, structure, format and leadership. As can be seen in Table 2, the Family Survivors of Suicide group (FSOS) is the only self-help group that is open and continuous, and is led by a peer facilitator. The other three groups are similar in terms of leadership, structure and format. These structural elements have impacted on the groups in a number of significant ways.

Setting/auspice

Setting and/or auspice has an impact on the groups in terms of accessibility, continuity, autonomy, leadership and symbolic meaning. These factors need to be seriously considered when selecting the setting for the group. The auspice has to be committed to group service in order to ensure adequate resources and support to the leader(s).

Table 2
Group profile

	Widows	FSOS	Hope and Cope	Childhood Cancer
Location:	Community agency	University	Secondary building of Hospital	Hospital
Structure:	Closed group Pre-determined number of meetings	Open-ended Continuous	Closed group Pre-determined number of meetings	Originally open/ now closed, pre-determined number of meetings
Format:	Themes Open discussion	Open discussion	Themes Open discussion	Open discussion
Leadership:	Professional/ peer co-facilitators	Peer facilitator/ professional consultant	Professional/ peer co-facilitators	Professional/ peer co-facilitators
Membership:	Women who have lost husbands	Any family member	Family member (no parents who have lost children)	Parents

The university setting of FSOS has provided for flexibility and autonomy. For example, the group was able to begin meeting just six weeks after the initial telephone contact between a bereaved mother whose daughter had committed suicide and the professional consultant. The bereavement group for childhood cancer, that meets in a hospital, took over six months to get started as it had to gain approval through many bureaucratic channels. The setting also had an impact on the type of group structure and leadership of these two groups. FSOS began as a self-help group under membership control while the hospital expected its bereavement group to follow a treatment format which included a professional leader.

It should be noted that the majority of group members from all four groups expressed satisfaction with the location of their groups. When asked about what an 'ideal' location for her group would be, one member of the widow to widow group identified a health spa.

Leadership

While the leadership format differed from group to group, most members liked their leaders whom they identified as 'warm, caring and available'.

The three groups with co-leaders (peer and professional) varied somewhat in terms of recruitment and training. In the bereavement group for childhood cancer (Parents) one member evolved into the role of co-facilitator. Volunteer co-leaders also emerged in the Widow to Widow Programme. The Hope and Cope Programme has the most structured recruitment and training of peer facilitators. They meet regularly with the professional before and after each meeting, and also participate in monthly meetings for volunteers. Members of these three groups noted in their responses that they valued the model of co-leadership of professional and volunteer. They identified, for example, the need for a professional leader to keep the group on track and to provide reassurance, while the peer facilitator was seen as serving as an important role model who provided hope for the future. As one parent remarked: 'The peer facilitator showed us that in time we too will be able to cope better and that eventually our lives will return to a semblance of order'.

The FSOS group differs significantly in the area of leadership. Members have always assumed the facilitator role, with the consultant present, but not participating, during the formal part of the meetings. The professional only intervenes when a member is perceived to be at risk. Despite this very limited role, the members value the presence of the professional as a resource person who has the skills to deal with a crisis.

Format

Three groups have adopted the support group format which includes a pre-determined number of meetings, and an expectation of attendance. Hope and Cope and the Widows groups also have pre-selected themes for each meeting. Hope and Cope respondents indicted that they would have liked their group to continue for a longer period. In contrast, the Widow to Widow Programme provides a full range of services for the graduates of its support group such as monthly social programmes and trips.

As the FSOS group is open-ended and continuous, without pre group interviews, members schedule their own entry and exit and may present unexpected challenges. In the five years that this group has been meeting the group has been run very competently by a core group with the help of the professional consultant. To provide continuity, the challenge facing the group now is to continue to expand the core to ensure the viability of the group as a member run self-help group.

Several FSOS respondents suggested the importance of establishing a more formal support system between meetings. They noted that people who go home alone to an empty house need someone to call or to call them after the very difficult work that takes place at the meetings. All attendees who request it can receive a bi-annual newsletter. One former member commented, 'I moved away from Montreal shortly after I attended one meeting so I am not familiar enough with the group to offer suggestions. I would like to thank you for the tremendous support that I felt the time I did attend. I really appreciated receiving the information you have sent me in the Newsletter and in some weird way have felt I was being supported and 'remembered' from afar and it really helped'.

Membership

The majority of respondents indicated a desire for groups which were homogeneous to problem but heterogeneous in terms of relationship to the person who died and to length of time since bereavement. This feeling of the need for homogeneity of problem was noted by members attending FSOS who had previously attended other groups for bereaved parents like Compassionate Friends. They stated emphatically that they could not disclose to the other parents that their child had taken his/her own life.

The strength gained by attended a group with others who have suffered the same experience was pointed out by a Hope and Cope respondent who said:

> 'You learn that you are not alone in your grief. You can share the pain, discuss, cry and help each other. This releases the guilt. You can ask questions and realise that there are no answers'. A FSOS member stated 'We can see that those whose loved one spoke about suicide a lot could no more prevent it than those for whom the suicide was out of the blue. All kinds of people kill themselves and all kinds of people are left behind'.

The usual criteria for group participation and/or exclusion are also relevant for these groups, e.g. people with pathological grief reactions need to be excluded and referred elsewhere for individual treatment.

Gender

While the majority of group participants were female (see Table 2), some men do attend these groups and their responses to several questions highlighted some significant gender differences. This was particularly evident in the question related to allotment of group time to specific issues (see Table 8). When asked to indicate their choice, men select items related to problem solving, coping and information gathering. Women select items related to sharing and feelings and rated information on bereavement very low on the scale. Responses to other questions, as well as professional observation, suggest that once in the groups gender is no longer an issue. A recent study by Dr Fred Tudiver of the Sunnybrook Health Science Centre in Toronto, Canada, discusses the success of a bereavement group for widowers. The group proved to be very valuable in helping the men develop coping strategies to deal with the death of a spouse.

Professionals need to be sensitive to how men/women perceive their needs and to utilise this knowledge in the pre-group phase of group publicity, membership selection and recruitment. It is very important that efforts be made to recruit male members as it appears that they are not being given the same opportunity to deal with their bereavement. This is particularly significant in the case of the death of a child from cancer or by suicide. The participation of both parents in a bereavement group will assist the couple in helping each other to cope with their loss, and may well help to sustain and strengthen the marriage during this vulnerable period.

Results: comparative data

The results suggest that all members who completed the questionnaire felt satisfied with their bereavement groups. Their responses to a series of questions about their vision of an 'Ideal' group indicated that they thought their groups were 'ideal'. They made frequent mention of the excellent quality of their group leaders who they felt were empathic, knowledgeable and helpful.

There were however, some specific items on which we would like to focus.

Reciprocity

'I myself feel better when I am helping someone else...usually a person whose loss is more recent than my own, although not always.' This statement underscores the importance of reciprocity in these groups. Interestingly, although the results of the questionnaire indicate that 55 per cent of all respondents felt that they received more than they contributed to the group, 40 per cent felt they received and gave equally, while 5 per cent indicated that they had received less from the group than they had contributed. This suggests that members may not realise when they are being helpful to others, or that the format does not consciously build in opportunities for reciprocity. Professional and peer facilitators need to emphasise that this model builds mutuality. They should reinforce helpful interventions by group members as this leads to restored self esteem and a sense of worth.

Involvement

In response to the question regarding their involvement in the group, it was interesting to note that a much higher percentage of Widows indicated great involvement. Hope and Cope members indicated that they were moderately involved, while less than 50 per cent of Family Survivors indicated great or moderate group involvement. This may well be related to the open ended, ongoing nature of the FSOS group as compared to the closed, specific number of sessions of the three other groups.

Reasons for joining

We ranked the reasons for joining their bereavement group from 1 to 13 for each of the four participating groups (see Table 3).

Table 4 indicates the three *most important* reasons selected for each group. You can see the similarity in the responses. Both Family Survivors and Hope and Cope members had the same three reasons, but in different rank order. The Parents group ranked three of the items equally important. These included two of the three chosen by the other two groups. The Widows indicated that their most important reason for joining a bereavement group was to make new friends. This was consistent with their responses to many of the other questions. Companionship appears to be much more important to the Widows than to any other group members.

We have also ranked the least important reasons for joining a bereavement group and these can be seen in Table 5.

Most valuable things gained

This was a write in question, but we tabulated the qualitative responses and they fell into the following categories (see Table 6).

Table 3
Importance of various reasons for attending bereavement groups

Reasons for attending	Widows		Family Survivors of Suicide		Hope and Cope		Parents	
	a	*b*	*a*	*b*	*a*	*b*	*a*	*b*
Gain information	43	5	36	8	48	5	0	12
Share experience	64	2	79	1	72	1	86	1
Satisfy curiosity	25	10	7	11	8	12	0	12
Share what I learned	68	1	40	6	44	6	86	1
I was depressed	36	8	45	4	40	7	14	8
Gain new coping skills	43	5	71	3	68	2	86	1
I was desperate	21	11	31	9	24	8	29	6
Gain comfort and reassurance	46	4	76	2	64	3	71	4
For advice	39	7	45	4	56	4	29	6
To help others	36	8	29	10	20	9	43	5
For something to do	18	12	2	13	4	13	14	8
No-one else to turn to	14	13	40	6	16	11	14	8
Make new friends	61	3	7	11	20	9	14	8

a = % 'Very important' b = Rank

Table 4
Three most important reasons for joining bereavement groups

Widows	Family Survivors of Suicide	Hope and Cope	Parents
To share with others what I learned	To share similar experiences	To share similar experiences	To share similar experiences
To share similar experiences	Gain comfort and reassurance	To learn new skills for coping	To learn new skills for coping
To make new friends	To learn new skills for coping	Gain comfort and reassurance	To share with others what I learned

Table 5
Least important reasons for joining bereavement group

Widows	Family Survivors of Suicide	Hope and Cope	Parents
No-one else to turn to	For something to do	For something to do	To satisfy my curiosity
For something to do	To make new friends	To satisfy my curiosity	To gain information
I was desperate	To satisfy my curiosity	No-one else to turn to	

Table 6
Six most valuable things gained from group

Widows	Survivors of Suicide	Hope and Cope	Parents
Made new friends	Not alone	Place to vent feelings	Not alone
Gained confidence	Not the only one	Chance to talk	Understood and supported
Shared with others	Someone understands	Opportunity to to share my grief	Share with others who understand
Gained hope	Shared my grief	Comfort not to be alone	Help each other
Gained strength and purpose	Not alone in my pain	Sharing, support	There is no right or wrong way to cope
Learned I can have a normal life	Learned I am not a bad person; others have similar tragedies	Similar to others	There is hope

Each of these responses was repeated a number of times. It is interesting to note that although all members felt that they benefited from the opportunity to share with others, the Family Survivors and the Parents who had lost a child repeatedly responded ‘important not to be alone’ while Hope and Cope members and Widows worded this as sharing and supporting others. This could be related to the fact that Family Survivors of Suicide are a stigmatised group in our society, and many people seem to have difficulty knowing how to respond to a parent who has just lost a young child.

Two other questions

Two further questions provided interesting data. The question which asked how uncomfortable or annoyed members felt when others talked too much, were extremely negative, were too dependent, gave advice or kept bringing up the same issues, showed that respondents were very accepting of each other, as none of these issues seemed very upsetting to any of the group members. The responses which were mentioned most frequently as being upsetting were when members talked too much or were extremely negative. Yet even these two items were mentioned by only a small minority. The male group members were not at all upset by any of these issues (see Table 7).

Programme

When members were asked how much time should be devoted to specific items, their responses were particularly interesting when related to gender. The female respondents gave first place to 'sharing feelings and emotions' while this ranked tenth among male respondents who selected 'learning how others solve problems like mine' (see Table 8).

The impact of this difference has already been discussed in the section on gender, but it is particularly striking and should be taken seriously by all who wish to get men to join bereavement groups.

From the data collected in this study we can conclude that while there are many similarities across groups there are also some differences. Further research with other bereavement groups in other settings will surely add interesting data and help group organisers and leaders to tailor their groups to the needs of their members.

Implications for practice

Results from this study confirm that bereavement groups offer their members the opportunity to accomplish grief work in an atmosphere that is both supportive and encouraging. The groups create an informal support network which is available on an ongoing basis. Family and friends, the traditional source of support, are often unwilling or unable to remain available and accepting over a lengthy period of time. They tend to expect the bereaved to 'get over' their

Table 7
Reactions of the group members

How uncomfortable were you when someone in the group:	Widows		Family Survivors of Suicide		Hope and Cope		Parents of Kids with Cancer		Males		Females	
	a	*b*	*a*	*b*	*a*	*b*	*a*	*b*	*a*	*b*	*a*	*b*
Talked too much	29	1	12	1	8	1	0	3	0		18	1
Emotionally upset	21	4	7	2	8	1	14	2	0		13	3
Negative or pessimistic	29	1	2	5	8	1	29	1	0		15	2
Too dependent on others	11	5	0	6	0	4	0	3	0		4	6
Gave advice	11	5	5	3	0	4	0	3	0		6	5
Brought up same issues	25	3	5	3	0	4	0	3	0		11	4

a -= % A lot b = Rank

Table 8
Issues which group members think a lot of time should be devoted to

	Widows		Family Survivors of Suicide		Hope and Cope		Parents		Males		Females	
	a	*b*	*a*	*b*	*a*	*b*	*a*	*b*	*a*	*b*	*a*	*b*
Information on relaxation	11	10	7	10	12	10	0	10	7	9	9	10
Shared feelings and emotions	43	4	76	1	72	1	100	1	6	10	67	1
Specific problems	21	8	33	7	32	8	14	8	28	7	33	7
Source of companionship	57	1	33	7	40	6	29	7	45	5	20	9
Talk with others in similar situation	50	2	64	4	56	4	100	1	60	2	60	2
Information on means of coping	46	3	64	4	60	3	71	3	60	2	47	6
Give/receive a sense of being loved	29	7	55	6	36	7	71	3	44	6	53	5
Learn how others solve problems like mine	32	6	67	2	64	2	71	3	67	1	54	4
Offer advice	14	9	29	9	24	9	14	8	27	8	22	8
Offer reassurance	43	4	67	2	56	4	57	6	60	2	56	3

a -= % A lot b = Rank

loss and 'get on' with their lives. This can be particularly true for widows. Disenfranchised mourners, like survivors of suicide and parents who have lost a child need the validation and acceptance they receive from other group members. This sense of isolation was expressed by several respondents in their qualitative comments. For example, 'My parents and brother don't know that my son died by suicide. They all live in the US'.

Normalisation is an important process for bereaved people. Seeing others with similar reactions helps members to recognise that their responses are neither crazy nor unnatural. (Visual or aural hallucinations are not uncommon.) One person indicated that the group demystified the bereavement process and helped her to feel normal. An FSOS member explained that:

> In the group I felt a sense of acceptance, of being among others who understand and therefore don't expect more of me than I can do. Especially the reassurance that I am part of a diverse and normal group of people who have in common the loss of a loved one by suicide. The reassurance that I am still an OK person...not a pariah. Our common experience of helplessness before another's suicide allows me to believe that I am not to blame...none of us are and I can go on with my life.

Another significant benefit of these groups was to assist members to gain a sense of control over their lives by developing coping strategies:

> I make a commitment to myself to get better, to learn more. I make a commitment to living a fuller life. If I didn't have this group where would I go? I would be stumbling around isolated.

Clearly, group members benefit through sharing experiences in a warm and accepting atmosphere which provides hope for their future. The research provides direction to practitioners and teachers to ensure the maximisation of these benefits.

Acknowledgements
The authors would like to acknowledge the financial support of the McGill Centre for Applied Family Studies. Thanks are also due to Kenneth Werk for his analysis of the data as well as his technical advice and expertise. A final thank-you to Cheh Cho, Trudi Friedman, Lorie Greenwood, Maureen McCrory and the members of their groups who so willingly participated in this research study.

References

Doka, K. (1989) *Disenfranchised Grief: Recognizing Hidden Survivors*. Massachussets: Lexington Books.

Gottleib B.H. (ed) (1985) 'Social support and the study of personal relationships', *Journal of Social and Personal Relationships*, 2, pp.351-375.

Gottleib, B.H. (ed.) (1988) *Marshalling Social Support: Format, Processes and Effects*. California: Sage Publications Ltd.

Irizarry C. (1981) 'Group services: a primary mode of hospital Social service delivery' in Goroff, N. (ed.) *Reaping from the Field from Practice to Principle*. Itebrun CT: Practitioner's Press.

Lindemann E. (1965) 'Symptomatology and management of acute grief' in Parad, H.J. (ed.) *Crisis Intervention*. New York: Family Service Association of America.

Parkes, M. (1972) *Bereavement Studies of Grief in Adult Life*. England: Tavistock Press.

Rando, T.A., (ed.) (1986) *Parental Loss of a Child*. Champaign, Ill. Research Press.

Rando, T.A. (1988) *How to go on Living When Someone You Love Dies*. Massachussets: Lexingham Books.

Schwartz-Borden, Gwen (1986). Grief work: prevention and intervention, *Social Casework: The Journal of Contemporary Social Work*, 65, pp.499-505.

Schiff, H.S. (1977) *The Bereaved Parent*. New York: Crown Publisher.

Taylor, S.E. (1990) *The Social Support Project Questionnaire*. Los Angeles, CA: Franz Hall/UCLA.

Videka-Sherman, L. and Lieberman, M. (1985) 'Effects of self-help groups and psycho-therapy after a child dies: the limits of recovery', *American Journal of Orthopsychiatry*, 55, pp.70-82.

Worden (1991) *Grief Counselling and Grief Therapy: A Handbook for the Mental Health Practitioner*. New York: Springer Publishing.

AN ASIAN MOTHERS' GROUP

LYNNE MUIR AND HARDEV NOTTA

This paper describes the setting up and running of a support group for Asian mothers in a children's hospice. All the mothers have one or more terminally ill children. A discussion on some of the issues arising from the group concludes this article.

Let me not pray to be sheltered from
dangers but to be fearless in facing them.
Let me not beg for the stilling of
my pains but for the heart to conquer it.
Let me not look for allies in life's
battlefield but to my own strength.
Let me not crave in anxious fear to
be saved but hope for the patience to
win my freedom.
Grant me that I may not be a
coward, feeling your mercy in my
success alone; but let me find the grasp
of your hand in my failure.

Rabindranath Tagore,
Fruit-Gathering

The decision to run a group is often fallen into, rather than being consciously chosen. So it was with the Asian mothers group. Five years ago a children's hospice was opened in Birmingham. The hospice provides a place where children who are chronically ill with a life-threatening illness can come for respite, emergency or terminal care. There is also limited accommodation for their families. After an initial period of settling, the issue of cultural separateness was raised by the only fulltime Asian care worker in the hospice. This worker identified a wider need in the hospice around support for Asian mothers. Bowlby says that one of the most painful experiences for any person is the loss of a loved one. It is both painful to experience and painful to observe (Bowlby, 1980). While many white workers think the Asian community is very self contained (Nathwani and Perkins, 1987), this is not always true. The experience of the

Groupwork Vol. 6(2), 1993, pp.122-132

imminent death of a child can be a harrowing situation for all parents but especially for parents in an unsupportive and isolated community. 'In all Asian traditions, the family is responsible for all the last offices, and they may wish to continue this in Britain' (Neuberger, 1987, p.20) but in the lead up time to the death the immediate family may welcome support from the community (Karseras and Hopkins, 1987). In addition, certain religious doctrines have associated disability with evil or 'a punishment for sin or misdeeds in a past life' (Fenton and Hughes, 1989, p.2) so some parents have to cope with the disapprobation of neighbours and extended family concurrent with adjusting to the situation of the terminally ill child. In the light of this situation it was decided by the hospice staff that a group meeting should be offered where families, but mothers in particular as the main carers, could give and receive support. However, while the careworker knew the families and spoke several Asian languages, she lacked groupwork knowledge. It was agreed, therefore, that she would co-work with a local groupworker.

While it was decided to use a systematic model of planning a group, the core philosophy was one explicated by Konopka who describes groupwork as a:

> ...basic grounding in a philosophy of respect for the individual, the skilful and gentle use of the positive aspects of the group process and the goal of enhancement of the individual's power and capacity (Konopka, 1990, p.14).

Each of the families in contact with the hospice have individual counselling and support available. What we wanted to offer was the collective strength available to group members through a positive group experience. Groupwork with white parents of chronically and terminally ill children has been extensively reported and is summarised by Engebrigtsen and Heap (1988). Groupwork with Asian parents is not so well recorded. While there are other Asian Support groups, such as the London group for mothers of disabled Asian children (Kelly, 1987) and the Asian Carers Federation at City Hospital in Nottingham, we could not find evidence of a similar bereavement group run solely for mothers.

Once the decision to run the group had been approved and agreed by the hospice team at the staff meeting, the two co-workers met to discuss and plan the group. Hodge (1985) stresses the importance of co-workers giving time to explore both group issues and personal values and approaches. Several meetings were held in which possible group goals and ways of working together were shared. Many group reports are of an anecdotal nature so we decided to plan and report this group through the various stages outlined on the following diagram developed by one of the workers.

Decision to run a group —Team meeting — Co-workers meet

↓

Define initial goals

↓

Referral of possible members

↓

Selection of members —Individual interviews

↓

Group objectives

↓

Group formation

↓

First group meeting

↓

Discuss and agree group objectives

↓

Group meetings

↓

Evaluation

Working to a model in this way focused the workers on the importance of planning, of setting initial goals and developing group objectives. The advantage of formulating specific group objectives at an early stage means they can be evaluated later in the life of the group. We wanted to avoid what Bloom (1975, p.177) has succinctly described as driving through a rear view mirror, we know where we have been but do not know where we are going.

Co-workers initial meetings

A major issue was language. Several of the mothers spoke no English and the Asian worker spoke Punjabi and Urdu. Should there be an interpreter for Hindi, Bengali and other possible languages? The advantages of clear interpretation were weighed against the disadvantages of additional workers in the group and it was decided to try to cope with mothers translating for each other. This has worked extremely well and although group discussions sometimes sound chaotic with several simultaneous translations going on, it has involved some mothers who are otherwise hesitant to participate. This has empowered the women by providing a situation where they have the resources and skills to help the group move forward. What should 'support' cover? We agreed we were not qualified to discuss medical information but would refer mothers to the appropriate source. All the parents know their child is dying but not all have told their children. Some of the adolescents know they are dying but the staff do not discuss it with them unless the parents agree. A number of the Asian mothers had independently expressed various concerns to the Asian worker. First, some women said that their extended families and particularly their husbands, refused to talk about the impending death of the child and the strain this put upon them of having to repress their feelings. Second, the wide range of beliefs, religious and otherwise, about death and the language used by the ill child and other members of the family to discuss the situation meant the mothers often felt they could not respond. Third, how are other children in the family helped to cope with a dying brother or sister and what pressures does this put on them? Lastly, the interest from neighbours can seem intrusive and ghoulish rather than supportive and helping - how can families deal with this? These were some of the initial concerns prompting interest in developing a group for Asian mothers.

Referrals

In going through the files at the hospice, 48 Asian families were identified. As this was too large a potential group membership, the arbitrary decision was made that the group would be for the 30 Asian mothers who had a terminally ill child living. It was agreed to also invite mothers who had already lost one child through death but who had another dying child. It was felt this latter group might facilitate discussion about death in the group as they had recently experienced it. An informal letter of invitation in Urdu was sent to interested mothers. This was followed by phone calls to the mothers, the aim of the group explained and an initial reaction as to interest, the best time to meet, child care and transport needs identified. Work with the co-ordinator of volunteers now began in earnest as she had agreed to arrange transport and child minding facilities for the meetings.

Selection of members

The two co-workers agreed on a policy of self-selection within their target group. It was recognised that this open policy could be problematic as a number of different beliefs, (Hinduism, Sikhism, Islam and Agnostic) and five languages (Punjabi, Bengali, Gujurati, Hindi and Urdu) were represented. The workers took the view that this mix could be dynamic and energising. The individual discussions with the mothers about their aims for the group also showed that the potential members covered a range of personality types. This reflected Bertcher and Maples (1977) view that group composition is enhanced by a mixture of people with different personalities and ways of behaving but with similar concerns, problems or life issues.

Pre-group planning and the first meetings

Before the first meeting of the group the two workers developed three general objectives. These were:

1. to meet with Asian mothers who have terminally ill children;
2. to provide a place where mothers can talk about their situation if they want to do so;
3. to initially plan a one-off meeting but to discuss with those who attend the possibility of regular meetings.

The administrative back-up, such as funds for postage, tea/coffee/ eats, room bookings, transport and child care, was arranged and a phone reminder given two days before the meeting to all the mothers who agreed to come. The two workers had a detailed plan of the morning - from greetings and name tags at the door, to clarification of languages spoken and who took responsibility for what to contingency plans if the mothers were all tongue-tied.

The meeting was held in a large committee room in the hospice and to a background of taped Asian music the volunteer drivers delivered the mothers. Out of the 12 who attended, two spoke no English, one spoke only English and most spoke or understood both Punjabi and English. It was therefore decided that a mixture of languages would be used with anyone acting as interpreter when required.

After a brief welcome it was suggested that mothers might introduce themselves and, if they wished, say something about their child. The floodgates were opened. The next two hours were taken up by mothers talking about their own situation, commenting upon the experiences of others and events often being described through tears. Several themes recurred: the load that other children in the family carry; the need to know how others cope and how circumstances shake religious faith.

Patterns for future meetings are often set in the first one. The workers were aware that many gatherings of people are not groupwork but really case work done in a group setting. Kurland and Salmon (1992) suggest that what distinguishes groupwork from casework in a group is an emphasis on the generalities of problems and situations and the accompanying similarity of feelings to which they give rise. It was on helping the mothers focus on the shared experiences that was the core of this first meeting. The only norm that was established was when the mothers were all talking at once and a worker suggested they take turns.

After a discussion on future meetings it was agreed by the mothers to meet monthly. This first meeting concluded with samosas and chutney with the group breaking into sub-groups of two or three for talk and showing a marked reluctance to leave when the volunteer drivers arrived.

The group then met monthly for the next year and specific objectives were developed for subsequent meetings from issues arising in the previous meetings. Some examples of these objectives were: to build links between the women to develop a support network; to practise several methods of relaxing; to raise the issue of male/female caseworkers and white/black caseworkers; to raise their expressed concerns about how a caring God could let their children die; to provide information on benefits and funding; to check out which mothers could provide their own transport and collect other mothers; to learn Indian dancing from each other and to mark the occasion of the one year anniversary of the group by using the occasion to publicise the work of the hospice and the existence of the group. The above objectives cover a period of one year and were used by the group members and the workers as a focus for different meetings. Each objective is stated in measurable terms and while a baseline was not established (so it was difficult to know at what stage each member was at for each objective), an informal exchange of existing knowledge or skills was done at each meeting and mothers often contributed their specialised input. For example, the speaker from the DSS on funds and benefits commented that she felt she had learned more from the group then she had given to them! Often planned objectives have been barely dealt with as current issues have arisen at the meeting. When this happens, at the end of the meeting the workers ask the mothers if they want to look at that objective another time or when the mothers are phoned about the date of the next meeting they are asked if they have any specific concerns for that meeting.

Evaluation

Evaluation is done in two main ways. First, through monitoring of the monthly objectives and second, through observation of behaviour. Some examples of planned objectives being met are the following. The question about the difficulty in maintaining faith when a child has died was a comment that frequently arose. As workers we explicitly raised this as a topic for discussion in the group on a number of occasions and it was an on-going theme. A second objective that was stated and then evaluated was providing information on benefits and the results of this are reported earlier in this paper. The second method of evaluating the usefulness of the group is that of observation and this has been reflected in several ways. The mothers now all take obvious care in their personal appearance for the group . This is a change from the beginning when mothers came in their everyday clothes. Now members dress up, wear jewellery and comment on one another's appearance. One member, whose child needs turning and moving every half hour through a 24 hour period. so he shares the conjugal bed, attends every meeting and says, 'it's very important to me as it is my time'. Another mother who is a single parent with three children, the oldest of whom is fifteen and in a wheelchair, says, 'it's the only time anyone looks after me. I can sit down and someone makes me a cup of tea. I feel cared for instead of always caring'. For the one year celebration of the group the mothers decided to sell hospice lapel badges as a fund raising event. With sales and donations they raised over £1,600 in a period of six weeks and presented this to a hospice trustee as a gift from the Asian mothers group. When surprise was expressed at the amount raised, several mothers said, 'it is a way of giving back something for the support received'. This also emphasises the value of being able to both give and receive through a group experience and strengthens both parties.

Issues arising from the group

Outside pressures on the group

New groups run the danger of becoming a fishbowl experience - everyone wants to visit and use creative reasons as to why they should. One social worker wanted to come with a Bangladeshi mother and an interpreter as no-one in the group spoke Bengali. One staff member wants experience of working with Asian clients. Several staff members have offered to explain their job in the hospice to the group. This puts a lot of pressure on the groupworker who is a staff member so the other groupworker (from the community) plays the hard role and refuses most visitors. A compromise was reached whereby some staff members have individually come into the end of a meeting and explained their role. Also, all staff were invited to share food at the December party and the first year celebration.

Effect of the group on families

While many of the women said their husbands refused to discuss the illness of their child or feelings attached to this, this was not always the case. Several of the mothers reported that their husbands wished they had a group. The use of symbolic talk and behaviour (Edmonds, 1988) has been used by others who find it difficult to express feelings. The husband of one pregnant member made and sent a bowl of jalebee (a sweet orange coloured confection) with her to every meeting. After the birth of the baby (who seemed to be healthy) a huge bowl of jalebee arrived and all the members ate some in celebration. Then it was discovered that the new baby also suffered the inherited terminal illness and the monthly gift of jalebee ceased.

The time needed to develop mutual support

A major aim of groupwork is mutual aid. Workers can define support through member interaction as one of their goals but unless the group members embrace this goal then it will be only rhetoric. As meetings progressed the workers noted that while members verbally and emotionally supported one another in the meetings, there was no contact outside the hospice. Then a breakthrough came. Around the ninth or tenth meeting a discussion on looking after yourself arose and one member, who goes to a health club, talked about its benefits for her. Another member expressed interest and the first member offered to collect her and take her as a guest to see if she liked it. Initially all members were collected by volunteers to come to the meetings but gradually those members who drive have offered to bring other members. Several weeks ago a family outing on a boat was arranged by the hospice and some of the mothers checked with others to see which group members were going and then arranged to go. This development of mutual support and networking has taken up to a year to begin and affirms for the workers the importance of time in order to allow alliances to develop.

Open access groups

Very often in the UK groups are time limited (six to eight meetings), have closed membership (particularly if they have a sequential programme such as alcohol education groups) and have a problem-solving focus (Brown, 1992, p.22). When it was decided to develop an on-going, open access group, a number of queries arose for the workers around the development of the group process. Open access has provided an opportunity for the members and an interesting dynamic in the group. It has allowed the longer-time members to talk and work through some areas of bereavement and loss and thus have energy available to offer newer members. Earlier in this paper we mentioned that at the first meeting of the group a number of members cried and while one or two would be tearful at subsequent meetings, it seemed to be an initial unloading reaction. This was evidenced several months ago when a new member arrived and told the group that her daughter had died in the autumn and she has another terminally ill child. The other mothers accepted her tears and were able to draw upon their own experiences as a way of giving her support.

Street credibility

Does a worker need to share the experiences of the group members? How far does empathy extend? Both workers are women but only the Asian worker has experienced severe traumatic bereavement. At the fourth meeting an articulate member said to the two workers, 'what experiences have you had that can help you understand our lives?' Silence fell, and all the members listened as the Asian worker recounted a difficult bereavement. It was then the turn of the white worker who did not have such a dramatic experience to tell and said so but recognised the challenge implied. When workers have not experienced a similar situation it may initially separate them from the group but it is not be helpful to either fabricate a situation or try to talk about other forms of bereavement. The member who had asked then turned away and the other women apologised for asking. There was a somewhat uncomfortable silence for a few minutes as the group norm of politeness had been broken. It is threatening for workers to be confronted in this way but it showed the growing strength of the group in being able to ask. This event also seemed to open other topics for discussion. While illness and death were talked about openly in the group in both English and Punjabi, physical violence in the home and thoughts of suicide tended to be discussed in Punjabi in small groups. The two workers discussed whether this was to exclude the white worker as a member of another culture or whether it was easier for the women to discuss these sensitive topics in their first language. The group members recently gave some feedback comments on the respective roles of the two workers which might illuminate this question. They said it helped to have an Asian worker in the group as 'she understands our culture and can get us help'. Their comment about the white worker was 'although she is not of our culture she listens and tries to understand'.

Gender and personal enhancement

From the beginning several women were refused permission to attend the group by their husbands. We realised this was a delicate area with a number of the women so progressed slowly. Some of the husbands saw the group as being concerned with care of the children rather than support for their wives so topics such as relaxation and stress control were introduced gently. They proved very popular topics and members wanted a regular relaxation spot in every meeting. Video and audio relaxation tapes in Punjabi from the local community health council were introduced and are available for mothers to borrow on their own. From this we progressed to a session in the hospice jacuzzi - with some mothers in bathing suits and some in shalwar and kameez (trousers and tunic). Interest was then expressed in learning to swim so the workers arranged private time in a local swimming bath with a female guard and female swimming instructor. This gradual expansion from personal to group to hospice to community is an effort to widen the links of the members to resources available to them as women and to new experiences possible for them.

The group is now well established within the hospice with a core group of regular members, a group of women who attend when they can and an open welcome to new members. Networking of a supportive and social nature operates amongst the women outside the hospice. A long term goal may be for the group to plan and organise their own meetings, using hospice resources as a back-up, but this description is an interim stage. The need for specialist support groups for minority community members is an area of work that groupworkers could well consider.

References

Bertcher, H. and Maples, F. (1977) *Creating Groups*. London: Sage.

Bloom, M. (1975) *The Paradox of Helping*. Chichester: John Wiley and Sons.

Brown, A. (1992) *Groupwork*. 3rd Edition. Aldershot: Ashgate.

Bowlby, J. (1980) *Attachment and Loss: Loss, Sadness and Depression*. Volume 3. London: Hogarth Press.

Edmonds, G. (1988) 'A good enough death', *Community Care*, 24 March.

Engebrigtsen, G.D. and Heap, K. (1988) 'Short term groupwork in the treatment of chronic sorrow: a Norwegian experience', *Groupwork*, 1(3).

Fenton, M. and Hughes, D. (1989) *From Passivity to Empowerment*. London: RADA.

Hodge, J. (1985) *Planning for Co-Leadership*. Newcastle: Groupvine.

Karseras, P. and Hopkins, E. (1987) *British Asians Health in the Community*. Chichester: John Wiley and Sons.

Kelly, C. (1987) 'Positive image', *Community Care*, 31 December.

Konopka, G. (1990) 'Past/present issues in groupwork with the emotionally disabled: part II, thirty-five years of groupwork in psychiatric settings', *Social Work with Groups, US*, 13(1).

Kurland, R. and Salmon, R. (1992) *Groupwork vs Casework in a Group: Principles and Implications for Teaching and Practice*. UK Groupwork Conference, London.

Nathwani, A. and Perkins, N. (1987) *Disability and Ethnic Minority Communities. A Study in three London Boroughs*. London: GLAD.

Neuberger, J. (1987) *Caring for Dying People of Different Faiths*. London: Lisa Sainsbury Foundation.

A CRUSE FAMILY CIRCLE

JOYCE RIMMER

This paper recounts the experience in setting up social support groups, in particular a Family Circle, of a branch of Cruse Bereavement Care in a large English city. The Children Act 1989 imposed legal requirements on the functioning of this Family Circle, the satisfying of which has made organisational and financial demands on the branch. Like so many voluntary organisations providing social support, the branch is inadequately resourced to carry an increasing load of work.

Through the driving rain, the figures approaching across the open spaces of a city housing estate looked very small. The mother was bent over the pushchair in which her baby was wrapped up. The girl clung to its handle, hurrying as fast as her legs could manage. It was Saturday afternoon and they were making their way to the Cruse Family Circle. 'I really did not want to miss it, and Susie loves coming'. This mother was widowed a few weeks after her second child was born. If she did not attend the Family Circle, she would see no-one except her children until Monday morning.

Cruse

Cruse is a voluntary agency, founded in 1959, which offers counselling and social support to bereaved people of all ages. It has 193 branches in the U.K. Originally it was an organisation for widows and, although it has been open to all bereaved people for nearly ten years, the name Cruse (from Kings I 17) may still give the impression that it is concerned only with widows.

Every branch is self-governing in accordance with the national guidelines. Bereaved people seek individual counselling, at no cost, from trained volunteers, or membership of social support groups. The branch with which this article deals had over one thousand new requests for help in 1992. Some people need individual help for a time and then join a group while they are still receiving counselling.

Among the objectives of Cruse are 'The relief of any persons who are in conditions of poverty or sickness arising directly from bereavement and the prevention of any sickness which might arise from bereavement', and 'To provide a service of counselling, advice and opportunities for social contact' (Cruse, 1991). Assessment of 'sickness arising from bereavement' is crucial in the first contact made by a counsellor with a 'client'. So too is assessment of 'poverty'. Groups are the means by which 'opportunities for social contact' are best met. However, it would not be appropriate for a counsellor to link up people he or she has been seeing just because their personal situations are similar or they live in the same area. Such linkage takes no account of the subtleties of class and education and the rate of mourning.

The network of Cruse branches is rather loose, partly because branches are very individual in character and do not necessarily have much common ground. Attempts are being made to help branches form local 'clusters' in order to share ideas. The network within the branch with which this paper is concerned is also rather loose; this is inevitable in a voluntary organisation serving a large geographical area. When the branch opened in 1975 there was only one support group serving the whole city and meeting in its centre. Sometimes more than one hundred people attended the monthly evening meeting; the venue had to be changed (from a large room in a church centre to an even larger room in a Quaker meeting-house) to accommodate them all. The group formed a social sub-committee, and arranged an attractive programme of lectures, demonstrations and games, and a yearly holiday.

It was always difficult to get men to attend this large group - they were put off by the sight of so many women - and it has also to be admitted that the programme designed by the social sub-committee was more interesting to women than men. In addition, many younger widows did not like to be identified with those over 60. The result was the formation of a group for widowed men and women aged under 50 (the Young Widowed Group), which began to meet in the bar of a nearby hotel. Subsequently, some people attending the large evening group became afraid of walking through the city centre subways and said they would prefer meetings nearer their own homes. As a result, four groups were set up in the suburbs and met in the day-time. Thus, in addition to the Family Circle, to be described later, there are six social support groups in the branch.

All six social support groups are open-ended and very informal. The aim of the groups is rehabilitation; people who want to meet other bereaved people can do so at their own speed. They will have been told the programme and the venue for the meeting by the group leader. They will be greeted by the group leader on arrival and introduced to other members, but they are under no obligation to continue attending or to take any responsibility for the running of the group. It is a kind of club. In fact, Cruse groups were called Cruse Clubs in the early days. If new members choose to meet other members outside the confines of the group, then it may be that the process of rehabilitation has begun. For some, though, rehabilitation takes the form of remaining with the group and helping to run it, as 'rescuers' (Berne, 1975, pp.186-88). Their first experience of committee membership may be the group's managing committee. Some move on from that to train as volunteer counsellors. But others remain as 'passengers' in the groups for a long time, neither getting much out of it nor giving much back.

It might be said that these people have not accomplished their grief work. Worden (1991, pp.10-19) gives four tasks which bereaved people need to work through:

1. to accept the reality of the loss;
2. to work through the pain of grief;
3. to adjust to an environment in which the deceased is missing;
4. emotionally to relocate the deceased and move on with life.

There is no set time scale for these tasks, but if a person after many months is still full of the acute pain of grief, there is clearly little possibility of moving on to the other tasks and so becoming rehabilitated. It has to be recognised that some people achieve status through a bereavement as, for example, some people who have a murdered relative (Victim Support, 1990), and may find it hard to give it up after many months of media attention. Some bereaved people are chronically sad and counselling is of little help to them; their depression is endogenous not reactive. Some are depressed as a reaction to their bereavement but see no point in seeking treatment even though treatment could help them. Some are made free by bereavement but dare not admit it (Pincus, 1978). It is for the counsellor or group leader to make a judgement about a 'passenger'; he or she might benefit from individual attention and counselling; or from being given a specific task in the group; or from joining a different kind of group altogether, that is, not a Cruse group. Ideally a Cruse group is a launching pad for getting back into activities pursued before the bereavement or for trying out new pursuits.

But the Family Circle is different. Bereavement affecting young children is long-term. Parents who lose their partners need the support of professionals and other parents until their children are in late adolescence. (It used to be said that parents needed a group until their children became financially independent - but nowadays that may be nearly impossible).

The family circle

In the late 1970s, a small group of widowed mothers in the city, including some with babies, met at the Cruse office once a month during school hours as a Parents' Support Group. The mothers talked with the group leader, a child care expert, about ways in which they and their children were coming to terms with the death of the husband and father. School children were not included in the group and the only time the group-leader saw them was during outings arranged in the school holidays. The composition of the group gradually changed as some of the mothers found part-time jobs. Some new members could not manage weekday meetings. Eventually the group became too small for fruitful interchange. A working party was set up, including some former members and counsellors who had attended the group, to decide on its future. The opinion of those who no longer attended was sought and they recommended meetings at weekends, often the worst time of the week for bereaved families.

By the time this working party was set up, the Children Act 1989 had come into force. If meetings were to be moved to weekends, children would attend them. Therefore the meetings would have to be in premises approved for health and safety and registered as suitable with the local authority, and the children would have to be supervised during the meetings by qualified play-leaders. These requirements gave an extra dimension to the task of the working party. Approved premises and paid sessional staff would have to be found.

Meetings of the working party were productive. A Day Care Officer in the Social Services Department examined the proposals and gave valuable advice about many aspects of the scheme. It was agreed that the new group, to be called the Family Circle, should normally meet monthly on Saturday afternoons. The objects would be to provide support by a counsellor for bereaved parents and supervised play for the children, as set out in the national Cruse guidelines for setting up a branch (Cruse, undated). It was not envisaged that bereavement counselling would be done with the children. Two bereavement counsellors were members of the working party. In accordance with Cruse guidelines, one of them was an academic with child care expertise (who had previously worked in the Parents' Support Group) and the other was a social worker.

These two counsellors contacted all the parents who had been referred to Cruse in the previous six months and found ten who wished to attend the Family Circle. Arrangements were made to use rooms in a purpose-built Family Centre, and some of the play-leaders already employed in that Centre agreed to work for Cruse for two hours a month. It was also decided to hire a group leader to run the parents' group, leaving the two bereavement counsellors free to help anyone who was too upset to remain in the group.

In the event, two group leaders were employed. The decision came about in this way. The working party appreciated that groupwork skills were necessary in addition to those of bereavement counselling. An approach was made to a local college to recruit a sessional group leader from among former students. Two young mothers who offered themselves stated that they would share the responsibilities and stand in for one another as both had family commitments. But they were keen to begin as co-workers in order that each should know the other's way of working.

The working party decided that the Family Circle should begin with six weekly meetings in order to consolidate the group, to work out a programme of activities and to form a managing committee. Although ten parents had said they would come, only three or four attended, and about ten children, and not all of them every week; some mothers came once and said they would resume when the Circle met monthly. Fares were paid so that no-one was put to extra expense. The Circle therefore made very little progress in 'forming, norming, storming and performing' (Brown, 1979, pp.65-71). A tentative programme of activities was discussed but could not be finalised as not enough people were present. There was some testing of the Branch Committee with an application for financial support for a camping holiday, a request that could not be granted since all fund-raising efforts were concentrated on finding money for the maintenance of the Saturday meetings.

The managing committee was formed, but not from the mothers attending during the first six weeks. They had too much else to think about. What they wanted was to be absolved from responsibility for a couple of hours - to have someone else look after their children and some 'personal space' for themselves. The group leaders, who were co-working during these six weeks, therefore began a programme of aromatherapy and reflexology with the mothers. This would have been disconcerting to any father who turned up, but as the venue of the group was not advertised, no-one was able to drop in and there was thus no risk of alienating a new member.

Once the Circle began to meet monthly, the group leaders agreed to take it in turns to lead the parents' group. (Grants which had been sought had not materialised and funding was tight). They consulted before and after each meeting and both attended the managing committee. The parents and the two bereavement counsellors said they were happy with this arrangement and it is understood that co-working will resume if funding improves. Gradually, as the parents began to trust one another and the group leaders and counsellors, they began sharing some of their concerns about their children and themselves. They asked for, and were given, books about bereavement for themselves and for the children; videos could also have been helpful but no equipment for this purpose was available in the Centre. The mothers shared their experiences over family matters and expressed relief at finding that other parents, not only those bereaved, had similar problems. The children too began talking about their bereavements with the counsellors and with play-leaders. (The senior play-leader had recently attended the basic training course for Cruse counsellors). Such unburdening does not take up much of the time in the parents' or the children's groups, but everyone knows that the opportunity exists if the need arises. Some parents have consulted the counsellors about financial problems and have been advised about welfare rights and about the resources administered on behalf of Trusts by the Cruse branch. A safe atmosphere at the meetings allows members to speak freely about whatever is troubling them.

The two social support group leaders who were members of the working party on the Family Circle persuaded their members to take an interest in the Family Circle. The Young Widowed Group gave a Christmas party for the Family Circle along with their own children. They also gave half the proceeds of their summer barbecue to the Circle. Another group held a coffee morning and raised funds. The other four groups were not involved in the foundation of the Circle; their members are all older and they are not likely to have contact with the members of the Circle as there is now no forum where all people in the branch come together. Slowly the Circle is getting bigger. All applicants are interviewed by one of the two counsellors before they are given details of the meeting place. The pace is slow but the counsellors think it better that some bereaved families should have individual counselling for a period before they join the Circle.

The branch of Cruse with which this article is concerned has a high profile for individual counselling. Because of the volume of work, the branch has to have an office and much of the counselling takes place there rather than in people's own homes. New counsellors may prefer to work on the office rota or to do home visits than to attend one of the social groups. Many other Cruse branches do not have the same emphasis on counselling and their activities are carried out chiefly in social groups. It is difficult to know the right balance of counselling and groups in a branch serving a population of nearly a million people. Ideally there should be another six social groups so that most of the city is covered. There ought to be four or five Family Circles so that parents do not have to make long journeys on public transport (as was necessary for the mother and children mentioned earlier in this article). But the branch depends almost entirely on voluntary effort and not enough volunteers can be found to service even the existing groups. New Family Circles would need to be serviced by professionals who already have more than enough to do. Like so many voluntary organisations offering social support, Cruse is under-resourced. As Charles Handy (1988, p.7) says 'The voluntary world is in the gift economy'. Bereavement is not a money-spinner. This has been the story for the past fifteen years; yet the branch not only survives but copes with a greater workload every year. The Family Circle is now established and the branch is committed to maintaining it

References:

A Cruse Branch: Its Formation, Structure and Service (Undated). Richmond: Cruse House

Berne, E. (1975) *What Do You Say After You Say Hello?* London: Corgi.

Brown A. (1979) *Groupwork*. London: Heinemann.

Cruse Annual Report (1991) Richmond: Cruse House

Handy, C. (1988) *Understanding Voluntary Organisations.* London: Penguin.

Pincus, L. (1978) *Life and Death: Coming to Terms with Death in the Family*. London: Sphere.

Victim Support (1990) *Families of Murder Victims Project*. Final Report.

Worden J.W. (1991) *Grief Counselling and Grief Therapy: A Handbook for the Mental Health Practitioner*. London: Routledge.

Coping with trauma

Frank Parkinson

Post-traumatic stress is now widely recognised as the normal reactions of normal people to abnormal events. The many disasters and accidents taking place around the world have made us keenly aware of the devastating effect these can have on human lives.

One method of helping devised in the USA by Jeffrey T. Mitchell and developed by Atle Dyregrov in Norway, called 'Critical Incident Debriefing', is increasingly used with victims, rescuers and helpers after many kinds of traumatic events. These include anything from major disasters, accidents and the experience of war to more personal events such as rape, robbery or any act of violence or loss experienced by an individual or group. Critical Incident Debriefing, outlined in this article, conducted about two days after the incident by trained personnel, can reduce the level of unnecessary psychological reactions and lessen the possibility of the development of Post-Traumatic Stress Disorder.

Any incident we experience which is sudden, unexpected and disturbing can result in emotional as well as physical trauma and shock. This can cause stress reactions which are usually identified as Post-Trauma Stress (PTS) or Critical Incident Stress and can follow any experience from a slight accident, or being attacked and robbed, to involvement in a shooting, an armed robbery, a hostage situation or a major disaster. The usual response of some authorities and organisations to victims and helpers is to offer immediate support followed by the services of a counsellor, psychiatrist or clinical psychologist, if requested. Natural defence reactions often result in the response: 'I'm OK. I don't need any help - least of all from a shrink or do-good counsellor!' However, a method called Critical Incident Debriefing (CID), can help any and all involved to surmount the problems caused by denial, fear of acknowledging stress and the peer-group macho image sometimes found in male dominated organisations and in a society which tells us that 'real men don't cry' or that 'when the going gets tough - the tough get going'. Critical Incident Debriefing is normally a group meeting of those involved, whether victims, carers or helpers, some two days

Groupwork Vol. 6(2), 1993, pp.140-151

after the event and it enables them to talk through the incident in a highly structured way. The aim is preventive in that it will reduce the possibility of deeper and more disturbing symptoms developing at a later stage.

Grief and trauma are the natural and normal reactions of normal human beings to the events of life. These events include the experience of birth, separation anxiety and growing through puberty, to making and breaking relationships, having children, moving home, divorce, unemployment and redundancy, discovering you were adopted, going into hospital for an operation, having a hysterectomy, retirement, growing old or losing a child, partner or friend through bereavement. Although these life events can be seen as 'normal', some do not happen to everyone. However, some 'normal' events such as getting divorced, being unemployed or made redundant can be shattering and traumatic experiences. Being in a traffic or other accident, being mugged, raped, beaten up, held hostage, involved in a shooting, bombing, war or armed robbery can be seen as 'abnormal' in that they are not usual 'for me'. They do happen to some people, either by choice, accident or design, and they usually comprise some element of fear and distress. What is certain is that these are all experiences of change and loss and in some cases and for some people the resulting symptoms can be similar to those of grief and bereavement and include reactions typical of Post-Trauma Stress. If the event is traumatic enough or life-threatening in some way and well outside our usual experiences of coping, the symptoms can develop into a condition known as Post-Traumatic Stress Disorder (PTSD), when professional help from a psychiatrist, clinical psychologist or counsellor will be needed. One problem is that many who experience Post-Traumatic Stress do not receive appropriate help, and deeper and unnecessary psychological symptoms may emerge. Even if they do not develop into PTSD, they can be extremely distressing and disturbing and may cause disruption or destruction of our lives. Post-Traumatic Stress reactions include the normal symptoms of grief and loss, but can also be defined in terms of three basic symptoms - *Re-experiencing, Arousal* and *Avoidance*. Although these are usually defined as symptoms of PTSD, they can also be symptoms found in Post-Traumatic Stress reactions.

In *Re-Experiencing*, feelings, emotions and symptoms associated with the event can come flooding into the present as though it was happening all over again. They can be triggered by external events, such as a balloon bursting or the smell of petrol or the anniversary of the event, but may also come 'out of the blue'. A man involved recently in a riot as an innocent bystander went to his car and as he sat trying to compose himself he began to hear the air-raid sirens from the Second World War and his old fears and feelings from the blitz returned.

In *Avoidance*, those involved may seek to avoid anything or anyone reminding them of the incident. In addition there can be a loss or lack of concentration or of some acquired skills with feelings of isolation and loneliness. Some will lose feelings of affection or love and be unable to show these to partners or family. They may lose interest in work or neglect themselves and might feel that they will not live very long. A soldier from the Gulf War said that he didn't see any point in getting out of bed in the morning and he found great difficulty in making decisions.

Arousal can be shown through an increased sensitivity to noise or relationships at home and work. Simple things can cause outbursts of anger or violence and a retreat into isolation. There can also be an inability to relax or sleep and some may become over vigilant. Strong feelings of shame, regret and bitterness can follow with survivor-guilt and symptoms of depression, claustrophobia or agoraphobia. There can also be changes in values or relationships. Some might lose or gain religious belief and speak of God, fate or bad luck operating in their lives.

When traumatic events occur, those involved need immediate support both at the time and later in order to cope with the feelings and emotions generated and to prevent the development of PTSD.

Critical Incident Debriefing (CID)

Critical Incident Debriefing, or Psychological Debriefing, is a method which can be used with individuals, but is especially effective with groups. The method was pioneered by J.T. Mitchell in the USA following his own work and involvement in many different accidents and disasters. Atle Dyregrov, from The Centre for Crisis Psychology in the University of Bergen, Norway, who took up and developed this method, defines Critical Incident Debriefing as:

> ...a meeting with one or more persons to review the impressions and reactions that survivors, bereaved and helpers experience during or following critical incidents, accidents and disasters. The meeting aims at reducing unnecessary psychological after-effects (Dyregrov, 1989, p.2).

The main elements in the debriefing are rapid outreach, focusing on the present and mobilisation of resources. The debriefing should not be done at the time of the incident or immediately afterward, but some 36-48 hours later. However, because of the shock and sense of unreality created and the denial by some of their real feelings, there will need to be a great deal of support and reassurance during and immediately after the incident. Many organisations have a planned system for helping and this is usually known as *defusing*. They will rely on the preparation, training and sense of comradeship of those involved to help them to cope and they will normally include a practical debriefing afterwards, usually done by a senior member of staff, which will sometimes involve some expression of emotions.

The problem here is that immediately after an incident, helpers and victims are often not in any fit state to talk logically or sensibly about their reactions and they are, as Dyregrov would say: 'thinking with their heads and not with their hearts'. It is usually about 48 hours later that people will feel able to talk in any reasonable way and put both their 'heads and hearts' together. In other words, they are trying to make some sense of the event and come to terms with their hidden or emerging feelings and emotional reactions and trying to understand what has happened and why. At a recent conference in Bergen (June 93), JT Mitchell said that CIDs could be conducted up to eight weeks after an event, but that with passing of time become less effective. Groups formed for such Debriefings can be from a number of different organisations or from none. They can all be policemen, firemen or ambulance personnel, or they can be the immediate victims from a car crash or a bank-robbery, who might be members of staff or people who are there by 'accident' in that they were fellow travellers, customers or bystanders. Where groups of people already exist in organisations, it is hoped that part of their preparation for a traumatic event would include training in awareness of possible post-traumatic reactions in themselves or others and the knowledge that Critical Incident Debriefing will be standard procedure for all. One major element is that the group is to be seen as mutually supportive with its own resources of training, preparation, experience and comradeship. In general, CIDs should be placed outside the normal medical or psychiatric organisations to prevent people from being labelled as sick, ill or in need of treatment. This raises the question as to whether or not CIDs should be compulsory. The response of many involved in Debriefing is to say that in times of crisis, intervention should be pro-active and everything possible should be done to encourage people to participate. This can be easier if they belong to a specific organisation and group because it can be expected and seen as something 'we all do after an event such as this'. Others would say that those involved should only take part through choice. The problem is that part of the normal response to trauma is to deny its existence: 'There's nothing wrong with me, I'm fine'. There can also be concern about the possible effect on relationships with peers or personal reports and promotion if 'they think that I am weak and not coping'. Having CID as accepted standard procedure should help to reduce this anxiety. However, where there are a number of people involved from different organisations or who are victims and helpers who just happened to be there, a more flexible approach is necessary and some will choose not to be involved. It is also practically impossible to organise debriefings when survivors come from many different parts of the country, as in the Zeebrugge disaster, or may be in different hospitals or in organisations where the policy over Debriefing is different. However, in the introduction to the Debriefing process, whether compulsory or with volunteers, members of the group are told that they need not say anything if they do not wish to. Ideally, everyone involved in any way with the incident can attend a CID, including partners or families. In practise, this will often not be possible. A CID would not usually be organised for people from different traumatic incidents although such a meeting could be organised using the same process and would almost certainly help those involved. It will help here if we look at what CIDs are trying to achieve.

The aims of the CID are:

1. to allow ventilation of impressions, reactions and feelings;
2. to help people to make sense of their experiences through creating a better understanding of the incident and by sharing similar or different experiences and feelings;
3. to utilise group resources and share experiences in order to reduce tension and any feelings or being 'abnormal';
4. to mobilise the personal, group, organisational and external resources available to help;
5. to prepare people for possible further or future reactions through giving information, looking at future needs and what Dyregrov calls, 'normalisation'. These are normal people who have experienced an abnormal event who are reacting in a normal way.

The method and structure of a CID

A CID needs to be open-ended in terms of time. The group debriefing of a team from the Manchester Prison riots was spread over two days. The debriefing of a family held hostage and a team of policemen from a fatal accident took three and a half hours. The debriefing of a man who had to shoot dead a gunman also took three and a half hours. Debriefing members of staff from a building society or bank can take about three and a half hours. Experience suggests that any CID, irrespective of the nature of the event and size of the group, takes at least two hours. The group should ideally be about 8-12 people and there can be one debriefer or two - a debriefer and a co-debriefer. Where there are large numbers of people, they should be divided into groups with a team of debriefers. In debriefing a group of 80 people held hostage, the team consisted of 16 debriefers working in pairs with about 10 people in each group.

A typical group might consist of helpers and survivors and, in some cases, bystanders, families or companions. The meeting should take place informally in a room where they will not be disturbed by telephone calls or other people and, if possible, they should all sit around a table. Sitting in an open circle could be threatening and feel like a therapy session. Coffee and tea making facilities should be provided. The debriefer must also be familiar with the nature and extent of the incident.

Introduction

The Debriefer then introduces the session and says what the object and aim is and gives an outline of his or her own experiences of debriefing. Stress should be placed on the fact that the debriefing is not counselling, but that it gives them an opportunity to talk about and share their experiences and will lessen the possibility of deeper reactions occurring. It is also explained that initially the object is to avoid looking at feelings, but to talk of the incident as though a picture was being painted or a script written for a play. Group members are encouraged to think of themselves as detached from the incident as though they had pushed it away and were floating above it. It should also be made clear that feelings can and will be expressed, but not until later and members should be told that deep personal problems are not appropriate for the session, but could be addressed privately and confidentially later if required. In addition they are told that the method is to go around the group asking each person in turn the same questions and that general discussion during the debriefing is not usual. The Debriefer then explains the Rules and asks all to agree to these:

1. nobody has to say anything other than who they are and what their role was at the time;
2. confidentiality within and outside the group should be agreed;

3. the focus is on reactions then and especially now;
4. the debriefing is not a forum for complaint;
5 people might feel worse before they feel better.

The Debriefer also says that if anyone wishes to leave they should do so quietly, but come back if possible and that the session could take three hours or more.

Expectations and facts

Each member in turn, going around the group, is asked to say who they are, where they were and what they were doing when they heard of the incident. These are the basic questions which all are encourage to answer. Further questions could be:

> 'What were you doing 10 minutes before the incident?'
> 'What was the weather like/road conditions, traffic etc?'
> 'What were you talking about or doing?'
> 'Have you had similar experiences in the past?'
> 'What did you expect had happened or would happen?'
> 'How prepared were you for the incident?'
> 'What were your thoughts at the time?'
> 'Did you expect dead bodies, violence, etc?'

The initial questions should gradually build up a picture of the incident and lead on to the 'facts' of the situation as seen or perceived by each person. Also, all the questions in each section are those appropriate and relevant to the event. Therefore, in different situations and events and with different people, questions will vary and need to be thought about and prepared in advance. For example, medical staff will probably have different agendas from policemen or clergy.

Thoughts and impressions

When 'facts' are being described, this usually leads to the questions:

> 'What were your first thoughts on being involved?'
> 'What did you do and why did you decide to do it?'

One advantage here is that 'facts', thoughts and impressions will be shared and encourage all to take part. Feelings are deliberately avoided to reduce any sense of threat or vulnerability. This helps people to put their own reactions into perspective and to gain a 'cognitive grip' on the situation. It also helps them to look at their own experiences and clarify their own and others' roles. Already, they should begin to see that they share many similar thoughts and experiences which enable them to have a wider picture of the incident. At this stage, the Debriefer would begin to ask specifically about sensory experiences.

'What did you see, hear, touch, taste, smell?'

Each of these should be asked separately. Facing these and expressing sensory experiences helps individuals to understand such memories if they emerge at a later stage and to control them when they do.

Emotional reactions

This is usually the longest part of the Debriefing. Questions about 'facts' and thoughts will usually lead to answers about feelings. 'What did you think?' usually evokes the response, 'I felt...'. Here the Debriefer should allow feelings to emerge and be expressed without comment and be able to cope with large amounts of emotion which are often expressed:

'What did you feel when you saw/heard/felt that?'
'What did you find most upsetting or disturbing?'
'When did you cry and why?'
'What were your physical reactions?'
'Were you angry and when?'

The Debriefer may be aware that some are suffering and if anyone cries or breaks down, someone from the group should be encouraged to help them:

'What happened when you went home/back to work, etc?'
'How did your partner/wife/husband/children/colleagues react?'
'What did they say?'
'Was this helpful and what do you feel about it now?'

In this part of the CID, there is often a sharp contrast between the shattering experience of the event and the seemingly trivial questions and answers given in the group. The Debriefer should be aware that some of the questions might appear to be irrelevant or obvious and that they need to be asked sensitively, sometimes with some explanation. Final questions can be:

'What do you feel now as you sit here in the group?'
'What are your main worries and anxieties now?'

The Debriefer should also be aware of any who might need special help, but this should not be mentioned in the group.

This section can be very difficult to handle, especially if the debriefer is not experienced in group work. Here the debriefer should remember that a CID is not counselling or psychotherapy and there is a danger of delving too deeply into personal problems or allowing group members to expose elements about themselves that are inappropriate for the group. It will already have been stressed in the introduction to the debriefing that the group is not there to solve personal problems, but to look at the incident and the reactions to it. As an example, in one debriefing the debriefer knew that one married member was having an affair and that this had been going on for some time, but it was not the object of the debriefing to deal with this. If this had been mentioned by the individual concerned, it would have had to be clearly said that this was not a matter for the group. However, there could be serious problems for the confidentiality of the group if deep problems are raised. The skill here is that the debriefer should be aware of the reactions in the group and not allow the group to develop into a counselling session. Keeping the emphasis mainly on present reactions can help.

Normalisation

Here the Debriefer stresses that the reactions and feelings expressed and shared are entirely normal and, with what has already happened in the debriefing, this should help people to begin to accept their own and others' reactions. A short presentation on other possible symptoms should be given - intrusive images, increased anxiety and feelings of vulnerability, sleep disturbances or nightmares, inability to concentrate, irritability, inability to show feelings, feelings of shame, guilt, helplessness or anger and possible changes in values or beliefs. This might evoke further comments from group members. It should also be stressed that reactions are usually normal and not signs of weakness and that some might find that similar or other feelings begin to emerge days, months or even years later. This also is normal. The possible effects on and reactions of wives, partners and children should be mentioned. A leaflet outlining these can be handed out.

Future planning and coping

Here the Debriefer mobilises all the resources available, both to the individuals and their families and to the group. Questions can be:

'What help and support do you think you need now/later?'
'What resources and help are available at work and home?'
'How will you deal with difficult people and situations?'

'Do any of your family need to talk things through?'
'What have you learned from others in this group?'
'Do you need to meet again as a group - where and when?'

The Debriefer can also outline all other sources of help, both internal and external and a list of people and organisations can be given out. It should also be noted that at this stage some people may feel worse and be in a very vulnerable state. Some will resist any offer of help. This is also a normal reaction and should be mentioned openly by the Debriefer.

Disengagement

The Debriefer asks if there are any questions and then gives a summary of the session. It is also explained that if any symptoms increase or do not decrease within 4-6 weeks, or longer, depending on the nature of the incident, or there is a loss of function or ability at home or work, or marked personality changes seem to occur, or people feel that they just can't cope, they should seek professional help and advice.

The session is then over and the Debriefer thanks everyone for taking part and will say 'goodbye'. Depending on the reaction of the group, the Debriefer will need to decide whether or not to stay and talk or simply leave. To stay can create the opportunity for some to talk privately or enable a mini-defusing and relaxing to take place.

Follow-up

It should be part of the Debriefing process that there is a follow-up at some stage, although this is not always possible. If there is to be a follow-up then this should be mentioned at the Debriefing and an explanation given. This follow-up would usually be about a month later and can take a number of forms, from an informal group or individual meeting to a questionnaire or number of questionnaires. These can vary, but usually include a series of questions about how people have reacted, how useful they found the CID and sometimes the use of the General Health Questionnaire. For such follow-up, permission is always obtained from those involved and some ask for a form of consent to be signed by those taking part. Some Debriefers have further follow-up at later stages, such as at 6 or 9 months and on the anniversary of the incident.

The benefits of such a Debriefing are many, although some might not be so obvious. Where budgets are short and money is tight, managers might be told that:

1. It can reduce any short or long-term distressing after-effects, especially the emergence of PTSD.
2. It can reduce the incidence of personal sickness or absentee-ism.
3. It can reduce personal, marital and relationship problems both at home and work.
4. It can reduce anxieties about how people might cope and about what help they might receive after an incident.
5. It can reduce anxieties for those who feel threatened or who might be embarrassed about asking for help.
6. It can reduce feelings that people are abnormal, weak, or going mad.

Where CIDs are conducted with groups, it builds up the solidarity and strength of the group so that they emerge with a deep feeling of mutual support and the knowledge that they are normal, that they have coped and that they can and will continue to cope. It also leaves them with the knowledge that further help is available if needed.

Conclusion

The problem is that CID is still in its infancy, especially in the UK, but the procedure is based on the belief that those involved need to be given the opportunity to talk about and share their experiences and to realise that they are normal and that their reactions are normal. It is also believed that the pain of grief and loss associated with trauma contains within it the seeds of healing and renewal. The method seems to allow the 'parent' in us to be in control and lay out the incident at a distance like a tableau. The hurt or damaged 'child' is then able to emerge in a safe environment, with safe people and, if necessary, cry 'with the parent present'. What a CID does do is address the problem that our sense of invulnerability has been challenged or called into question by the incident and turned upside down the belief that our lives have meaning and purpose, especially when there are deaths or injury. The loss of self-respect or feelings of self-worth can result in anger, guilt, regret, resentment, bitterness and intense feelings of failure. A Critical Incident Debriefing is instrumental in looking at all the emotions and feelings generated by these and will help those involved to express them, put them into context and begin to come to terms with them.

We should let JT Mitchell and Atle Dyregrov have the last words.

> Clinical experience gained from providing follow-up debriefings for disaster workers in this and other accident and disaster

situations highlights the need for confronting the event following the disaster work. While distancing is most helpful at the scene, the reverse seems to be most helpful afterwards. By actively confronting one's impressions and reactions through meetings and conversations with colleagues and others, the helper is able to manage the after effects of trauma work in the best possible manner (Dyregrov and Mitchell,1992, p.16).

References

Dyregrov, A. (1989) 'Caring for helpers in disaster situations: psychological debriefing', *Disaster Management,* 2.

Dyregrov, A. and Mitchell, J.T. (1992) 'Work with traumatized children - psychological effects and coping strategies', *Journal of Traumatic Stress*, 5.

Further reading

Dyregrov, A. (undated) *Critical Incident Stress Debriefing*. Paper published by the University of Bergen.

Parkinson, F.W. (1993) *Post-Trauma Stress.* London: Sheldon Press.

From group meeting to therapeutic group

Bernadette Duffy and Brian McCarthy

In residential care, much of one's life is spent in group settings. There is a danger that the potential of group experiences can be taken for granted, and as a result valuable opportunities for achieving goals important to clients may be lost. This article reviews the conversion of a routine house meeting in a hostel for teenage girls to a therapeutic group with more emphasis on personal growth and relationships. The aims and development of the group are outlined with comment on the implications for staff-client and staff team relationships. Some theoretical aspects of work with adolescent groups are considered and the need identified to use a model of group behaviour which not only analyses the interactions and atmosphere of group sessions, but also relates to the system of interactions in the agency as a whole.

Context

There are groups that have identified treatment goals and can be described clearly as group therapy. There are other groups which 'offer experiences which are not intended to be therapy but which may often be therapeutic'. (Aveline and Dryden, 1988, p.2-4). It is to the latter category that the work described in this article belongs.

Most residential agencies have regular meetings which have the function of organising living arrangements and duties, reviewing recent events, sharing information, and dealing with disciplinary issues. Such meetings have a value in their own right and serve the purpose of achieving organisational aims. It is the authors contention however that those meetings often have the potential for a more developed use as a key element in the life of the agency. This is much more clearly the case in those organisations which are explicitly described and developed as therapeutic communities; here the therapeutic group can be seen as a central therapeutic force.

In the case of group homes and hostels, sensitive decisions and planning are required to make better use of group meetings while at the same time not converting a residential centre into a treatment centre. This article traces the development of a house meeting in a residential hostel for adolescent girls from the stage where it was simply a functional meeting in the weekly cycle of events to the point

Groupwork Vol. 6(2), 1993, pp.152-161

where it had become an important forum for the expression of feelings and conflicts and had a significant role in the lives of both staff and clients.

The setting is in a residential hostel for adolescent girls , some of whom have lived rough; some have come directly as a result of intolerable circumstances at home, others have been referred by social workers. About twelve girls live in the hostel at any one time. Problems of depression, moodiness, anxiety, excessive use of alcohol, solvents or drugs are common , and behaviour can be aggressive with occasional out-bursts of violence. The principles and methods of work are closely related to reality therapy as outlined by Glasser (1965), with particular emphasis on the taking of personal responsibility, the challenging of unrealistic behaviour and the development of commitment to relationships. A house meeting was held regularly; it was short, mainly administrative and tended to be squeezed in between dinner time and favourite television programmes.

Aims

The idea of working with the group meeting in a different way was stimulated by a few factors. Social education groups had been held in the hostel for some time with the purpose of social skills training and discussion of personal problems. This programme had made use of role-play, drama and relaxation exercises, as well as structured discussion. However, the sessions were usually run by an outsider and attendance was voluntary. There was agreement that a more intensive group meeting was required, involving all members of the hostel, clients and staff, with one outsider, in attendance. Thus the idea developed of using the existing structure i.e. the weekly house meeting, but with new aims and methods.

The new style of meeting was planned to encourage clients to verbalise conflicts. They had a tendency to resort very easily to shouting and violence. To go through the process of talking conflicts and problems through, would constitute important learning for them.

Difficulties with staff should be aired, staff were often construed as authority figures and could be associated with the sources of much anger and resentment. The emphasis in discussion would be to encourage alternative perceptions.

Through the pressure of the group, unrealistic behaviour could be challenged. In line with reality therapy principles, there would be analysis of current behaviour with encouragement for clients to take responsibility for their own actions and consequences. In this way, the group might become a forum for reality testing. They might test their opinions and views of themselves and others. They were never slow to offer such opinions; but to give opinions constructively and with some sensitivity could have useful application in many of their relationships.

The review of the preceding week and planning of the week ahead should play a part, but unlike previous meetings they should be used to make sense of the past and facilitate thinking beyond the present moment, something that many adolescents are uninterested in. One could make use of role-play, drama and relaxation exercises etc. as before, but more as required by the situation than as part of a programme. Above all the clients should in time have a sense of the group meeting being 'their' time, with a sense of participation and a sense of safety and security.

Clearly some of these aims could be in conflict at times, and in these circumstances the priorities of particular situations would have to take precedence.

Development of the group

The early meetings centred on allowing the culture to change. This required staff to become less directive and resulted in discomfort and questioning by the clients. These meetings tended to highlight the staff-client, us and them division. The more staff stood back, the more clients claimed their new-found role and used it to accuse, attack and indicate injustice. 'I was blamed in the wrong', 'punished in the wrong'; was a regular cry. A period of testing the limits occurred; how far a staff member should be pushed ; how much bad language could be used. This created a difficult dilemma for staff. To open the possibility of the group becoming 'their's' in any significant way, requires a certain laissez-faire attitude; to move clients towards taking personal responsibility requires some direction; to encourage people to be sensitive to each other, requires that staff make observations and give feedback.

In this instance, the dilemma was resolved by different staff members taking on different roles, as agreed at staff meetings. This stage of the group can of course be a period of defensiveness and ambiguity for a team who are not familiar with each other.

The content of the early meetings tended to focus on domestic issues- mealtimes, duties, who did and did not do their share; issues of discipline, especially house rules, now that there was a new forum to question them. These domestic debates could quickly move to more serious or significant issues or provide the possibility of dealing with issues of power.

Ann: 'I don't know if this has anything to do with the meeting, but I am not cooking dinner again. All I get are insults from certain people'.
Mary: 'If you are hinting at me would you say it to my face'.
Ann : 'Don't you start me - it's not the first time you did it. You are always insulting others as well. If you don't like the dinners you don't have to eat them...or else cook them yourself if you are so smart and see if you like being insulted'.
Mary: 'How can I cook dinner if I am at work all day. I would not give your dinner to my dogs'.
Staff: 'Would somebody like to tell us what is going on'.
Mary: 'It's not fair me working all day and then having to come home and eat that! I hate mince'.
Staff: 'We don't have mince every day Mary'.
Mary: 'Yes, well I wish I knew when we were having it so that I could buy my own dinner'.
Theresa: 'Well how are we meant to know what's for dinner? We don't know until the house-parents give us the meat just before we cook it'.
Ann: 'Maybe it's a menu you want!'.
Mary: 'Well it wouldn't be a bad idea!'

This resulted in a decision to organise menus themselves and was an early indication to them that discussion could resolve issues.

An important development occurred after six weeks. Because some of the meetings had become unwieldy with everybody shouting together, an idea emerged that a chairperson was required; further, that the chairperson should be one of the girls. This role of chairperson came to assume importance; it rotated and in time the person in the role was accorded considerable respect. A book for meetings, where people would enter an issue they wished to discuss, happened as a result of further discussions.

The emergence of a chairperson, the 'minutes' notebook, and rules about listening and talking one at a time, marked a move to a new phase of the group. The range of issues discussed grew wider and showed greater depth of feeling and thought. Given the chance and the time to talk, some individuals began to verbalise their aggression especially in relation to fights with other house members and in relation to drinking and 'sniffing' (which was very popular at this time). On one occasion a client described having arrived back at the hostel drunk, as a result of which she had been 'grounded' for a week. The discussion of this incident led to the conclusion that they would prefer to be refused entry, to have to survive the night, rather than 'get grief from the staff'. This issue of being drunk or high and the related one of making decisions and taking responsibility, came up at nearly every meeting. At least the group was leading to realistic discussion of the problem and the fights and violence that might ensue.

A discussion on bad language led to some restrictions on its overuse in the group. The girls initiated a fine system at one point which would operate during the week and was administered entirely by themselves. This did not last for very long, but was evidence of a type of initiative; it was the operation of peer pressure rather than a behaviour management programme.

The theme of authority, power and the role of staff continued to arise. On one occasion this led to the opinion that the house would be a very happy place to live in, if the staff were not there. They pointed out how 'the fight the other night finished as soon as you (staff) left the room!'.

> *Staff*: 'So you feel that by us paying attention to the fight, it goes on longer?'
> *Client*: 'Yes, nobody would want to give in to you, they can sort it out themselves'.
> *Staff*: 'Okay, say the staff decide for the next week not to call you or ask you to do jobs, what would you say?'
> *Client*: 'You mean you would sit in the office all day?'
> *Staff*: 'We would be in the house, but we would not be telling you what to do or checking on you'.

It was agreed to try this experiment. Things ran smoothly for three days; staff were then 'invited to come back on duty'.

There was some change in the membership of the group from time to time. A practice developed whereby a group member would have the responsibility of 'initiating' a new client both to hostel life in general and to the group in particular. This was accomplished with considerable maturity by most and where it was neglected, the group member was challenged and censured by the group.

With the group now working for about six months, it moved subtly into a third phase. This was most clearly marked by the commitment people felt to be present. To miss the group meeting was to miss two hours where 'anything might happen'. Thus, curiosity alone provided good reason to be there. In the course of one very volatile session, an individuals behaviour had become so unruly that she had to be asked to leave the room; she remained in the hallway, trying hard to listen and interjecting comments in a relevant and reasonable way (in contrast to earlier behaviour). The need to be there was strong.

The group meeting at this stage could be a barometer of the atmosphere and level of tension or excitement in the hostel as a whole. A meeting might begin with all ten clients sitting bundled together on one couch, clearly and distinctly away from staff; other meetings began with very civilised, polite adolescents, spaced appropriately about, and ready to solve whatever problems might come their way. For staff prepared to listen and observe there was feedback, verbal and non verbal on all aspects of hostel life.

Discussion about the hostel itself was a recurrent theme; sometimes this would occur because of some particular complaint or bad feeling about the place. More often it arose from a need to discuss the image of the hostel or as a vehicle for trying to make sense of why they were actually living here at all.

Mary: 'Let's talk about this place'.
Staff: 'Well would you like to tell us what you think of the hostel?'
Ann: 'Don't ask me that question - I don't know anyway'.
Sonya: 'I think it's gear- great crack- forget it, I didn't mean it, I said forget it- you turned on me straight away!'
Staff: 'Why is it gear?'
Sonya: 'Forget it- I said'.
Staff: (turning to others) 'Why are you here?'
Nuala: 'I have no place else to go'.
Staff: 'So it's a house that you can sleep and eat in if you have no place to go?'
Nuala: '*No*, it's my home, it's all our home'.
Staff: 'If I asked you to tell me about the hostel, just say I was never here before, what would you tell me'.
Sonya: 'I'd tell you to mind your own...business'.
Kathleen: 'Don't look at me like that I don't want to talk about it- Right'.
P*atricia*: 'I'll tell them the truth, you all annoy me if you don't like it here, go home and let us alone'.
Sonya: 'Don't start me, you big-mouth!'
Staff: 'Do you like it here?'
SONYA: 'Oh, here she goes again, always me...of course I like it here, I'm here aren't I?'

In this dialogue we can see the way in which a sense of victimisation or an opportunity to insult can be integrated with any discussion; staff had to learn to notice but not necessarily react.

The issue of confidentiality took on a more serious meaning. Lengthy arguments occurred about clients respecting stories or information outside the hostel. This was interesting as it showed a developing sense of privacy and respect for their own affairs. With time, the level of confidentiality did improve, resulting in mature and often quiet personal discussions of sexuality, marriage, pregnancy, personal hygiene and habits of excessive drinking etc. It was during these interactions that some individuals became aware for the first time of their patterns of excessive drinking. Suggestions and advice from other group members were valuable and could carry more weight than staff comment.

The role of staff members in the group

Staff members tended to avoid 'being Solomon' on matters of right and wrong and systematically tried to comment more on the group processes as appropriate. This had interesting effects. Some of the girls became more alert to the mood of the group. This would often lead to discussion of the reasons for particular tensions, angers or depressions. One such discussion led to an acknowledgement of the frequency of bad humours, aggressive outbursts and generally negative feelings. A practice developed of asking each member of the group to recount one pleasant event or feeling. This was an example of a practice which allowed staff to introduce exercises to identify and explore feelings e.g. exercises from the Gestalt Therapy literature (Perls et al., 1972). Opportunities like this would be used, where possible, to highlight the 'here and now' and to anchor their awareness in the present where they might compare each others feelings and reactions.

There were times when they tired of observations being made about the group. One client commented: 'You're always saying things like that about the way we say things'. In its way, a very succinct description of group processes.

Another function of staff members was to be the group memory. It could be useful to remember a piece of dialogue or a sequence of events from an earlier meeting; this could be relevant to issues of taking responsibility or to the origins of a specific quarrel. Some people have a flair for retaining the storyline; it is a valuable asset, especially where there is not the time to listen to tape-recordings of group meetings.

The confronting of inappropriate or unrealistic behaviour was accomplished frequently by the group itself; this was the preferred method of achieving the aim. There were inevitably occasions where it fell to a staff member to do this; to confront without becoming the ogre of authority was a delicate balance to hold. Again a solution was for members of staff to alternate this role, while others moved towards intermediary or supportive roles.

The atmosphere could change rapidly; one minute easygoing and trivial, next minute highly charged and serious; the beginning of a session inactive and lethargic, later active and creative. This demands of staff an ability to move with abrupt and often inexplicable shifts of mood. Awareness of one's own temperament, and more precisely, one's humour and level of flexibility on a given evening, is valuable.

There is no doubt that involvement in this group had implications for staff roles and behaviour. Some staff felt quite vulnerable at the early stages of the group, especially on evenings where the group seemed interested only in attacking members of staff. It can take time to develop the resilience needed to weather these storms with the small comfort that more civilised discussion would eventually emerge. The sense of 'clearing the air' did however usually outweigh the discomfort and this played a part in reducing barriers. Staff-client communication was thus enhanced both within and outside the group meetings. It was noticeable that staff roles often changed in the context of the group itself. A staff member who ordinarily tended towards being strict could take on different roles within the group e.g. being supportive, more open, devil's advocate etc. This was interesting in that it could help change stereotyped views clients might develop of staff. It also contributed to staff learning to expand their repertoire of possible roles.

The group meeting has continued to be a feature of life in the hostel. It is now run almost entirely by staff which raises the issue of the use of an outsider as consultant. It is a matter of constant debate whether more can be gained from reflections on group meetings when an alternative perspective is available. While the value of consultation is appreciated, limitations on funding restrict the use of extra resources. It is generally felt however that the group meeting has proven itself and should continue to provide a forum for discussion and resolution of issues.

Some theoretical considerations

Various theorists of group behaviour have considered the question of whether groups develop through recognisable stages towards maturity. Tuckman (1965) surveyed therapy groups, training groups and groups within laboratory settings; he delineated four developmental phases which he termed 'forming, storming, norming and performing'. Yalom (1975) posited a model whereby psychotherapy groups were seen to move from a phase of orientation through conflict and rebellion to a stage of cohesion and closeness and finally to issues concerned with termination. Spitz and Sadock (1973) described a pattern of change from an initial stage of guardedness and anxiety to the group moving through a period of group interaction with the growth of trust, to a period of disengagement, separation anxiety and positive feelings towards the leader.

Bennis and Shepard's model (1965) suggests that power relations are important in the early stages and need to be explored and confronted before interpersonal issues can become part of the agenda. Reitz (1981) provides a model which is an amalgamation of some of these approaches; this view emphasises the latter point that issues of power tend to precede the development of cohesiveness and the capacity to deal with interpersonal matters. This model provided a useful frame of reference to review sessions. The issues of power and authority, dependence and independence did not however disappear. The developmental stage of the client group is of course relevant here, insofar as most teenagers would be concerned with these issues on a regular basis. A point did come when power issues were less salient; perhaps the period where the clients deemed the staff 'redundant' marked the change most dramatically. Certainly interpersonal issues were discussed more thereafter. This pattern fits the broad thrust of theoretical accounts of group development.

Inevitably the movement of group sessions was fuelled by adolescent energy or stagnated by adolescent lethargy. James Anthony described the regressive and progressive 'movements' of adolescent groups and the need to treat 'members as potentially mature adults, with the right to regress on some occasions. Too much should not be expected nor disappointment shown when the group fails to live up to expectations'. (Anthony and Foulkes, 1957, p.221).

These words are still relevant to such groups and highlight the demands made on staff adaptability and energy. Mapping the changing cultures of the group presented an interesting challenge. Just as Bion (1961) described the group culture changing from theocracy to playgroup in the case of adults, so the adolescent group could switch from street corner to household to court-room. To capture the essence of that culture and feed it back to the group, represents one of the important skills of the group leader. It was often after a group meeting that significant aspects of changes in atmosphere were appreciated; to feed this back to the group closer to the moment, would be more valuable. Further development of this type of groupwork skill would be useful.

It is ultimately of most importance to relate the group events and atmosphere to the overall context of the hostel and to the lives of the individuals. A systems approach might better facilitate an analysis which can relate the micro-events of the group meeting to the macro-system of relationships and patterns of living in the hostel.

Conclusion

This account of a specific set of group sessions is inevitably a brief survey of the many, complex interactions that occurred. If it makes one point, that there is potential for growth and development in the routine spheres of an organisations life, it will have served its purpose. In commenting on how people learn from groups, Smith (1980) makes the point that learning occurs 'where two paradoxical messages impinge on the learner, the messages being identified as support and confrontation. Where this occurs, the learner is seen as able to take greater personal responsibility for actions and therefore able to sustain changes subsequent to the group' (p.78). Certainly both of these messages were there at various times in the group meetings; whether they occurred in adequate or appropriate form can only be assessed by relating future life experiences of the clients to these interventions.

References

Anthony, E.J. and Foulkes, S.H. (1957) *Group Psychotherapy*. Middlesex: Penguin, p.221.

Aveline, M and Dryden, W. (1988) *Group Therapy in Britain*. Milton Keynes: Open University Press, pp.2-4.

Bennis, W.G. and Shepard, H.A. (1965) *Group Development : Human Relations*. Volume 9, pp.415-457.

Bion, W.R. (1961) *Experience in Groups*. London: Tavistock.

Glasser, W. (1965) *Reality Therapy: A New Approach to Psychiatry*.' New York: Harper and Row.

Perls, F., Hefferline, R.F. and Goodman, P. (1973) *Gestalt Therapy*. Middlesex: Penguin

Reitz, H.J. (1981) *Behaviour in Organisations*. Illinois: R.D. Irwin.

Smith, P.B (1980) *Group Processes and Personal Change*. London: Harper and Row, p.78.

Spitz, H. and Sadock, B.J. (1973) 'Small interactional groups in the psychiatric training of graduate nursing students', *Journal of Nursing Education*, (12), pp.6-13.

Tuckman, B.W. (1965) 'Developmental sequence in small groups', *Psychological Bulletin*, 63, pp.384-399.

Yalom, I.D (1975) *The Theory and Practice of Group Psychotherapy*. New York: Basic Books.

GROUP THERAPY WITH ADULTS WITH LEARNING DIFFICULTIES WHO HAVE COMMITTED SEXUAL OFFENCES

ELISABETH CORMACK

This article focuses on the under-researched area of group therapy for adults with learning difficulties who have committed sexual offences. It examines some relevant aspects of psychoanalytic theory and then describes a hospital based group run by the author. A description of the preliminary assessment process and the profile of the group membership is followed by a detailed exploration of three areas: the group process, important group themes and the transference and countertransference. The conclusion is drawn that people with learning difficulties should not be excluded from group therapy.

Introduction

It has been within the last decade that group therapy for people with a learning difficulty has been recognized as a treatment modality with potential. This change has gone hand-in-hand with the growing movement, in British psychoanalytic circles, to offering individual psychotherapy to this client group.

The conclusions in the early literature are that group therapy can provide a useful forum in which adults with a learning difficulty can express their feelings and begin to come to terms with the issues that affect their everyday lives. In addition, there is an increasing conviction that group analysis has a part to play in encouraging the creative emotional development of adults with a learning difficulty.

The ubiquitousness of sexual offences has finally demanded much public attention and this is reflected in the mounting expertise developed in Britain of treating sexual offenders. This has included extensive use of groups.

As described by Murray Cox (1973), group therapy for sex offenders is invaluable:

> It was in a group setting that the patient originally established a deviant identity and ipso facto a group setting may also provide the redefining process on which the patient's self-definition may

be changed in the direction of greater personal fulfilment in socially acceptable patterns

Yet group therapy with sex offenders with a learning difficulty has rarely been written about in the English language psychiatric literature. An extensive computer search revealed a dramatic lack of research on this topic, indicating a degree of clinical distrust of such therapies with people with limited verbal and cognitive skills. Typically, group therapy for sex offenders uses severe learning difficulty as an automatic rule-out criterion when selecting patients.

Before I give an account of a group that was run for people with a learning difficulty who had committed sexual offences, I want to examine briefly the origins of their behaviour as arising from within early relationships.

Relevant aspects of psychoanalytic thinking

Mervin Glasser (1988), looking at the common pathology of sexual deviation, has defined a set of interrelated factors, forming the central pathological nucleus, as 'the core complex'. The driving force of this complex is a wish by the individual to achieve a form of union with the love object. However, the danger of such union spells annihilation of the self, a belief that he will be taken over totally by the object to the point of disappearance. He has two ways of reacting to this danger: Firstly, narcissistic withdrawal, which regains him safety. However, this position brings with it unavoidably profound isolation, feelings of worthlessness and depression, suicidal ideation and intent. This again leads him to seek secure closeness with the object, which is the very closeness which he can not bear. Secondly, aggression is the other way of reacting to danger of annihilation. Aggression has the aim of negating anything which threatens the physical or psychological survival. It uses control and domination to negate the annihilatory dangerous object, the very object from whom he is seeking gratification of his most intense needs.

In an attempt to solve this conflict the individual uses sexualisation to convert self-preservative aggression into sadism. The aggression carried away with him in narcissistic withdrawal is turned onto the self, sexualised and transformed into masochism. The sexualisation allows him to interact with the object at a safe distance in sadomasochistic terms, and through this avoid intimacy and trust. The purpose is to gain psychic equilibrium, the crime is an attempt to adapt intrapsychically.

Conditions which determine the development of sexually abusive behaviour are laid down in early childhood experiences, disturbances in the parent-child relationship, the early family group, being of critical importance. Through sexual abuses the original victim becomes the victor.

Factors in the psychotherapy of adults with a learning difficulty

The importance of loss for an adult with a learning difficulty has been emphasized especially by Professor Joan Bicknell (1983) and her colleagues. Due to failure to resolve the grief, 'the loss' has the potential to produce a multiplicity of problems, like rejection of the child with a learning difficulty and chronic grief for the parents, interrupting the delicate stage of the attachment process in the infant and young child and setting up psychopathological difficulties with external and internal objects. The loss, which may be evident at birth, will certainly confront both the individual as well as the parents and siblings at all developmental stages.

What is lost is intelligence, but in addition also the symbolic loss of the idealised intelligent child. Maud Mannoni (1973) attacks the problem from the viewpoint of mother's pathology, which becomes crucial for any understanding of the child with a learning difficulty. During the pregnancy the mother fantasises about the child of her dreams. This dream child will allow her to get in touch with the deficiencies of her own childhood and help her to work through them. A child with a learning difficulty arrives on the scene, getting her in touch with her own early traumas and frustrations. Being so identified within mother's fantasy unconsciously, the child faces additional hurdles to negotiate the complex task of separation and individuation. As Pierce Clark says: 'The ego of the subnormal patient is not separate from the mother'. This results in stunted self-esteem and self-regard, as it is the integration of the whole personality that relates to the quality and quantity of self-esteem with adult sex offenders. E. Welldon's experience is that 'often these people would still be subjugated to an overpossessive mother, who did not allow them to develop any independence and individuation'. I would suggest that this conflict is indeed almost insurmountable with an adult with a learning difficulty who has committed sexual offences. These factors amalgamate and merge with the original intellectual disadvantage, producing likely consequences of severe personality disturbances and maladjustments. The experience of having a severe learning difficulty then is not defined by the IQ figure of 70 and below, but by something that involves feelings of pain, loss, and attempts to accommodate all that in the personality.

Setting up the group

The preliminary work involved selection of patients. In informal discussions we identified 8 male patients, all residents in a hospital for adults with learning difficulties, with a mix of sexual disturbances. Our intentions were to have a closed group running for six months, a group session lasting for one hour. A male staff nurse and myself were the therapists. The group was to be structured loosely. Estela Welldon believes preparation to be essential for minimising early dropouts, for providing information on the group rules and for encouraging the patient to pursue therapy. Once we had selected our patients I saw each of them for a two hour individual preliminary interview. This served various functions. It was intended to establish a relationship between the patient and me, the therapist. It provided him with information about the reason for establishing this group, making it clear that all members have difficulties expressing their sexuality in an acceptable way and hopefully fostering a sense of belonging to this group. It stressed that the nature of the commitment was mandatory, the fairness of this was not questioned by any of the participants. Through using two questionnaires on each group member I hoped to open up channels of communication about their sexuality and desensitise them to some extent to the open discussion of the group on sexual matters that were to follow. It also served the purpose to standardise the initial interview and as a therapeutic tool encouraging the patient to talk and elicit information that he might have been reluctant to give.

Sex offenders live in two worlds, presenting 'normality' to the people around them and a 'deviant' world they keep quiet about. The offender's presentation of information is self-serving and often lacks objectivity. Much of the individual's energy at the time of evaluation is directed towards self-protection rather than designed to provide clarification. At least to some degree the sexual behaviour is egosyntonic, the hallmark of offenders is defensiveness. Therefore effective assessment and therapy require a degree of scepticism and cynicism on the part of the professional, whose normal mental health approach emphasises client support, discourages authoritative and controlling silence.

Ray Wyre (undated) sees his 'assessment questionnaire', which we modified to make applicable to our patients, as a tool for breaking into this deviant world. He suggests approaching the offender as though one knows everything about him. As he says: 'You know he fantasises, masturbates, you know his likely sexual experiences and the fact that the offence is just the tip of the iceberg'. The questions start in the safe area of known facts: age, sentence, present offence, previous offences, sexual and non-sexual, to the patient's perception of his own parentage, relationship durations, religious beliefs, the abuse of alcohol and drugs, and then moves towards the more difficult areas of sexuality, masturbation frequency, sexual contact in childhood and adolescence, sexual practices past and present, patterns of offending and undisclosed offending, masturbation and offence fantasies and victim perception. The style of interviewing the offender is through leading questions, like 'when you masturbate' or 'I expect you masturbate at least five or six times a day'. This enables the patient to tell.

The second questionnaire was Brook's Sexual Knowledge Questionnaire, an illustrated questionnaire designed for use by the therapist to gain some indication of the level of knowledge and understanding which exists before sex education classes. Used after completion of the course, it gives an idea of the amount of knowledge acquired. The questionnaire checks on the understanding of human relations, body parts, changes at puberty, sexual relationships, pregnancy, contraception and so on.

Profile of the group members

In my group of eight patients the pathology previously described was obvious. All of them had deeply disturbed backgrounds: four men gave a history of sexual abuse as a child and adolescent, involving exposure, forced masturbation, incest abuse by father, mother, siblings, group sex and exposure to pornographic literature. Parental pathology involved alcohol abuse by three fathers, suicide attempts by two mothers, and for most men the experience of physical violence in childhood by the hand of their parents. They generally perceived their parenting with ambivalence, except for two young men who saw their parents as 'bad people', and only one man who perceived his parents to be perfect. Yet his father was impulsively violent towards his son and his wife, and the patient himself expressed quite extreme aggression towards his mother when he was a child.

Four men had a criminal record involving manslaughter, theft, robbery, break-in and entry, grievous bodily harm and arson. They all shared a very low self esteem which, in two people, was defended against with a facade of arrogance. IQs of men in the group ranged from 46 to 70. All eight patients had a history of court proceedings for indecent assault on children. In addition, three indecently assaulted adult females, and five committed incest abuse. The mean age at which they started offending was 17. The length of stay in hospital varied between 2-13 years, with a mean of 4.6 years.

Before hospital admission, 50 per cent of the men drank regularly every weekend or more, 25 per cent less frequently and two patients did not admit to alcohol use. The only other substances abused were glue and cannabis by one patient. Only one perpetrator had a history of self harm, in the form of wrist cutting and drinking a bottle of shampoo.

Sexual knowledge was rudimentary in most patients. Responses ranged from 'a woman can get pregnant through kissing' to pathological attitudes like 'the child has to hold the man back' from abusing her. Masturbation was viewed generally as immoral, resulting in physical ailment i.e. blindness, bodily weakness, renal problems. Two men failed to distinguish between girl and woman and boy and man regarding the ability to marry.

As a consequence of trauma, abuse, neglect, abandonment, exploitation during their formative years, the patients' development was adversely affected. The pain, distress and anxieties require to be given a forum for expression, in order for these deep-seated and constantly recurring problems to be tackled head on. The expectations are that the individual establishes his typical conflicts and behaviour patterns in the group, endowing the therapist, group members and the group as such with properties of persons in the past and present life. They become personifications of his inner objects, namely transference objects. The transference of individual therapy is diluted in the group and worked through in the interactions of group members. It is also easier to see in others what one cannot recognise in oneself: the mirror phenomenon. Having confronted the other person and understood their behaviour, the member may begin to recognise the trait in himself. Another view frequently expressed in the psychoanalytic literature on groupwork with offenders and individuals involved in sexual abuse emphasises that the therapeutic task is to facilitate a movement towards acting less and suffering more, whereas with neurotic patients it is to help them to suffer less and to act more.

Life of the group

Experiencing very much the growing pains of the beginner I set out to work with this group, which comprised 8 perpetrators, a male staff nurse and myself. We met weekly for 1 hour for 26 sessions. The group was intended to be exploratory, both in the methods employed and the content addressed. However, an educational component needed to be included to correct misconceptions about sexuality.

I want to explore three areas in particular in my examination of the group:

1. the group process and how it compares to groups of adults who do not have severe learning difficulties;
2. important themes of the group relating to the core complex issues, as well as exploring the psychodynamics associated with learning dfficulties;
3. evolving analytic concepts of transference and countertransference, and how those are influenced by the pathology of 'sexual deviation' combined with learning difficulties.

Joining and establishing group processes

The first five sessions were taken up with various themes like establishing rules, the issue of confidentiality, getting to know each other, and a commitment to the group, all very much highlighting the joining process.

This early period was characterised by little spontaneous conversation, where group members talked, almost without exception, to the two leaders only. The issue of confidentiality recurred frequently, emphasising the high level of anxiety and insecurity experienced by all members.

Surprisingly very emotional disclosures were made by two patients in the second session. One man admitted to the group his great fear of being let down when approaching adult females in a social setting, like asking them for a dance. In his own words: 'I am very shy with women, if one lets you down, you see it in your mind when you ask another one. If I don't ask, I won't be let down.' Another man responded: 'I only dance by myself, when I go to the community centre.' It transpired later that this second patient imposed on himself a ban of any future sexual relationships following his offence.

Being let down and rejected remained a prominent theme throughout the discussions in the group. This would relate to the core complex issues dating back to childhood, the longing for intimate gratification and security, the anxieties of annihilation and abandonment. When abandonment and rejection become a reality in adult life, it resonates with the traumas of infancy and childhood. The emotional loss of the mother, engaged in her own difficulties, coping with the reality of the 'damaged child' by chronic grief, unable to solve her own castration fears, has become distant from the child's needs. She cannot act as a container. Present-day rejections recreate a similar loss of psychic equilibrium and remain tragically the core complex issues, to which the perpetrator of sexual offences is so sensitive. The rejection and humiliation with resulting loss of self-esteem can be guarded against by phobic avoidance, resulting in the unhappy solution of narcissistic withdrawal and isolation, as this young man so vividly showed.

During this stage especially, the loose structure of the group requested spontaneous contributions from its members. Their discomfort with this appeared as the suggestion that I should structure the sessions with a preselected topic and 'fire questions at them'. They wanted to make it into an education class, rather than a therapeutic group. I was empowered and pressed to lead, to make decisions, to resolve conflicts, to ease tension. Silences were frequent and embarrassing, and I found myself in the role of the overly active group conductor.

This first stage of development seemed like any other group. Initial anxieties about the conflict to attach and belong, but yet the fear of rejection and the urge to remain separate was clearly evident both in the behaviour and verbal content of the group. Those are also the core complex issues. How was cohesion in the group formation going to be influenced?

Towards group cohesion

Very gradually changes evolved as the group established some cohesion. Painful childhood memories of the drunk father hitting mother were brought up. One patient in particular made the clear connection between his drinking and his sexual and non-sexual crimes. The most defensive patient, who up until then had not even admitted being a sex offender, for the first time participated actively.

He recounted an incident, when he was driving his car after a drinking bout, suddenly wanting to drive over somebody unknown to him in a fit of rage. The group responded with incredulity and laughter. One man expressed his disbelief in this statement, pressing him for details of why he felt so angry with an unknown person. The patient in the hot seat was under considerable pressure and stopped responding with his usual defensive style. He disclosed how he was raging before leaving the house because of a heated argument with his mother.

The group members had started to interact with each other without dependence on the therapist in a confrontationally revealing manner. However, this happened infrequently. The usual tendency was a slavish reliance on the therapist.

In Session 8, and from then on, the focus became more and more the crime, the effects on the perpetrator as regards labelling him, and, in some patients, the admission that preventing reoffending was not going to be easy.

The level of anxiety became intense when they approached the subject of being no-hopers incarcerated in hospital. Two members took it upon themselves to pacify those emotions by drawing attention to one patient who already worked outside the hospital grounds unsupervised and another young man who had transferred residence in the early stages of the group to a hostel.

During the middle stages of the group more cohesion between members was in evidence. Themes arose which had a unifying quality, issues of being labelled and being treated differently from other patients. However, slavish reliance on the therapist was evident throughout, and they found it difficult to rely on each other for solutions to their common problems.

Ending

The theme of dissolving the group ran throughout the group's life, anticipated ambivalently as a relief to evade anxiety provoking conflicts, at other times with a grieving response. This took the form of frequent suggestions to re-establish another group after termination, focused however not on sexuality. On a number of occasions the group was denigrated by members as useless. This tended to occur after natural breaks due to holiday times. The group is often represented as the mother, the breast, a nurturing entity. The absence of this supporting environment was missed, but this needed to be defensively denied. The content of material towards the ending of the group dealt again with a sense of rejection and being let down. The members requested to celebrate its termination with a meal. Democratically they elected organisers. No references were made about their feelings of loss until I addressed their defensive attitude. Leaving and with it an implied rejection remained unresolved issues, resulting in three members making themselves unavailable for the party. However, the impression left was an appreciation of a setting where they were allowed to express and explore feelings within a context of emotions being valued and given importance.

Key themes relating to core pathology and learning disability

Various themes tended to recur, taking centre stage as the main preoccupying conflicts of the group, especially the issue of death and loss.

At the beginning of one group session a young man found it very difficult to join. He was distressed, having come from the funeral of an older female patient from the hospital. A deathly silence developed. The members were unsure of how to console him, feeling awkward in expressing care and concern. Defensive remarks were made, like 'we shouldn't talk about the dead, it doesn't do any good . Can we not talk about something else? Let the dead rest.' Addressing the defensive posture and affective intensity of the group slowly opened up the discussion. One patient projected his own fear onto another member: 'He thinks a big hand comes out of the grave and pulls him down. Death comes to everybody's door. Sometime we have to go ourselves'. One previously very hesitant and restrained man became quite agitated, shifting in his chair, looking to the floor. His friend, drawing the group's attention to him, elected himself the facilitator, helping him tell his story. Gradually the dramatic event of his father's sudden death was revealed.

Some sympathised with his feelings: 'It's a queer shock to the system. It could have killed him, the shock of it all'. Being understood allowed him to expand on the consequences on the family of his father's death. He explained how his mother reacted with disbelief and 'she never recovered after that'. With his father's authority gone, the family fell apart. The intense rage with his father for leaving him was soon to be acted out in the sexual sphere by sadistically abusing a young child. The abusive act served as a plea for togetherness and containment of his narcissistic wound, and the sexualised attack for the failure to be provided with it. He was greatly at risk emotionally during the object loss and defended against it in the abusive act. This young man was also very unsure about his masculinity due to an anatomical abnormality of his genitalia. When his externalised superego figure abdicated all power through death, his psychic economy became so unbalanced that he needed to act out his uncertain masculinity to bolster his self-esteem.

Murray Cox (1973) describes those deep disclosures as third level disclosures. They occur if the abusive behaviour is a self-esteem regulator. It is then likely that the deepest disclosures will not be about the offence, but refer to those areas of experience where self-esteem was fragile or shattered.

This emotional disclosure fostered an openness about expressing feelings. It released the inhibitions of others who were then willing to discuss their own dramatic life events. The revelations dealt with key group issues, loss, grief and getting in touch with their own mortality. It also confirms some aspects of the psychoanalytic theory of sexual deviancy.

Very infrequently did any discussion deal with learning difficulties as an issue in an overt way, and clearly a defensiveness surrounded this taboo subject. Over 26 sessions, on only one occasion the words 'mentally retarded' were used by the patients to describe themselves. The label served them as a relief of responsibility for their sexually inappropriate and abusive actions. 'Retarded is like defective. If you do these things (abuse) you are not responsible for them. My social worker said I am retarded'. The intellectually most capable member who often dominated communication and regularly spoke for other people, invoked the label of 'morons' as an explanation when longish silences ensued and the atmosphere was charged with emotions. Defences evolved rapidly to prevent any escalation or discharge.

This has been termed 'moving in and out of damaged states of mind' and reveals itself as a common defensive manoeuvre in the psychotherapeutic relationship with people with learning difficulties. This loss of intelligence requests acute therapeutic intervention, as they find it hard to process that state by themselves. In the face of a painful situation intelligence is obliterated. I believe that this also showed itself in the wish expressed by some group members of wanting me to be an educator who preaches at them, tells them and teaches them. If they can passively hand over all the ability to me, make me the focal point who provides solutions, they would not have to bother to reflect on extremely painful and anxiety arousing issues threatening them psychically. They could inhabit my mind. To act 'stupid', to be 'stupid', became a safety net to escape difficult issues, feelings, responsibilities.

There is a sense in which the sex offender suffers from an inbuilt deficiency as perceived by himself. One patient drew attention to this through various statements to the group. 'There is something wrong with my brain. It makes me do things to children'. This perception of a fault is then used as an explanation for his paedophilic actions. He described it as a primitive urge: 'Something then comes over me, and I do things to children'. One function of psychotherapy with sex offenders is to delineate that fault in terms of the core complex issues and to find alternative means of regulating self esteem, not through aggressive sexuality.

The experience of being valued in a group, having a forum for discussing intimate traumatic experiences, is in itself a healing process.

Transference and countertransference

Symington (1981) found that his client with a learning difficulty showed a more immovable dependence and idealisation of the therapist. On the whole, my patients never expressed verbally any negative feelings about me. The presence of negative transference was conveyed in a more elusive and shadowy way. I was held idealised. Throughout the group's life, but to a lessening extent, I was empowered to present solutions. Most members were quite demanding of individual attention from 'the good enough mother'. The patients were able to split: I was generally the all good mother, whereas outside the therapeutic space, their responsible doctors, nursing staff, the world as a whole, was mostly all bad. The outside world was condemning, prejudiced, jailing and restraining, I, the therapist, understanding and helpful.

However, even this usage of me as 'the good enough mother' for identification has with these patients, to be perceived as an invasion by an object, with the consequence of narcissistic withdrawal or sadomasochistic defensive engagement. Both situations were played out!

I had to cancel one session at short notice. The next group meeting was extremely disruptive. Some men had refused to accept coffee or tea before the start of the group. I felt a sense of hostility towards me, but not my co-therapist. The group fragmented into smaller sub-groups and it was painfully difficult to hold the group together. I got the cold shoulder and was excluded. Only when I interpreted my sense of rejection to them and my belief that they were angry with me for cancelling the session the week before, did this exclusion process terminate. They started to talk about being undervalued, stood up and rejected by objects in the past. They were wounded and withdrew to sever the perceived power I had over them. The intense fear of abandonment originating in childhood had been reawakened.

In group Session 17, for which my group co-therapist was unavailable, the transference became sexualised and I felt disempowered to contain the group. I was unusually anxious and defensive in my role as the surrogate victim, unable to maintain an interpretive, therapeutic stance. Never did I feel so closely in touch with the disturbed parts of those patients' ego. The perverse transference had become clearly visible but I was unable to make therapeutic, interpretive contact with it.

The idealisation of the transference presented a defensive manoeuvre, to protect me from the deeper, sadistic part of their self. The idealisation was magnified by the presence of the male therapist, who maintained external control and dampened any impulses to act out. In my group of patients this dependence and idealisation may also have been a side effect of institutionalisation.

Transference onto the group as a whole was acted out especially by one patient. He used the group to abreact his masochistic guilt and blame. 'I am worse than a murderer for what I have done.' Despite his obvious plea for mercy, he received no placatory reassurances, no subduing comments. Instead, he became the personification of conscience in the group. He persistently drew attention to his masochism to distract from viewing his sadism. This process appeased his powerful superego, which he externalised onto the group.

For me, sometimes overwhelming countertransference feelings proved to be difficult defences. I acted in an overprotective manner towards the members. Especially at the beginning, they could not tolerate much anxiety. My preconceptions and prejudices about people with a learning difficulty persuaded me to act motherly. By being too gentle I did not facilitate them to transfer their aggression onto me. Through this stance I also discouraged, to a degree, the development of independence and taking responsibility for themselves in the group. I avoided being construed as remote and critical.

Another transference-countertransference issue arose with regular frequency. I often perceived a dull feeling, as if my thinking was stuck. It occurred when remarks suddenly changed the direction of the thought content of the group. Difficult feelings were about to erupt, but quickly they were squashed and cancelled out. When I tried to allow those feelings some development, all I received was diversion, an abandoning of intelligence.

Conclusion

It is my conclusion from working with these patients that psychotherapy groups are valuable for people with learning difficulties who have committed sexual offences. Limitations in abstract reasoning and the members' cognitive abilities are mitigating factors affecting the tempo, with which the group can progress, gain insight and change. My experience with those patients has convinced me, that emotional intelligence is often independent of intelligence quotient. I have the hope that the experience of acceptability of each member, as well as their often tragic and painful life events, has furthered their personal development and their fragile self-definition has to some extent been redefined.

Acknowledgements
The author wishes to thank Dr. Maria McGinnity, Consultant in Mental Handicap, for her support and enthusiasm for this project; and John Devine, psychiatric nurse for his assistance as co-therapist.

Note
The co-editors and the author recognise that the language used in some of the bibliographic titles and texts would be questioned by contemporary publishers on grounds of anti-discrimination.

References

Bicknell, J. (1983)'The psychotherapy of handicap', *British Journal of Medical Psychology*, 56, pp.167-178.
Brook Advisory Centre (nd) *Questionnaire on Social and Sexual Behaviour*.
Bungenor, J. (1992) *Exploring Disability: Individual Psychotherapy with the Mentally Handicapped.* Unpublished paper.
Clark, P. (1933) *The Nature and Treatment Amentia*. Bailliere: Tindall and Cox.
Cox, M. (1973) 'Group psychotherapy as a redefining process', *International Journal of Group Psychotherapy*, 23.
Glasser, M. (1988) 'Psychodynamic aspects of paedophilia', *Psychoanalytic Psychotherapy*, 3(2), pp.121-135.
Hodgetts, D.A. (1986) 'Psychotherapy group for people with mental handicaps', *Mental Handicap*, 14(3), pp.121-123.
Mannoni, M. (1973) *The Retarded Child and His Mother*. Tavistock Publications
Symington, N. (1981) 'The psychotherapy of a sub-normal patient', *British Journal of Medical Psychology*, 54, pp.187-199
Welldon, E. (date unknown) 'Group analytic psychotherapy to sexual deviancy' in *Spheres of Group Analysis*.
Wyre, R. (nd) 'Working with sexual abuse', *Workshop - Gracewell Clinic.*

Reviews

Groupwork, Third Edition
ALLAN BROWN
Ashgate, price £8.95 ISBN 1 85742 087 X

It is with great humility that I approach writing a review of this book. *Groupwork* through its first and second editions has become a standard introductory text, the bible for successive groups of students writing about, or taking up, practice opportunities in groupwork. It is invariably an item in booklists, is frequently cited in articles and longer works, and is one of the few British texts to have earned respect among the discerning and somewhat exclusive North American groupwork audience. From its first edition in 1979 the book has expanded from barely 100 pages to well over 200 reflecting, I believe, the author's own continued learning and development, as much as the expansion of groupwork experience and theory. In particular the latest edition reflects, throughout, an attention to contemporary concerns for equal opportunities and promoting anti-discriminatory and anti-oppressive practice.

Parts have been substantially re-written and there are two new chapters: on anti-discriminatory groupwork and on working with groups in day and residential centres. The very helpful bibliography has been expanded and updated and is, in my experience, the most comprehensive and up to date resource of this kind. It is a mine of information for advanced as well as basic studies and a good starting point for research work. The highlighting of key texts inevitably invites argument but in my view is balanced, practical and representative of the discipline.

If all this reads like a eulogy then that is correct. *Groupwork* is in my view a very good book. But perhaps it should be! By the third edition the author has had ample time to take account of earlier criticisms and to smooth down the rough edges.

Groupwork is set into a logical structure. The first chapter, which fixes groupwork in the context of contemporary practice, policy and theoretical developments, stakes out what makes groupwork distinctive, where it can be helpful (or not), and what approaches might come beneath its umbrella. In particular increased attention is given to self-directed/social action/empowerment models which had but passing reference in the second edition. However at this point of the book I get already a sense of struggle from Brown, perhaps reflecting his own development, between whether he should reorientate the work towards a statement explicitly committed to groupwork based on anti-oppressive principles or to maintain the more neutral overviewing approach which succeeded so well in the first two editions. More about this later.

Chapters two and three covering planning, and the factors this involves, and leadership, particularly the lengthy section on co-working, are full of useful information, ideas and practical tips and hints for both new and experienced groupworkers. One of the commendable features of Brown's writing is that he never slips into the 'practice manual' mode but always discusses underlying issues. Where he has not worked out an answer for himself he is honest enough to leave matters open - and space perhaps for the next edition!

Chapter four on group programme, group process and stages of development, and group activities and techniques is the one I find, personally, least satisfactory. The problem for me is the tendency to over generalise creating the impression that the features outlined can apply to all the different types of groups described in chapter one. Insufficient attention is given to the vital significance of purposes and values out of which, in my view, flow different group histories/processes and attendant activities. As an external examiner I have found too often that students who have not had adequate college teaching or practice supervision latch on enthusiastically to the frameworks and activities outlined in this very chapter. Grasping them as 'the answer' to expectations that they demonstrate their work to be structured and disciplined, they undiscriminatingly frame any group they describe in these terms.

Chapters five and six on working with groups in day and residential centres and on anti-discriminatory groupwork focusing in particular on race and gender, are newly written for this edition. Chapter five is based on material developed in greater detail in *Groups and Groupings: Life and Work in Day and Residential Centres* co-edited with Roger Clough (1989). By its inclusion in this general text, the usual assumption being that general practice is fieldwork, this chapter makes an important contribution to bringing day care and residential work into the 'mainstream' of groupwork. Indeed, as is strongly emphasised, these are settings in which groups, and therefore groupwork, are a norm. They should have central, not marginal positions in the development of our theory base and repertoire of skills.

Chapter six on anti-discriminatory groupwork is thoroughly researched and carefully written. Commendably Brown is not afraid to admit his own limitations, confusion and pain. I found the analysis of anti-discriminatory groupwork enlightening and the practice guidelines a practical and substantive beginning. Brown seeks to move beyond American literature rooted predominantly in the social psychology of attraction and difference into exploring the foundations for a groupwork which will address oppression both as a 'state of affairs' ingrained in social structure, and also as a 'process' expressed in personal relationships and revealed through the exercise of power. The chapter ends with a framework for empowerment in groupwork. As it stands this section is rather marginal but yet it seems to represent, perhaps, the inevitable outcome of such a reflective and self critical approach - a challenge to reconceptualise groupwork within a discourse committed to empowerment and change. As such this questions for me the very framework of the book established in its first edition and rooted in the assumptions of respectable scholarship of that time. The framework merits further development - a task for the fourth edition? But it will require reconstruction rather than 'adding on'.

The final chapter has an expanded section on consultation and supervision, a subject area to which Brown has made over time a particularly worthwhile contribution. It is absolutely vital that greater attention is given to this aspect of work, if standards of practice are to become better and more consistent.

The third edition of *Groupwork* is worthy successor to its predecessors and easily maintains the standards set by these. In my view it provides both a helpful guide and tool for practice and an authoritative overview of the discipline. Brown achieves a good balance between summary and clear guidance, and critical reflection and challenge. However, I wonder if edition number four will look anything like the same?

Dave Ward, Senior Lecturer, Head of Social Work Programme, University of Nottingham

The Small Group Trainer's Survival Guide
BIRGE D. REICHARD, CHRISTIANE M.F. SIEWERS, Paul RODENHAUSER
Newbury Park, Calif., London, Delhi, Sage; 1992, price £12.50 (pbk)
0-8039-4740 -2 (hbk) ISBN 0-8039-4757-7 (pbk)

This is a practical book, clear and succinct. It is concerned with a form of groupwork to which the American authors give the generic name 'laboratory education', though they also speak of 'affective', 'emotional', 'experiential' or 'non-cognitive' education - in short, groupwork events where participants learn about themselves and about groups in the here and now by lowering their defences, accepting disarray and vulnerability.

The introduction offers a concise account of the development of the National Training Laboratory method (the original 'T-Groups') starting with Lewin in 1946. It recognises the shift from 'group dynamics' to 'a more individual and psychological emphasis' after Lewin's death. The authors' experience is with the NTL and with this intra- and inter-personal American tradition which has a strong reliance on the psychiatrist as back-stop. I was struck by the contrast between this and the Grubb-Tavistock Group Relations tradition with which I am familiar; here the psychiatrist is not the solution but is rather - like everyone else - part of the problem, and the staff will strive to interpret a 'casualty' in terms of what an individual may be 'carrying' for the group, via projections, rather than as a consequence of personal history.

However, the book does describe the continuum of different learning groups. It also gives handy basic summaries of the various processes (projection, splitting...) which can occur in any of them. Specifically it shows that distress can occur in an encounter group, in a T-group, in a role-play for salespersons or even, I would add, in a creative writing workshop or a university seminar. Wherever learning is not purely cognitive there is risk. And where there is risk a guide is welcome.

This book claims to be such a guide and the claim is justified. There are check-lists; the application of the Johari window is useful for distinguishing levels of awareness; there are good references. However, whether it was appropriate to call it a survival guide is debatable (the word appears on the title page and nowhere else). I wonder too if it is a *trainer's* survival guide: the book itself focuses very clearly on the potential distress of *participants*. The survival of the trainer would seem to be dependent on limiting casualties among participants. To this end he or she is required 'to be available for out-of-group talks...The trainer's job is a 24-hour one'. The problem of trainer survival is, if anything, understated, and the whole question of power and authority, central in the Tavistock tradition, is left relatively unexamined. In particular, distinctions are rarely drawn between individual staff and directors of events.

It might be objected that the authors' insistence on the danger of casualty is over-done and even counter-productive. Is it really necessary to have application forms specify previous psychiatric treatment, to have psychiatric support available, to have all the staff scanning members in the first session for 'subtle clues' to stress? May this not create a role of casualty which some participants will be eager to fill? Will it not move the focus from the educational model to the therapeutic or the clinical? The occasions when I have been involved with 'casualties' have been for me ambiguous. On one occasion the disturbed and erratic behaviour of a 'casualty' could have been interpreted as 'distress' or madness but was also seen as a powerful act of self-liberation, and as offering crucial data about institutions; the participant remained until the end. On the other hand, I recall a workshop where the fact of a participant bursting briefly into tears was seen by other (academic) participants as proof that the staff group was behaving recklessly. Each context is different and the response to distress will depend on the assumptions of staff and participants.

But it is true that whenever one describes this type of learning to people who have never engaged in it, it emerges that the fear of emotional damage fuels their resistance. This book is courageous in that it deals openly with that fear. The objections I listed above are serious ones: it may not be necessary in every context to invoke the possibility of psychiatric intervention; some stress is inseparable from certain important kinds of learning and most people experience this as positive. But the general point about openness with respect to risk seems to me to be a sound one. The guidelines (screening applications, attention to individuals, contingency plans) are really no different from those which a professional canoe instructor would follow: 'We don't expect things to go wrong but they might and we are prepared'.

Those who are chary of this kind of learning need this reassurance about the strength of the container. Most of us have had educational experiences which are purely cognitive: we have learned powerful defences against self-disclosure. We know that 'unfreezing' will be risky and we need trainers whom we can trust to let us melt at our own speed and to cope if we boil over. For most passengers the cabin crew's safety demonstration represents reassurance rather than confirmation that flying is a high-risk activity.

If 'laboratory' learning is to expand, practitioners will have to be able to allay fears and one way is to be open about the risks and to be reality-based and discriminating as to their severity. While, as the authors point out, this book is not a manual and no substitute for supervised experience, it still constitutes a useful resource for a wide range of groupworkers.

Colin Evans, Reader in European Studies, University of Wales, Cardiff

Training Techniques in Groupwork (3 Volume Pack)
PENNY HENDERSON AND GAYLE FOSTER
The Effective Trainer Series, National Extension College, price £49.00

In many ways this has been a difficult review to write since the authors of this training pack, together with the help of members of a post-qualifying groupwork course, have thought of just about every aspect of introductory groupwork training.

The training pack aims to 'provide sufficient ideas and materials for you to be able to mount a successful short course, workshop or short session on the theme of working with groups'. We think that this pack offers the reader much more.

The pack is attractive, well designed and straightforward. It has been produced with much care and attention to detail. The contents are readily accessible to the reader avoiding unnecessary jargon and the pack is both open and welcoming to the new groupwork trainer. The description of groupwork method can be easily understood by trainers and most participants alike. Though there is perhaps an assumption that course participants have all reached a similar academic standard. Many groupworkers, who would want and would benefit from training, having already gained a lot of 'hands on' experience, may not have perhaps had any professional training and even little formal education. This pack would, therefore, put many, potential groupworkers at a disadvantage if a course placed too heavy an emphasis on literacy skills. It may fail to address and value other skills that participants may bring.

An unusual feature of this publication is its division into three parts; a course leader's guide, a participant's guide and a series of resource sheets which the authors invite the trainer to copy for use during the training course. All of these fit neatly into a handy and durable folder - useful for busy trainers.

The course leader's guide and the resource sheets provide excellent training material although at £9.95 a copy, the participant's guide may well be beyond the resources of some users in current circumstances. This would be a loss since its inclusion offers participants the opportunity of taking responsibility for their own learning and this sharing of information reduces the 'mystique', so called, of groupwork.

All sections of the pack address in clear terms the how, what and when of running groups, making a strong statement about its anti-discriminatory, equal opportunities framework and offering useful material specifically about multi-cultural issues.

It covers the whole linear process from the planning stages through to ending and review. It undoubtedly offers a useful framework when thinking about and designing a basic groupwork course, for example, under the heading 'what to look for in groups'. The course leaders guide offers a clear introduction followed by an explanatory note about content and process. This links well with the resource sheet No. 4, which is a group observation check-list. This is similarly supported by the participant's guide under various headings, for example, participation, influence group tasks, group maintenance, atmosphere, membership, feelings and norms. It offers a good mixture of well organised structured exercises intended to be used in an experiential way making use of course members' first-hand experiences. Not only does it cover the whole aspect of groupwork practice training but much of the information is transferable to running training courses on any subject giving emphasis to the how, in the structured context, of what actually happens in groups.

This pack undoubtedly achieves its aim and as experienced groupwork trainers, we are able to dip in and out of the material, mixing and matching possible course content, adapting to the needs of particular course members with whom we are working.

Although flexibility and sensitivity is encouraged by the authors, it would be tempting as a new trainer to follow a more prescriptive path skimming over issues and avoiding some of the more fundamental and challenging situations. By organising the material so well, the compilers may have made the process of teaching groupwork appear simpler than it actually is, perhaps failing to prepare the inexperienced trainer for the emotional disclosures of course participants which frequently occur. Such disclosures often act as good preparation for groupworker course participants when dealing with the unpredictability of group behaviour. They frequently look to the trainer for modelling on how to handle such situations.

This is offered merely as a warning of something that might happen as we would have no hesitation in recommending this pack for use by experienced and inexperienced groupwork trainers alike. Old ideas are refreshed by a new approach, organised differently. There are many new structures for old successful themes. In a busy world, it can take out a lot of the hard work of course design leaving more time to contemplate and plan for possible outcomes of course sessions.

A very useful addition to any groupwork trainer's library.

Ann Walford, Independent Groupwork Trainer, Consultant for the London Borough of Lambeth
Kathy Darby, Group and Organisational Analyst, Groupwork Consultant for the London Borough of Enfield

Post-Trauma Stress
FRANK PARKINSON
Sheldon Press (Insight), 1993, price £8.99, pp.176, ISBN 0-85969-662-6

Disasters have always afflicted mankind, many on a catastrophic scale. Because of our rapid communication system it feels nowadays as if these catastrophes occur more frequently. Not necessarily so of course - it just feels that way. In the past you survived or you didn't. It was, apparently, as simple as that. Now we demand, particularly in Western societies, that whether the disaster is very personal like bereavement, or very public like being taken and held as a hostage, help should be offered to manage constructively the stress that is almost inevitably a concomitant of shock. As those of us with long experience of counselling know and as Mr Parkinson, author of *Post-Trauma Stress,* reminds us, stress is often denied and help rejected.

Frank Parkinson has worked for many years with the surviving victims of disasters, their families and those often forgotten heroes and heroines, the helpers who also witness dreadful scenes they would like to forget.

The great strength of Mr Parkinson's book is in the description he gives, backed by apt and moving case histories, of the personal consequences of the sufferings following disasters. These cover a very wide range from shocking car accidents, the East Midlands air crash and violence of all kinds, to personnel from the Falklands and Gulf Wars and from Northern Ireland involved in situations beyond individual control. His understanding of the stress suffered is based on his wide experience of his professional role in psychological debriefing.

For anyone not familiar with counselling Mr Parkinson's book gives very valuable insights into the damaging effects of stress, particularly if help is not forthcoming or if the stress is denied and the symptoms ignored. As an experienced counsellor, however, I was looking for clearer guidance on the model and methodology used in psychological debriefing. I am left with the question, 'for whom is this book intended?' The general reader interested in the subject will gain much from careful reading; I am less certain of its value to the professional who already has a clear understanding of the symptoms of stress, the damage these can cause and the counselling techniques required to help the sufferer overcome the difficulties. A more rigorous analysis of the methodology of psychological debriefing and how this differs from short-term focused counselling would have greatly enhanced the value of this book. What is made clear is that the debriefing must take place immediately, within 24 hours is possible, of the catastrophic happening.

The cover is a somewhat unconvincing photographic mock-up. It detracts from the serious manner with which Mr Parkinson has dealt with the anguish of post-trauma stress.

Jean Griffiths, Honorary Lecturer, Department of Continuing Studies, University of Birmingham.

NOTES ON CONTRIBUTORS

Elisabeth Cormack is based at a Young People's Centre in Northern Ireland.

Bernadette Duffy is a social care worker who has worked for many years with adolescents, especially in residential settings. A study she did in Dublin focused on aspects of the groupwork described in the current article.

Sheila Finlayson works for the City of Birmingham Education Department as an Area Senior Social Worker in the Child Advisory Social Work Service. She is also an independent trainer and counsellor.

Estelle Hopmeyer is an Associate Professor at the McGill School of Social Work, Montreal, Canada, teaching in areas of groupwork and lifethreatening illness and bereavement.

Brian McCarthy is a Lecturer in Psychology with the Dublin Institute of Technology. He was previously a clinical psychologist with the Health Board and has worked with adolescent groups in a variety of settings.

Lynne Muir was a Lecturer in Social Work, with a particular focus on groupwork, at Birmingham University. She now directs an MEd programme in the Practice of Community Education and is an independent trainer.

Hardev Notta is a member of the community team at Acorns Hospice for children in Birmingham. She specialises in work with Asian families.

Frank Parkinson was an Army chaplain for twenty-five years and now works as a private consultant in counselling and trauma.

Joyce Rimmer was a Lecturer in Social Work at the University of Birmingham for many years and is the founder of Cruse in the Birmingham area. She was given an OBE in recognition of her services to the voluntary sector.

Annette Werk is an Associate Professor at the McGill School of Social Work in Montreal, Canada. She has been working and teaching in the area of violence against women for the past ten years.

NOTES FOR CONTRIBUTORS

Articles are welcome from all who have an interest in work with groups (whether as practitioner, trainer, researcher, user or consultant) and who wish to contribute to the development of groupwork theory and practice.

Types of Articles

The journal will publish two main types of articles:

i. PRACTICE-BASED PAPERS

These articles will be based directly on groupwork practice experience, but written in a way which is evaluative as well as descriptive. We recognise that many practitioners may not be familiar with writing for journals, and we wish to suggest the following guidelines to assist in this process:

(a) A brief summary of the contents of the article (100-150 words), drawing attention to any particular theme or emphasis.

(b) Background to the group, the context, e.g. agency setting, type of group, workers and members; group aims and objectives; and the theoretical/philosophical perspectives i.e. any particular principles or values central to the approach taken.

(c) A brief review of the group, content, methods and process.

(d) Outcome and analysis, specific topics of interest relevant to the focus of the article, e.g. key issues arising from this piece of practice; and evaluation of the group drawing out learning points for other practitioners.

ii. THEORY-BUILDING PAPERS

Each issue will carry several theoretical papers ranging over groupwork concepts, theory, research, issues and values. Papers on the following topics would be especially welcomed:

(a) The current 'state of the art' of groupwork.

(b) Papers analysing the significance for the groupwork process of race, gender, class, culture and other social factors.

(c) Papers analysing key group concepts and issues.

(d) Papers from different countries, sharing current developments and theoretical concerns and preoccupations likely to be significant for groupwork practice in Britain and elsewhere.

(e) New sources of research evidence.

(f) Groupwork training and skill development, consultation/supervision.

Length of papers

The normal range will be 2,500-4,000 words, with practice accounts normally not longer than 3,000 words. Exceptionally, longer articles will be accepted and there will be a place for briefer contributions on new developments, responses to previous articles and other material of special interest.

Form of Submission

Articles should be submitted in one of two ways:

i. typed on A4 paper, 3 copies, double-spaced with wide margins

ii. on computer disc. Authors who have prepared their material by word processor are asked to provide a copy of the computer file on disk. Most Macintosh, IBM-PC compatible and Amstrad word processing programs can be read.

References

These should be quoted in the text by giving in brackets the author's name and year of publication. They should then be listed in alphabetical order at the end of the article as follows. *Books* - author's surname, initials, date, title of book, place of publication, publisher's name, page if relevant.

Articles - author's surname, initials, date, title of article, title of journal, volume and number. Only those references which occur in the text should be listed. Where appropriate, additional resources may be listed separately as further reading.

Assessment for publication

Articles submitted will normally be passed to members of the journal's panel of assessors, and decisions as to publication made by the editors in the light of the assessors' comments.

Enquiries

Allan Brown, Dept of Social Work, University of Bristol, 8 Woodland Road, Bristol BS8 1TN. Tel: 0272-303030, ext.853/Nano McCaughan, 12 Barr Beacons, Canonbie Road, London SE23. Tel: 081 699 8438

GROUPWORK

Volume 6 Number 3 1993

SUBSCRIPTION, ADVERTISING AND BUSINESS ENQUIRIES
Should be addressed to the publishers, WHITING & BIRCH LTD, PO Box 872, Forest Hill, London SE23 3HZ. TEL: 081-699-0914 (Int'l +4481 699-0914). FAX: 081-699 3685 (Int'l. +4481-699 3685)

SUBSCRIPTION RATES
British Isles £35.00, North America US$80, Elsewhere £45.00
Special reduced rates apply as follows:
Individuals to private address: £19.00 British Isles, North America, US$35 Elsewhere £25.00. Special reductions available for members of AASWG and Groupwork Exchange Network.
Groupwork is published three times a year.

PAYMENT
Should accompany order. Cheque or banker's draft (made payable to WHITING & BIRCH LTD) may be in any convertible currency to the relevant amount. Direct transfer can be made to our Girobank account (no. 5440564). The following credit cards are also accepted: Access/Mastercard, Visa, Diners Club, American Express. Quote card number, expiry date and give cardholder's name and address if different from delivery address.

GROUPWORK is cited in: *Applied Social Sciences Index & Abstracts, Sociological Abstracts, Bibliographie Zeitscriftenliteratur aus allen Gebieten des Wissens, Social Work Research & Abstracts, Special Educational Needs Abstracts*. and *Studies on Women Abstracts.*

PUBLISHED BY WHITING & BIRCH LTD, LONDON. ISSN 0951-824X
Printed by Short Run Press, Exeter.

EDITORIAL

The articles which appear in this last issue of volume six give us particular pleasure for two reasons. The first is the strong emphasis on practice, with most of them being authored by practitioners directly out of their own experience of working with the groups they write about. The second is being able to publish in one 'general' issue three articles about groupwork associated with disabled people (learning and physically disabled), a much neglected topic in the groupwork literature. A further feature is the significance in three of the accounts of the author's own personal experience for her ability to identify with group members' needs and concerns in her facilitation of the group.

In the first five years of publication of this journal hardly any articles on groupwork with people with learning disabilities — or their carers — were submitted. We always suspected that the groupwork was going on, but for whatever reason (the marginalisation of learning disabled people until recent years?) it was not being written up for publication. The situation is now changing quite dramatically, with articles published in 5(3) and 6(2) - both from Ireland - in addition to the two in this volume - both from England. We hope this trend will continue as there is still some catching up to do to provide practitioners and group members with the accumulated wisdom and experience of others running similar groups.

Kavita Kohli movingly describes how her awareness of herself as a deaf black woman was aroused by her contact with a social worker for deaf people, and how this led her to meet and work with deaf Asian women in groups. Her paper also demonstrates the linking of the personal and the political, as this empowering group provided evidence of members' triple oppression and the lack of suitable services. This was then passed on to the agency for action.

Stigma and loss are central themes in Helen Gobat's article about groupwork with the parents of learning disabled adolescents. Following on the Irish issue (5:3) and the special issue on bereavement and loss (6:2), we are seeing how central loss is to the lives of group members in so many groups, and what a strength to those groups it can be when the worker is able to draw on personal experience to empathise and motivate group members.

The third article concerned with disability is a fascinating account by Dorothy Atkinson of how a group can change as the members take ownership of it. This group for older people with learning disabilities started off as an individually-focused research project to elicit and share life histories. As the group developed over two years, the members became enthusiastically engaged in documenting their own collective experience in a group publication *Past Times*. In the process of group empowerment, the worker's role changed dramatically from 'central person' to resource as 'scribe'.

A discerning common contribution in the other three articles is a sharpening of our understanding of the importance of specific and creative methods and techniques in the facilitation of group goals. Miriam Dumbleton and Oded Manor help us to understand the difference between activities and growth games, and their appropriate use at different points in the 'wave' of a group session. Olive Otway describes how the use of art therapy in a group for working class women can be a creative empowering process strengthening self-esteem, and increasing life choices. We learn that art therapy has application in a wide range of groups, and is not dependent on having prior skills in drawing or painting. Two probation officers, David Henchman and Susan Walton, write about their use of critical incident analysis in groupwork with offenders. This method shows the value of focusing in great detail on a specific offending incident, as a way of helping group members clarify and question those values and lifestyles which influence offending behaviour.

Finally, as we plan for volume 7, we hope that the papers in this and previous issues will inspire those readers who are on the brink of putting pen to paper, fingers to word-processor, or mouth to dictaphone, to take the plunge and write. We look forward to hearing from you!

Nano McCaughan and Allan Brown, Editors

CRITICAL INCIDENT ANALYSIS AND ITS APPLICATION IN GROUPWORK

DAVID HENCHMAN AND SUSAN WALTON

Since 1991, Bath Probation Team have adopted a groupwork method of supervising offenders. All probation clients attend Offending Behaviour Groups in accordance with the Agency's aim of reducing the likelihood of offending. This article focuses on the work of two members of this team who have developed a method of Critical Incident Analysis which harnesses the resources of the group and enables a thorough assessment of offending. In completing this process clients are helped to improve their cognitive skills and in doing so increase their knowledge and understanding of their own behaviour. The group leaders are able therefore to plan effective intervention. Illustrations of the Critical Incident Analysis as part of the assessment process are given and the authors outline their development of the method and its application in groupwork to increase victim awareness, risk assessment and anger management.

The groupwork system

Two years ago Bath Probation Office decided that groupwork should become the primary way in which Probation clients would be supervised, and therefore an integral part of all Probation Orders. This move from individual supervision to a groupwork model is based on our belief that groupwork provides a more effective forum for clients to examine their own offending, to challenge and be challenged and to take positive action to change. We also think that groups provide an opportunity for the empowerment of clients and an invaluable sense of support that is difficult to achieve in one-to-one contact.

All clients attend a first stage group which is a closed group consisting of twelve weekly sessions, and which typically would have six to eight members. The objectives are:

1. to clarify the extent of their offending;
2. to clarify the reasons for offending and the patterns of behaviour that lead to their criminal activity;

3. to clarify the consequences of their offending for others and themselves;
4. to develop strategies to help clients to change their behaviour;
5. to develop clients' cognitive skills and in particular their ability to conceptualise the consequences of their behaviour.

There is no set programme to achieve these objectives but group leaders choose from a range of exercises and methods to ensure that the above are met and the needs and abilities of group members are taken into account. Clients subsequently attend second stage groups, such as Alcohol Crime and Education Groups (ACE), Anger Management Groups and Employment Groups, or receive individual counselling to address in more detail the problem areas highlighted during stage one.

The purpose of this groupwork approach is to reduce offending by encouraging clients to recognise their behaviour, develop an understanding of it and take responsibility for what they have done. By doing this, they are more able to acknowledge and accept control over what they do and can make informed choices for their future. Therefore the model of groupwork adopted is broadly that of Offending Behaviour Groups as outlined by McGuire and Priestley (1985).

Offenders do not come to us as a matter of free choice, but following a pre-court interview when a probation officer will have written a report for the court assessing amongst other things the seriousness of the offence, and the offenders attitude to his/her offending, and the risk of re-offending. If the offence is considered to be of sufficient seriousness and there is evidence of a pattern of offending that the offender wishes to address, the probation officer will discuss with the potential client the legal and the day to day requirements of a Probation Order, including group attendance. If the client agrees in principle, the report writer can then make a proposal to the sentencing court for a Probation Order with a condition to attend groups. If the sentencing court agrees that a Probation Order would be an effective sentence the defendant will be asked whether he/she agrees to the making of such an Order. Therefore, whilst there is an element of choice, we would argue that when the alternative to a Probation Order may be custody the choice is far from a free one. Having agreed to a Probation Order, attendance at our groups is then compulsory and this has obvious implications for our subsequent work with clients.

We realise that for groupwork to be effective, group members need to be motivated, and because of the structural restraints upon our groupwork system imposed by compulsory group attendance this motivation cannot always be assured. Consequently it is even more important that the content and exercises that are used are flexible, accommodating of the group and responsive to individual needs. The motivation of clients is an issue in all supervisory contact, but we find that the power of a group can be an effective tool to motivate clients who are attending only because they have to or who, for other reasons, are not fully motivated.

If offenders are to change their behaviour they need to take responsibility for their actions and an essential process for this to occur is for clients to recognise that they do have some choice and control over their behaviour. We acknowledge the power that is implicit in the probation officer's role, especially as the client has to attend appointments. Groupwork can assist in recognising this power imbalance and provides a forum in which anti-authority feelings produced by the system can be expressed and addressed. We do not expect to redress the power imbalance that our clients experience in society but what we try to do is equip them to deal with the implications of this imbalance and to encourage them to make rational choices about how they achieve this.

The problem

In order that we can work effectively with clients, we need detailed information about what they do. Whilst we have access to witness statements, summaries of prosecution evidence etc, we are primarily reliant upon clients' versions of their life events. Eliciting this information is usually very difficult and our work with sex offenders makes us particularly aware of a whole range of complex manoeuvres the individual deliberately or otherwise makes to avoid or block self awareness. As we see it there is a tendency for offenders to distance themselves from what they do, and this prevents any useful examination and ultimately any impact being made on the patterns of behaviour which lead to offending. At the initial stages of working with clients on the detail of their offending we are often met with comments like: 'I can't remember', 'it just happened', 'it happened so quickly', 'I already told the police what I did'. The group becomes an effective means of drawing out the detailed information and breaking down the blocks. We have found that group members are more likely than us to share an understanding of these life events and therefore are able to challenge an edited version of an offence.

What we require is a detailed 'script' of real events, so detailed that the group could almost have been at the event described, as we believe that it is important that group members should come to understand the interplay between thoughts, feelings and actions, and the subsequent effect all three have upon each other.

We recognise that up to the point of group attendance, each offender has been forced to play a passive role in an elaborate, complex and alien court room drama where professionals in the criminal justice system are centre stage. The group now provides the arena where, through the collective power and support of the group, offenders take the centre stage and are given the opportunity to move away from a professional interpretation of their reality and to express their own version of events and its importance to them. In facilitating this, group members are able to feel recognised and valued collectively and individually. As the research done by Ross, Fabiano and Ross suggests (1986), in influencing behaviour it is vital to understand, and work on, how individuals receive and integrate information about the social world and how this information affects their behaviour. This research establishes such work as a major factor in successful intervention in criminal behaviour.

Critical Incident Analysis (CIA)

The problem having been defined, we decided to use an incident analysis that produced the very detailed information we required. Initially we used the McGuire and Priestley model (1985, p.29) and then from this we subsequently developed our own model and its application. By completing the Critical Incident Analysis (CIA, Figure 1) group members are encouraged to detail each stage of a particular event, not only focusing on the action but the feelings and thoughts that accompany and influence these. The group is encouraged to recall the time scale of these incidents as a means to ensure as full an account as possible.

The information that this exercise elicits is significant, and subsequently the whole group acquires a different perspective on an individual's behaviour. For example, one client who normally presented as a timid person described uncharacteristic behaviour when he had been in a pub and had subsequently assaulted someone outside. Having completed the CIA exercise we were left with a vivid account of an entirely different incident whereby John had been one of a group of people outside the pub, and when he was himself pushed to the floor in the course of the fracas, so fearful was he of becoming a victim himself that he joined in the group assault (Figure 1).

Figure 1

THOUGHTS	ACTIONS	FEELINGS	TIME
	Arrived at the pub - Saturday	Happy and relaxed	6.50
	Sat down by door	Happy	7.20
Someone to talk to	Met friend and bought him a drink	Happier	7.30
What's that noise?	Playing darts, then a man came in and threw things about	Annoyed	7.50
Showing himself up	Yelled "shut up"	Pissed off	8.00
"Shut up will you"	Man disturbed	Feel angry	8.15
Lets have some peace and quiet	Man was getting more stupid and so told him to shut up	Anger building up	8.17
Going to hit him. this is getting serious	Said "Lets take him home and get him out of the pub"	Worried Excitement Nervous	8.25
This is getting bad	Two people in front push him to the ground, one kicked him, another punched and here I joined in	Scared, Worried	8.25
I'm going to get hit too	I was pushed forward by 2/3 people	Really scared	8.30
How am I going to get out of this	I'm at the side of him	In pain. Frightened (of getting hurt)	8.37
It's time I had a go punching him	Join in punching him, half-a-dozen times	Glad Excited	
Glad it's over	Stopped hitting him, went back to pub	Felt good to be with the lads	

Initially, groups find it difficult to complete this analysis, understandably so as without doubt we can all recognise from our own experiences of confrontational and emotional situations how difficult it is to recall a clear sequence of actions, let alone thoughts and feelings. At first the group leaders initiate questioning but group members quickly learn the kind of information required and the questions that provide this. In fact the group are able to direct more appropriate questions due to their understanding of the situations being described. With encouragement and the questioning of group leaders and group members all clients have been able to complete this process and have overcome their confusion about the distinction between thoughts and feelings and their interplay.

In evaluating our groups, feedback from group members indicates that they appreciated the opportunity to think in detail about what they have done and whilst at times this was a challenging experience, they felt supported by the group who were able to relate to the processes described. The challenge and support of the group is essential and therefore this form of analysis can only be done with a cohesive group who have developed a trusting and safe environment through a series of exercises which gradually lead individual members from talking about offending in general to focusing on their own offending.

This detailed analysis tells us a great deal about the individual offender, and repetition of the CIA exercise on other events enables us to elicit the complex patterns of behaviour and cycles in which these events occur. In addition it enables us to clarify exactly what the 'pay off' for the offender is. For example, working with one group member (Sam) who had a history of assaulting his wife, the CIA enabled him to see that in fact his initial statement of 'she makes me hit her', was far from the case and that a cycle of behaviour had developed whereby he would upset his partner in such a way that he knew she would react, in order that he could justify (to himself) hitting her whilst not having to take responsibility. The analysis elicited the complex power relationship that existed (Figure 2).

If people are going to break out of a cycle of behaviour and thought, the CIA provides a real and effective way of helping them to assess themselves, probably for the first time, and thus start the process of understanding themselves and taking the responsibility for control. The block of 'it just happened' is inevitably removed and with encouragement from group leaders and members the complex stages of an event are revealed. It has become apparent that clients do not necessarily wilfully and intentionally fail to think through

Figure 2

THOUGHTS	ACTIONS	FEELINGS	TIME
He's not pulling his weight	I was arguing with my husband about saving money	Frustration and anger	6.30
He's better get his act together - he's stupid	He said "I wanted to buy cannabis with the money - not sensible things"	Anger	
Any minute he is going to put one on me, I've got to get away - get out of the house	He lashed out - he got up dead fast and said "I say how to spend my money" He was shouting, gritting his teeth, red in the face. I left	Jumpy, on edge, overcome, scared, worried	
I hope he doesn't get me	He ran after me, got me on the stairs, shouted my name	Terrified	
He's not much of a man. He's using me for a punch bag. He might do worse.	I stopped, he was at the top of the stairs, came towards me shouting, "why are we arguing, it's my money". I said "I don't want to be around you while you're like this. You ought to spend your money on sensible things." He came towards me, grabbed me really right, it really hurts, he kicked me on the shin. I start to cry.	Victimised, used, sick (mentally) Hurt, nervous, scared	

what they are doing, but rather they often do not possess the skills that enable them to do this:

> Many offenders have a deficit in a number of (cognitive) skills and training in cognitive skills is an essential component of effective correctional programmes (Ross et al., 1986, p.1)

The CIA thus addresses one of the major objectives of the group, to enable offenders to learn to think in a different and broader way whilst providing us with the information we need to plan subsequent intervention with the client.

Development of the model

Having used this method to establish what really happens we have been able to use the same process to enable groups to consider the events from the victims point of view. In the past this has proved particularly difficult, the typical response being a wall of silence, and our experience suggests that many clients do not have the thinking skills to imagine how it must be to experience an event in the shoes of another. However, with the help of the group they have been able to do this. In the example of Sam (Figure 2), he was able to appreciate the fear that his behaviour created in his wife and thus acknowledged that she was the victim rather than himself. The group were particularly challenging of Sam and by this stage were able to take the predominant role of conducting the analysis. Sam was able to accept this confrontation from the group and we question if this would have been the case had an individual Probation Officer taken this role. Being challenged by his peers was a completely different experience for Sam and he was more able to accept this challenge in the context of a supportive group who were all participating in the same process.

Focusing work on the victims of crime also enables us to ascertain the risk of re-offending. For example, work with a paedophile, using the model to detail the thoughts, actions and feelings that formed part of a current fantasy, highlighted the fact that despite assertions to the contrary he was still not taking full responsibility for the events that occurred. The CIA from the victim's point of view demands that our clients see their victims as human beings who have thoughts and feelings like themselves and who are affected by crime in a multiplicity of ways in the immediate and longer term.

The CIA is also proving to be a useful basis for the development of techniques of self control. In our Anger Management Group, clients having completed the CIA have been able to link sequences of thoughts and feelings to the physical symptoms of anger and thus they can begin actually to recognise when they are feeling angry - an essential factor if they are to learn to prevent incidents escalating. Similarly, CIA's have been used to encourage clients to become aware of the role of self-talk (the internal conversations that we have with ourselves) in escalating violent situations, and subsequently to consider alternative positive self-statements at each stage of an incident. The group have been encouraged to develop self statements for each other that are real for them, that reflect reality and which they can own. As one client (Michael) said: 'You have to block out your conscience otherwise you wouldn't do it'.

In the course of critically analysing the events, self-talk such as 'go on there's nothing to worry about, you can do it!' enabled him to do just that. The group can help individuals recognise the techniques they employ to block thinking and escape from the reality that they are always making decisions and choices about their behaviour. The group can provide practical suggestions for self-statements which do not allow the blocking to continue, and so for Michael (previous example) self-statements such as, 'It's dangerous, you're going to get caught, you've only got yourself to blame' are devised.

In the case of a small group of young offenders who had committed burglaries a further application of the CIA was highlighted. It emerged that they saw their offending as a career in which they took professional pride and which involved very rational decision making at every stage: for example as part of planning a burglary, one group member would check gardens around the target house for evidence of dog faeces. A decision to proceed with the burglary would be made if no signs of a dog were evident.

The CIA also demonstrated the contradictions in their attitudes and values towards burglary, and has revealed important areas of work still to be done with the group. Again from the same group, one young man strongly expressed a general view that while it was acceptable to commit a burglary he would never take anything from a child's bedroom. The CIA revealed that in the course of one particular burglary this principle could be compromised when what was in a child's bedroom was an expensive video camcorder, the rationalisation being that it must have been a gift from a relative who could afford it.

This model is proving to be a very powerful tool which leaves users questioning their values and lifestyles. However, having reached this point the alternatives available to them in terms of housing, education, employment etc are often very limited. We are aware that this has structural and policy implications which as individual practitioners we cannot address, but we recognise our responsibility to ensure that these implications are not ignored by our own organisation and the wider community. Inevitably this work has made us aware of the importance of our own values in every aspect of our practice and therefore provides a useful component in the development of anti-discriminatory practice.

The use of Critical Incident Analysis in groupwork is very time consuming and for its successful completion requires skill and enthusiasm from the practitioners using it. The resource implications are therefore a factor for practitioners and management. However, it is proving to be an invaluable tool for assessment and the subsequent groupwork that we do with clients. We will continue to use the CIA and develop the range of ways in which it can be applied. It has increased both our own and group members' knowledge and understanding of their real behaviour which is an obvious pre-condition if clients are to reduce or stop their offending, and we are therefore confident that it will facilitate more effective intervention.

References

McGuire, J. and Priestley. P. (1985) *Offending Behaviour: Skills and Stratagems for Going Straight.* London: Batsford.

Ross. R.R., Fabiano, E.E. and Ross, R.D. (1986) *Reasoning and Rehabilitation: Handbook for Teaching Cognitive Skills.* University of Ottawa

Life history work with a group of people with learning disabilities

Dorothy Atkinson

This paper describes and analyses a life history project with a group of older people with learning disabilities. Originally set up as a research project primarily to test a method, the group eventually became an entity in its own right. My own role as researcher became that of group scribe, as the participants increasingly sought a means of documenting their individual and collective memories. This account traces how the evolving product of the group's work came out of, and in turn began to shape, the group process. These changes are illustrated by extracts from tape transcripts, diary accounts and the group's own booklet Past Times.

Introduction

> People welcome the opportunity to look back, reflect and make sense of what has gone before - and to plan what happens now and later.

This was one of the conclusions which I, and my co-editor Fiona Williams, came to as a result of compiling the anthology, *Know Me As I Am* (Atkinson and Williams, 1990, p.244). The anthology is a compilation of written, spoken, signed and painted accounts by people with learning disabilities about their lives and experiences. It provided the inspiration, and the motivation, for the group-based research project which is the subject of this paper.

The anthology helped set the scene for the research project in three ways. It demonstrated the value to people with learning disabilities of involvement in *life history* work. It contained examples of vivid and insightful accounts which had been compiled by *groups of people* working together. And, as a published book, it represented a highly prized and valued *product* for its contributors, an outcome which people were proud of.

My subsequent project, explored in this paper, combined these three distinctive features. Thus, I set up a 'history group' (as it became known) with nine older people with learning disabilities. We met regularly and frequently over a period of two years, focusing on the individual and collective memories of group members. The *process* of sharing and discussing life histories was important, but so too was the group's *product*; a written booklet entitled *Past Times* (Atkinson, 1991).

This article looks at how a collection of individuals, initially brought together for research purposes, over time became a functioning and self-determining group. There were two main phases in the group's lifespan. In the first phase my role is that of a researcher, finding out about people's past lives and experiences. In the second, I find I become the servant of a group with a history and identity - and aims - of its own. How did this happen? The discussion which follows aims to shed light on the major change of direction and emphasis which occurred within the lifetime of this group.

Background

My project involved life history work with people with learning disabilities in a group setting. I know of no comparable project which has combined these elements. There are, however, some published accounts on the separate factors in this equation. In this section I will outline, very briefly, some of the existing literature which has some relevance to my own field of inquiry.

There is a growing interest in, and literature about, qualitative research in relation to people with learning disabilities. Considerable work has been done to find ways and means of engaging people's interest and involvement in research about their lives (see, for example, Edgerton, 1984; Flynn, 1986; Atkinson, 1988; Jahoda et al., 1988; Wilkinson, 1989). Most research in this area has tended, however, to be based on interviews, or other one-to-one work with individuals, and focusing on the present rather than on the past. There have been relatively few reports of life or oral history-type projects, and few accounts of research work conducted in groups.

By way of contrast, the use of recall and reminiscence with older people more generally has been well-tried, and documented, especially over recent years (recent examples include: Coleman, 1986; Bornat, 1989; Gibson, 1989; Fielden, 1990.) It is rare to find documented accounts of similar work with older people with learning disabilities. One such rare example is the work of Potts and Fido (1991) where the authors chart the history of a long-stay hospital through the memories of 17 of its present and previous residents.

Research work involving groups of people with learning disabilities is equally rare. An earlier project of mine included research interviews with people living together in group homes (Atkinson, 1988; 1989), but these were with residential groups. A more effective use of group interviews, in combination with individual interviews, was reported by Walmsley (1990) in an account of her work with members of a self advocacy group. Whilst most contributors to the anthology, *Know Me As I Am* (Atkinson and Williams, 1990) were individuals, the book also contains a significant number of accounts produced by groups of people working together. The Women's Group and the Experiences of Handicap Group, for example, contributed striking observations and insights into the hitherto hidden worlds of their members.

It was with these observations and insights in mind that I chose a group format for my own project. The challenge, as I saw it, was to provide a supportive group setting where individual life stories could be recounted. This was an attempt to combine two approaches in one; to aim for the richness of individual accounts, but to do so within the more insightful and reflective mode of a group setting (Thompson, 1988).

The project

The group

The group had a membership of nine people; seven men and two women. The age range was 57-77, with most people in their late 60s or early 70s. I was introduced to potential members by day and residential staff who were working locally with older people with learning disabilities. We met informally and individually, and I personally invited people to join a series of group discussions based on their memories of past events and experiences.

In inviting people to join the group, I had two research aims in mind. One aim was to collect narrative accounts of people's lives against the background of key legislative and policy changes in the learning disability field in this century; to co-construct a history 'from below'. A second and inter-linked aim was to explore a method. Could people with learning disabilities use recall and reminiscence to produce oral life histories and - more importantly - could they do so in a group? This paper looks not only at how these invited individuals were able to recall past events *in* a group but also how they later came to do so *as* a group. Although my intention at the outset was to use the group as a vehicle for my own research, in fact it later became a driving force impelling us towards an emerging third aim - also the subject of this paper - of transforming these oral accounts into a written document.

Group members had three things in common. Each person was currently linked with special day and/or residential services so everybody already knew, or knew of, at least one or two other members of the group. Secondly, group members were all living in the same county and seven (of nine) had always done so. The same seven people had lived for much of their lives in long-stay hospitals. The county address proved a tenuous link in practice, as everyone had lived in different villages and towns in their younger days. The hospital link did prove important, though, as it led to the sharing of many memories of institutional life.

Although initially I had envisaged the project lasting only a few weeks, in fact it spanned almost two years. The group's life was extended because it became apparent that it provided a forum where experiences could be remembered, re-lived and shared. The weekly, and later fortnightly, group meeting quickly became a popular event in people's lives. It gave them an opportunity - which they grasped - of recalling, and reflecting on, important aspects of their personal pasts, and of making sense of those experiences. The group format made possible the sparking-off of individual and shared memories between people.

The group met on 28 occasions and all the hour-long meetings were, with permission, tape recorded and transcribed. As well as an opening session, where group members began the process of recall, and a closing session, where we said our goodbyes, there were two main phases in the group's life. The first of these (14 sessions) I refer to as the *research phase*, and the second (12 sessions) I refer to as the *group-as-an-entity phase*. I will explore both phases in more detail, drawing on illustrative extracts from tape transcripts, my diary accounts and the booklet, 'Past Times'.

Phase 1: The research phase

In the early days of the group my intention was to introduce themes of a universal kind for people to respond to. My rationale for introducing what I thought of as relatively non-threatening topics was that this would help the group get started on its task. My initial list of themes thus included memories of childhood and adolescence in terms of *where* (the type of house and neighbourhood), *how* (home and community life) and *with whom* (family life and relationships) group members lived. Discussion of hospital life, in particular, was left until later in the group's evolutionary cycle.

In this first phase, I saw myself primarily as a researcher, relating to individuals but within a group setting. In that capacity, I addressed group members rather than the group: asking questions, seeking clarification and reflecting back their answers. Not surprisingly, then, this first phase was characterised by group members speaking, on the whole, directly to me rather than to one another. They might also address a member of staff directly, especially if I was having difficulty in understanding the content of their speech. (I was accompanied by one or two members of staff on every occasion. They each knew at least some group members well and were invaluable in helping to interpret and translate people's responses. They helped in numerous other ways too, for example, in organising transport, offering reassurance and support, and joining in with their own memories.)

The following extract (Extract 1) is taken from the transcript of the second meeting of the group. It is really a question-and-answer session between myself, 'D', and 'Enid', 'Godfrey', 'Bob' and 'Barry', with 'Angela' - a staff member - later coming to my rescue (no real names are used in this account).

Extract 1

D. I tell you what I'd like to know, 'cos I'm not quite sure of people's ages, and how far back we're going. I don't know if anybody can remember which year they were born?

E. 1932 I was

D. You're 1932....

G. (interrupts) 'Scuse me....

D. Hang on, hang on a minute, (writes) 1932. [Background noise of several people speaking at once.] Slow down a bit.

Bob. 1920 I was

D. 1920?

Bob. Yeah.

D. Right..(writes) Barry, what were you saying? February? You got as far as February. Do you know which year?

B. Erm....

A. (staff) Let me just think, I'll try and work it out.

A second characteristic of this phase was the willingness, readiness even, of group members to talk about their individual and personal pasts. The types of memories varied, and included some period details of the time. Examples of this type included memories of coal fires and candlelight, childhood games of marbles and hopscotch, and descriptions of wash-tubs and mangles. But other sorts of memories were revealed often, to my surprise, including the disclosure of painful or traumatic events. The following extract

(Extract 2), also taken from the transcript of the second meeting, is an example of such revelations. Again, these confidences are addressed to me; they are Godfrey and Barry's earliest memories of death.

Extract 2

G. (interrupts) I had one little brother, but he died.
D. You had a younger brother did you, Godfrey?
G. Yeah, he died.
D. How old was he then? He died as a child?
G. Well, he died in his mother's....you know....
D. As a baby?
G. Yeah
D. Oh, that was sad. Any other brothers and sisters?
G. No.
D. Just the one?
G. Only one, yeah,
B. ....one brother and three sisters. I used to have a younger brother, but he died, in the water. He got drowned, he did.
D. He got drowned?
B. Yes.

In this phase of the group's life my research aims were to the forefront of my mind. My role was twofold; to keep the group to its task of recalling personal pasts (a task-focusing role) whilst, at the same time, trying to make the group a safe and comfortable place to be (a group maintenance role). My task-focusing role included introducing themes from childhood, schooldays and adolescence; asking questions, and reflecting on what was said. This was not always easy. Whilst sometimes my topics struck an answering chord, often they did not. Consequently group sessions often left me feeling out of control and powerless, as themes were sabotaged through side conversations, stage whispers, loud yawns, interruptions, and the accomplished telling of extended anecdotes (on rival themes).

As well as struggling with keeping people to task, I also felt responsible for the group's social and emotional well-being. Thus, I attempted to create and maintain a friendly and informal atmosphere, where group members would feel relaxed and valued. I also felt responsible for keeping the group going, and maintaining people's interest, including - as I ran out of themes - acquiring reminiscence aids such as tapes, slides and photographs to act as memory triggers.

In practice, of course, both roles were interconnected. People kept to task when they seemed interested and motivated. And the group felt a good place to be when its members were fully engaged and participating. The following extract (Extract 3) is taken from my diary account of the third meeting. It illustrates the difficulties I encountered in my dual role.

Extract 3

> I felt it was laboured tonight. There were two new people. They both started by saying they couldn't remember anything (though they joined in later). We also missed 'Jean' (staff). We did the 'house-as-you-remember-it' theme. Some memories got people going; tin baths, wash-tubs, flat irons and old wireless programmes. Sometimes everybody spoke at once, and I heard nobody. At other times I was forever fishing and probing, getting nowhere.

It is interesting now to look back at this first phase of the group's life in terms of theories about group development. This was a structured, task-focused group with a closed membership. It existed, as I saw it, to achieve some specific research aims, and yet my attempts to impose control on its direction and purpose could not prevent it taking on aspects of the 'classical linear model'. (Brown and Clough, 1989, p.39). The 'forming' stage had not proved problematic. However, the prolonged 'storming' stage (Tuckman, 1965) where I felt, as I described earlier, both out of control and powerless, threatened to undermine my research aims. This was no docile gathering of people, willing to reminisce to order, but a group classically engaged in early struggles over roles and influence.

Phase 2: The group-as-an-entity

In the second phase of its life the group became an entity, with a life and a momentum of its own. This happened because during the course of our first 15 meetings it became apparent, as transcript followed transcript, that in spite of everything we had a product in the making. During the summer of our first year we took a break from meetings to give me time to compile the fragments, vignettes and anecdotes into a coherent whole. This document was made into a large-print reprographed and stapled booklet, with a coloured cover, and was given the title *Past Times*, (Atkinson, 1991). Each group member was given a personal copy of this booklet, and it became known as 'our book'.

The first draft (as it turned out to be) of 'our book' acted as a catalyst for a dramatic change in the group dynamics. The delight in the book as it was, and the desire to make it bigger and better, proved to be potent forces. The book thus became a trigger to its own contributors, and I spent much of my time from then on giving readings from its contents. As the readings continued over the months that followed, and the layers of memories steadily peeled away, 'our book' became 'our second book' and, later, 'our third book'.

There is no doubt that 'our book' was extremely important as a written document in its own right, but it had a deeper and more symbolic significance. For 'our book' one could almost read 'our group', although this was never articulated. The coming together of the book symbolised the coming together of the group, to become 'our group' with common goals, a sense of identity and interaction between members (Brown and Clough, 1989). We had moved, at last, from 'storming', to the 'norming' and 'performing' stages of the group's life (Tuckman, 1965).

The second phase of the group's life was strikingly different from the first. Somehow the ownership of the project had shifted, and I had become its servant rather than its instigator. Group members spoke to one another, as well as to me, and collective memories began to emerge. Support during painful moments of recall often came from peers rather than from myself or staff. The group, it seemed, had 'come of age', and had taken at least some control over its destiny. My role combined several interrelated tasks; reading, listening, recording, transcribing and writing. I had, in fact, become the group's scribe.

I will now illustrate these points with extracts. The changed nature of group interaction, where people speak to one another as well as to me, and where peer support is offered and accepted, is illustrated in Extract 4. This is taken from the tape transcript of the eighteenth meeting, where members of the group are recalling their wartime experiences - these were memories, for several people, of wartime in 'Talltrees Hospital'. The conversationalists in this extract, as well as myself, are Godfrey, Marjorie, Barry and Jim.

Extract 4

G. They dropped a bomb, and it fell somewhere near Talltrees.

D. Oh, I think I've got that story.

M. Yeah, we see that, we see that bomb, it come over F1, and we was all in the cloakroom. We see this bomb go over the top.

D. Were you scared?
M. No, I wasn't scared....
B. Poor Marjorie (putting a hand on her arm)
M. ....the board had come down from the window, so we put it back up.
D. Yeah, we've got a little bit about that in here as well, when the board came down.
G. I should think you remember it, don't you Jim? Do you remember that bomb that come down near Talltrees when the war was on?
J. Yeah, in the cornfield.

Extract 4 also begins to illustrate the interactions between group members which led to the development of shared memories. Although individuals remembered, and felt keenly, their personal losses of home, family and friends, nevertheless there was also a sense of collective loss. The causes of these individual losses were already known to other people as they had suffered them too. Long-term hospitalisation brought in its wake separation from home and loss of family and, in their sharing of these memories, group members were beginning to reclaim a collective past. Extract 5, below, is taken from *Past Times*. It is Marjorie's account of leaving home, but it is a story which most people in the group could identify with, and 'match' with their own.

Extract 5

> When I was a little girl I was put away. I was 14 and a half. I went to 'Red Roofs' to live because they said I was backward. My dad refused to sign the papers for me to go, but the police came and said he would go to prison if he didn't. I cried when I had to go with the Welfare Officer.

As I said earlier, my task in this phase was, essentially, to serve the group - to facilitate and record its discussions in order to extend and enhance 'our book'. This proved liberating. As group scribe I had a socially sanctioned role but, better still, I was also able to shed some of my erstwhile responsibilities. The group was itself highly motivated to keep to its task and, as memories became deeper and more painful, so the support and humour within the group grew stronger. I illustrate these changes in the following extract (Extract 6) taken from my diary account written in the early weeks of this second phase (meeting 17).

Extract 6

> A good session. My tiredness evaporated as people came in smiling. No Fred, but Arthur was there. Apparently he talks a lot *outside* the group nowadays. Bob returned! He looked fine considering what he's been through. He was in a wheelchair but very active. He contributed a lot, especially about hospital days.[...] It was relaxed and fun. They were proud and pleased about how far they'd come, and how much they knew. It felt a good place to be![...] They haven't made a formal decision, but maybe they don't need to. Maybe they're doing it by their commitment to the work in hand. Who's in charge? Not me, it seems!

The second phase of the group's life was characterised by its new-found *identity as a group*. This had found expression, and symbolic recognition, in the production of *Past Times* in its various drafts. As a group, people came to share common goals (to create 'a bigger and better book') and there was a shift towards more interaction between members. My role was transformed by these changes in group dynamics. As a group culture became established, and members increasingly took responsibility for the group and its 'performing' role, I became - of necessity - more of a supporter and less of a leader.

Conclusion

This project begins to shed some light on the use of groups in the process of recall and reminiscence. I chose a group format because that way, I felt, lay the richness and diversity of accounts and the sparking off of ideas between people. As a researcher, I saw the group setting simply as a forum in which experiences could be recounted and shared. The group provided that forum in the end, but it took months of struggling - or 'storming' - to get there. At the time, I operated on the basis of research aims not on the basis of groupwork theories. Somehow I had assumed that the research focus of this group would protect it from those unconscious forces let loose in other people's groups. How wrong I was! Research in groups, no less than groupwork itself, requires an understanding of how groups operate, and some knowledge of what to expect.

It also became clear, in the course of this study, that life history work - and the processes of reminiscence and recall which this involves - can be of great value to people with learning disabilities. Although this was designed to be a research project to chart the lives and experiences of group members, and to find the ways and means of doing so, it had other unintended but beneficial outcomes.

Reconstructing lives, and reclaiming individual and collective pasts, brought about a greater sense of self esteem as group members increasingly came to see themselves as the holders of historical knowledge. This growing consciousness was further enhanced both by the group process itself, and the product of the group's work. Looking back, it is apparent that the process of remembering, and sharing memories, had proved hugely enjoyable to group members. However, it was the emerging and evolving *product* of the group's labours (*Past Times* in its various drafts) which transformed the group's dynamics and my own role.

This booklet was the source of individual achievement and collective pride. It was also an inspiration to its contributors to go on with their work. My original research aims became subsumed into the group's own long-term and overriding aim; to keep working together to produce 'a bigger and better book' as documentary evidence of their own hidden history.

Acknowledgements
I wish to thank all the people who took part in this project. This includes both the group members themselves, and the staff who worked alongside them. My thanks are to everyone for their generous investment of time, energy and enthusiasm into this project.

References

Atkinson, D. (1988) 'Research interviews with people with mental handicaps', *Mental Handicap Research* 1(1), pp.75-90

Atkinson, D. (1989) 'Group homes for people with mental handicap: key issues for everyday living' in Brown, A. and Clough, R. (eds.) *Groups and Groupings. Life and Work in Day and Residential Centres*. London and New York: Tavistock/Routledge

Atkinson, D. (1991) *Past Times*. Unpublished.

Atkinson, D. and Williams, F. (eds.) (1990) *'Know Me As I Am'. An Anthology of Prose, Poetry and Art by People with Learning Difficulties*. London: Hodder and Stoughton.

Bornat, J. (1989) 'Oral history as a social movement: reminiscence and older people', *Oral History*, 17(2), pp.23-31.

Brown, A. and Clough, R. (1989) 'The mosaic of groups and groupings: some theoretical concepts' in Brown, A. and Clough, R. (eds.) *Groups and Groupings. Life and Work in Day and Residential Centres*. London and New York: Tavistock/Routledge.

Coleman, P.G. (1986) *Ageing and Reminiscence Processes*. Chichester: John Wiley.

Edgerton, R.B. (ed) (1984) 'Introduction' in *Lives in Process: Mentally Retarded Adults in a Large City.* Monograph No 6. Washington: American Association on Mental Deficiency.

Fielden, M.A. (1990) 'Reminiscence as a therapeutic intervention with sheltered housing residents: a comparative study'. *British Journal of Social Work,* 20(1), pp.21-44.

Flynn, M.C. (1986) 'Adults who are mentally handicapped as consumers: issues and guidelines for interviewing', *Journal of Mental Deficiency Research*, 30, pp.369-377.

Gibson, F. (1989) *Using Reminiscence: A Training Pack.* London: Help the Aged.

Jahoda, A., Markova, I. and Cattermole, M. (1988) 'Stigma and the self concept of people with a mild mental handicap', *Journal of Mental Deficiency Research*, 32, pp.103-115.

Potts, M. and Fido, R. (1991) *A Fit Person To Be Removed.* Plymouth: Northcote House.

Thompson, P. (1988) *The Voice of the Past.* (Second edition.) Oxford: Oxford University Press.

Tuckman, B.W. (1965) 'Developmental sequence in small groups', *Psychological Bulletin* 63(6).

Walmsley, J. (1990) 'The role of groupwork in research with people with learning difficulties', *Groupwork*, 3(1), pp.49-64.

Wilkinson, J. (1989) 'Being there': evaluating life quality from feelings and daily experience' in Brechin, A. and Walmsley, J. *Making Connections. Reflecting on the Lives and Experiences of People with Learning Difficulties*. London: Hodder and Stoughton.

ART THERAPY: CREATIVE GROUPWORK FOR WOMEN

OLIVE OTWAY

This paper explores an innovative way of working with women, in which the author describes setting up an art therapy group for working class women, in a local community centre. Common themes emerged in the women's paintings such as, self blame, racism, sexism and body image. The group illustrates how the creative process, mutual support of group members and utilisation of the women's own abilities helped resolve some of the difficulties they experienced in their daily lives. It is particularly aimed at practitioners.

History of the group

It is clear from statistical analysis of service users, that women are the main consumers of social service facilities (Brook and Davis, 1985). We also know that tranquillisers are excessively over prescribed to women and that admission to psychiatric wards are significantly higher for women than for men (Miles, 1990). Alternative treatment is not freely accessible particularly for working class women, and free counselling services are few and far between. At the same time, in a climate of restrictions on local government expenditure and budget cut backs to the voluntary sector, the dearth of community based supportive facilities is becoming more noticeable (Manning and Page, 1992).

Given the present situation of financial constraint and lack of resources, how can social services respond to women in a creative way, which possibly avoids unnecessary admittance to a psychiatric ward and repeated demands on an over-loaded duty system?

Too often there is pressure on social workers to deal with crises on an individual basis, concentrating time and energy on the symptoms of the problem rather than the causes. This paper reports on a different approach, one which used the medium of art to help women utilise their own problem solving skills.

Why art therapy?

Art therapy through the use of painting and drawing to produce visual images, can assist an externalisation of thoughts and feelings that may have remained unexpressed. Such images can have a

Groupwork Vol. 6(3), 1993, pp.211-220

diagnostic and therapeutic value as they provide a record of the session, and can give pointers to other problematic areas that could be explored in further meetings (Waller and Gilroy, 1992). It is a misconception to hold the view that this medium is only available to those who are 'artistically gifted'. If anything, the reverse is true. Those with formal training may be too conscious of the quality of the painting rather than the feelings it is attempting to evoke.

Once any initial inhibition is overcome for those not familiar with this way of working, the benefits and enjoyment of the materials can be immense. Art therapy can offer a gradual method of exploring feelings due to the versatility of communication at different levels. Individuals can work at a pace and depth that feels safe for them (Otway and Ellis, 1987). We may find it difficult to articulate our true feelings, fearing that the expression of these may be overwhelming and/or destructive. Through the use of images in art therapy, and a build up of trust in group members, feelings can be expressed with greater safety. This may be attributed to the frame of the paper literally containing such feelings, and so they are experienced as less dangerous and overwhelming than initially feared. Through painting, the women can rehearse the expression of their feelings before taking the risk to verbalise them to others.

Why use groupwork?

Liebmann (1989) suggests nine advantages of art therapy in groups:

1. Much of social learning is done in groups; therefore groupwork provides a relevant context in which to practise.
2. People with similar needs can provide mutual support for each other, and help with mutual problem-solving.
3. Group members can learn from the feedback from other members.
4. Group members can try new roles, from seeing how others react (role-modelling), and can be supported and reinforced in this.
5. Groups can be catalysts for developing latent resources and abilities.
6. Groups are more suitable for certain individuals, e.g. those who find the intimacy of individual work too intense.
7. Groups can be more democratic, sharing the power and responsibility.
8. Some therapists/groupworkers find groupwork more satisfying than individual work.
9. Groups can be an economical way of using expertise to help several people at the same time.

There are, however, some disadvantages:

1. Confidentiality is more difficult because more people are involved.
2. Groups need resources and can be difficult to organise.
3. Less individual attention is available to members of a group.
4. A group may be 'labelled' or acquire a stigma (Liebmann, 1989, p.7)

Getting the group started

The two groupworkers described in this paper were an art therapist and a social worker. The author of this paper, as a social worker, was keen to widen the range of responses to women service users. Adult Education and a local charity provided the funding which enabled the group to run, with creche facilities, for a six month period on a weekly basis.

A lively, active community centre was to be the setting for the sessions. The venue had a number of advantages;

1. It was local.
2. It was not attached to a social service office, so possibly avoiding the stigma that can accompany a client of social services.
3. There was a separate room for the creche on a different floor.
4. Refreshment facilities and toilets were close by.
5. Materials and equipment could be locked away when not in use by the group.
6. The room was free on the day we had set aside. Finally, it was affordable.

What the group could offer

Since women are generally expected by society to take care of others it is often extremely difficult for them to recognise or admit their own need for support (Hanmer and Statham, 1988). Afraid too of being unable to articulate feelings and of possible stigmatisation, women may be hesitant to approach a statutory organisation to talk over their fears and anxieties about their own well being. Publicity for the group was therefore intentionally displayed in a wide variety of settings, with the expectation that there could be self referrals and no direct link with a statutory agency.

Many women can find that their roles in society as carers and nurturers prevent them from recognising their own need for time and support for themselves. As women, we may have been taught to think of ourselves as second-best, to see difficulties arising from this as 'our fault'. Through accepting ourselves more, we may begin to feel that taking care of ourselves can be a valid and necessary activity. Therapy can be a powerful tool helping us to understand what is happening in our lives, and to deal effectively with the issues and problems we face (Ernst and Goodison, 1984).

As feminists, we believe that many women's experiences were a product not of individual failure but of the contradictory demands that society makes on all women. The resulting depth of gender conditioning can hinder efforts to change. Through the institutions in a patriarchal society many women are brought up to be submissive and supportive of others, to be seductive, manipulative and passive. Women are rarely actively encouraged to decide what we want and to seek openly to achieve it, to be angry, powerful, demanding. We may experience pressure to deny our own needs by putting the needs of men and children first. By unlearning this conditioning we can bring to the surface some of our suppressed feelings and learn to tap into previously submerged strengths and resources.

In our experience, therapy had been mainly available to middle class women who had the power to purchase it. What had been traditionally available to working class women was purchased through medical prescriptions in the form of tranquillizers or in/out patient treatment in psychiatric wards (Roberts, 1985). For this reason the group was targeted at working class women and was to be free.

Group members

We sent our publicity to social services, local nurseries, library, general practitioners, health centres, women's refuges, and relevant voluntary agencies. Where possible we spoke to people directly too, explaining who we were, what we wanted to do and why. Referrals were received from social workers as well as from women themselves who had seen the publicity leaflet. All women were contacted and seen at home. At the initial meeting we used the time to introduce ourselves and what we hoped to offer by running the group. We shared anxieties and discussed practical arrangements. Not everyone who we saw initially joined the group. This was for a variety of reasons, from lack of motivation to obtaining employment, and not being available on the day the group was to run.

Six women agreed to join the group after meeting with the two facilitators. In a closed art therapy group in which membership is fixed, and attendance throughout the life of the group is expected, six to eight participants is generally viewed as the optimum number (Schaverien, 1992).

Those who did join were from different ethnic groups, of different ages, and presented initially different concerns: for example, relationship difficulties, poverty, lack of confidence and unemployment. The women described themselves in terms of ethnicity as follows: two were white UK European, one Irish, one Jewish, one African/Caribbean and one Scandinavian. Their ages ranged from 17 to 40 years. Two women had part time employment.

Structure of the weekly sessions

The first session was used to explore introductions, discuss worries, share expectations and establish ground rules. Those with children introduced the young people to the creche and workers, spending time settling the children and helping them to get to know their surroundings.

In the following weeks the sessions lasted for two hours. Each meeting began with a discussion about anything the women wished to raise. The subsequent 45 minutes was the time for individual painting/drawing, followed by one hour's talking as a group about the feelings that emerged in the women's paintings and how these related to what was happening in their own lives.

As facilitators, we aimed to enable the women to identify their own needs and feelings, the source of these feelings and the possibilities for change. We also encouraged the women to explore how these feelings were reflected in their relationship to the group at the present time. It was each woman's choice as to how much and when she contributed to the conversations, but as the weeks went by the women grew in trust and confidence resulting in a reduction of the role of facilitator during discussions. The group members moved away from directly addressing the groupworkers and moved more towards each other, using observations, questioning and interpretation. Through participating in group discussions and exploring ideas a heightened awareness of some of the emerging themes was reached, with possible strategies to enable change.

As feminists, we also attempted (when appropriate) to place individual issues in the wider context of the expectations and constraints women in our society face (Dominelli and McLeod, 1989).

Common themes that emerged over the sessions

Self blame

All the women shared feelings of missed opportunities and regret about their past and decisions that had resulted in their present unhappy circumstances. As they were working class women there was little choice concerning opportunities around education, paid work and quality of life style. They talked of self-blame, finding it difficult to acknowledge their own strengths and ways they had coped and struggled in adverse situations. It was often hard to talk of successes. When possible, we tried to reframe their personal experience and place it within a socio-political perspective examining structural oppression. For those women with children a common area concerned the internalisation of how society devalues women's work in the home (Gittins, 1987).

The group provided the space and opportunity to discuss the choices they had made and to recognise that these were often all that was possible in the circumstances, and to re-evaluate their feelings of ' failure'. Through talking with each other about their painting and feelings, some women became aware of the needs they had and how these could or could not be met in their present situation, and how they could develop different coping strategies in the future. Awareness was raised about how to challenge, confront and question their predicament. Through sharing their 'stories' the women were attempting to break down the loneliness and isolation experienced outside the group. For many women the support and encouragement received by others was a completely different experience to the devaluing of self which happened outside the sessions.

Racism and sexism

For some of the women, talking of their childhood experiences enabled them to understand the source of their present feelings and how this could impinge on their present situation and relationships. Through looking at a culture that has particular expectations of women, the group members were enabled to feel less self-accusing, and this facilitated the recognition of a link between the external world and their emotional experiences (Sayers, 1986). For the women who were from minority ethnic groups, the group offered them a place to explore their experiences of the multiple oppression of racism and sexism (Bogle, 1988). White members of the group recognised how at times they acted on the internalisation of racism and its oppressive attitudes. The discussions that followed explored coping mechanisms and strategies for recognising and challenging both racism and sexism. Being able to identify the sources of low self-esteem helped to illustrate the potential for change.

The painting time in the first hour of the session provided women with a much needed space for themselves to focus on their own individual experiences, without the pressure of others' demands. Women were able to look at some of the feelings of guilt evoked at receiving this attention for themselves.

For instance, one member had never left her 14 month old child since his birth and found it extremely difficult to separate from him. Using the creche became a source of stress and conflict. She defined herself solely as 'a mother', to such an extent that she could not envisage any other identity. Through her paintings she uncovered another reflection of herself as a woman, and with the group's support and encouragement she was able successfully to leave her child in the creche and allow herself two hours away from him. She used the time for herself to look at her own feelings of anger and hidden longing to be nurtured, loved and cared for. She was also able to value her skills as a carer and to explore her strengths and positive qualities. In the past she had tried to cope with negative feelings through compulsive eating (Dana and Lawrence, 1988).

Body image

Questions of body image and sexuality are recurrent themes for women, and feelings about those issues can be expressed directly through visual imagery and the physical and tactile qualities of paint. An anorexic woman in the group used the painting time to explore the unconscious meanings attached to her body image and eating patterns. Through her painted images she recognised the extent to which she used her body as a metaphor for her attempts to gain control over her life (Dally and Gomez, 1980).

By drawing herself alone on a desert island protected by the sea, one woman expressed her hidden wish to free herself from the bombardment of other's demands. In feeling supported by other women in the group who had similar experiences, this young mother trapped in a violent relationship, gained information, self-confidence and self-valuing, enabling her to leave the relationship.

Shared experiences

Through recognising as women that they shared common experiences, their sense of personal blame, responsibility and isolation began to diminish. Within the group they shared their feelings towards each other and how these related to their experiences of other relationships. The group was able to offer a place to explore new ways of relating.

For all, anger was a particularly difficult emotion to express. Afraid that it would be overwhelming and uncontrollable they hid their rage to protect others and possibly themselves. By using their paintings as a tool they slowly became able to communicate their anger and release feelings they had long suppressed. Over the weeks they began to feel safe enough to express their anger with one another. This enabled them to see how anger might be a source of their own power to gain more control over their own lives.

Supervision

As co-workers and individual professionals we recognised and valued the contributions of a supervisor/consultant. Realising the specialist nature of the group, we sought the services of a woman psychotherapist who we knew of and respected. We felt that her contribution was essential to our working together effectively, to ensure a good quality of service to group members (Richards et al., 1990). The supervision provided a valuable forum to explore our different roles, styles of working, perspectives, conflicts and backgrounds. It also aided our exploration of the difficulties of groupwork with women in a community setting. Supervision took place weekly throughout the life of the group.

Conclusion

Experience in this group demonstrated the extensive potential of enabling women who have no previous art experience to gain access to their own creative processes. Since women in particular have been denied possibilities for creative expression outside their nurturing role, art can be a facilitator in enabling them to discover their own creative power and to increase their awareness of their own needs and feelings (Miles, 1990). Art can offer women a language for what is 'unnameable', increase self esteem, articulate their needs and hence empower women to increase the choices in their lives.

We did not formally follow up what happened to the women afterwards, but we do know that one woman left an abusive relationship, one gained her first job for several years after having a child, one began an access course and one began a degree. Another member decided that she wanted to continue with art therapy and so joined the subsequent group. Several of the women ceased having contact with social workers and therefore appeared to be developing and drawing on their own coping mechanisms.

Success could also be measured in attendance at the group which was high, with no one leaving the group except for the woman who left the area on ending the abusive relationship with her husband. Six women began the group and five were still attending when the group ended. As groupworkers we were convinced of the usefulness and need for such a resource, as were the group members themselves.

Another group quickly followed which did not need publicity. This was due to other women seeing the information regarding the initial group and contacting groupworkers for details. This is a way of working that is accessible for a range of 'clients', in individual work or in groups: for example, groups for children who have behaviourial and relationship difficulties (Clerkin and Knaggs, 1991), children and young people who are differently abled and whose main way of communicating may not be through the spoken word (Froude, 1989), and children who are in care (Gillespie,1986). There is also potential for its use in residential settings when working with older people. The potential and use is therefore vast and would benefit from further research.

In the past there has been resistance to research into art therapy. However there now appears to be some acknowledgement of its value and the need for research. Research could improve practice, enhance training and the credibility of this form of therapeutic intervention (Waller and Gilroy, 1992). Research that attempted to look at the efficacy of art therapy as a 'treatment' model could place it along side more traditional models and so give 'clients' more choice as to the way they discover their own solutions to their predicament.

Acknowledgement
Thanks are due to Mary Lynne Ellis, art therapist.

References

Brook, E. and Davis, A. (1985) *Women, the Family and Social Work*. Tavistock Library of Social Work Practice.

Bogle, M. (1988) 'Brixton Black Women's Centre: organising on child sexual abuse', *Feminist Review*, 28(3).

Clerkin, E. and Knaggs, B. (1991) 'Working creatively with children', *Groupwork*, 4(1).

Dally, P. and Gomez, J. (1980) *Obesity and Anorexia Nervosa: A Question of Shape*. Faber and Faber.

Dana, M. and Lawrence, M. (1988) *Women's Secret Disorder. A New Understanding of Bulimia*. Grafton.

Dominelli, L. and McLeod, E. (1989) *Feminist Social Work*. Macmillan.

Ernst, S. and Goodison, L. (1984) *In Our Own Hands: A Book of Self-Help Therapy*. London: The Women's Press.

Froude, C. (1989) 'Teaching special children, and the art of therapy', *Social Work Today,* 16 March.

Gillespie, A. (1986) 'Art therapy at the familymakers project', *Adoption and Fostering*, 10 (1).

Gittins, D. (1987) *The Family in Question*. Macmillan.

Hanmer, J. and Statham, D. (1988) *Women and Social Work - Towards a Woman Centred Practice*. Macmillan.

Liebmann, M. (1989) *Art Therapy for Groups*. Routledge.

Manning, N. and Page, R. (1992) *Social Policy Review*, 4. Social Policy Association.

Miles, R. (1990) *The Women's History of The World*. Paladin.

Otway, O. and Ellis, M. (1987) 'Painting their way out of the blues', *Community Care*, 9 April.

Richards, M. et al, (1990) *Competencies in Supervision: Identification and Assessment*. National Institute of Social Work.

Roberts, H. (1985) *The Patient Patients: Women and Their Doctors*. Pandora Press.

Sayers, J. (1986) *Sexual Contradictions, Psychology, Psychoanalysis and Feminism*. Tavistock Publications.

Schaverien, J. (1992) *Revealing Image*. Tavistock/Routledge.

Waller, D. and Gilroy, A. (1992) *Art Therapy: A Handbook*. Open University Press.

GROUPWORK WITH PARENTS OF LEARNING DISABLED ADOLESCENTS

HELEN GOBAT

This is an account of two groups for parents of children with learning disabilities, which focused on issues around their adolescence, and were based on a psychotherapeutic model of groupwork. They were short-term workshops, yet achieved a great deal for the participants. This article explores the special nature of the cohesiveness in these groups, the analogue for the therapeutic relationship in individual therapy. The author explores her own experience of having a chronically sick child, and how this and other factors may have affected the cohesiveness in these groups.

Introduction

This is an account of two groups for parents of children with special needs, which I offered as workshops at a school for children with severe learning disabilities. I have worked for many years as a specialist social worker in the field of learning disability, and found in all the parent groups with which I have been involved, whatever their expressed purpose, that there is a special intensity and cohesiveness which occurs very quickly. In this short space, I cannot examine at depth all aspects of the group process and its effects on the individual, but will explore the nature of this cohesiveness and the dynamics which influence it.

Background

The focus on 'issues of growing up' was based on the premise that the time when a child with special needs becomes adult in body, is one of the most critical times for both parents and the child. On the one hand, the hope that there would be a magical cure, that after all the disabled child could become a 'normal' adult, is seen finally as an impossible fantasy: 'I somehow felt that when he grew up, he would get better' (parent). The child's emerging sexuality is a confirmation of an adulthood that will be unfulfilled in many ways, and encourages fantasies that it may have been a bad sex act which resulted in the child's birth (Sinason, 1992). On another level, it arouses fear that the child will reproduce him or herself, so it is best to deny sexuality altogether: ' It's not for her'. ' I'm sure he does not have sexual feelings' (parents).

For the child, there are new feelings which are hard to understand and new expectations of them as a 'grown-up' person. Behaviour that was acceptable in a child, is no longer acceptable for an adult, whatever their cognitive level.

There is desperate sadness for the young adult who may not have the opportunity to experience adult love, to pursue further education or to lead an independent life of their own choice. This is yet another stage of grieving. I have been much influenced by William Worden's (1983) theories of grief therapy, particularly around the issue of chronic loss. Parents of disabled children no sooner pass through one loss than another emerges which has to be tackled. If there are stages and processes to be gone through with loss as Worden suggests, then each new loss revives the feelings of the previous losses, and the same set of defences are called upon to deal with the accompanying grief. If the losses are never acknowledged , the grief remains unresolved, and each new loss remains unresolved. By the time a disabled child reaches puberty, there are well established lines of defence in each parent, both functional and dysfunctional.

The parents in these groups were able to identify critical stages which had already occurred - diagnosis of the disability, statementing for a special school, and of course losses incumbent upon each of these stages, before puberty came along.

The groupwork

The groups were held for one and a half hours at weekly intervals for six sessions, and then eight sessions for the second group. The number of sessions was agreed at the beginning, and was governed by finance. The parents contributed £1 per session, and the balance was provided by the Parent Staff Association. My inspiration came from a parents' group set up by Mary Ryan, at the Special Needs Sexuality Project in Lewisham. This project was instigated by parents and subsequently supported by both statutory (Lewisham) and voluntary (Mental Health Aid) finance. This indicated to me that there is both an expressed and perceived need, and I felt that the model could be used again. I called the groups 'workshops' deliberately - to enable the parents to direct the work themselves, and to suggest that learning would take place.

The *aims* of the workshops were thus twofold. Firstly, to enable a set of parents to explore issues which concerned them about their adolescent children, and secondly, to allow them the opportunity to do this in a safe environment with others who shared their experiences. For almost all the parents, this was their first experience of a group of this kind. The headteacher gave her support all the way, initially sending out letters of invitation to all the parents of the older classes, then helping to ensure that a room was found which was kept exclusively for the group at the appointed time. We were only once interrupted. I have found that the model with which you begin a group will stay with it. These groups were considered precious and private, and respected as such from the start, by worker, parents and the school staff.

The *objectives* of the group were not specifically to promote change. They were of too limited a life. However, one objective was the development of greater insight into issues which troubled these parents and the defences they used to cope with them. Another was to help parents to recognise their own ability to handle difficult issues with their growing children, to acknowledge their existing skills and explore new possibilities.

I used a psychotherapeutic model of groupwork, such as Brown and Pedder (1979) outline. Conditions must exist in the 'treatment setting' so as to build relationships of trust, leading to honest talk and communication in depth. These interact with dynamic processes in the individual, leading to increased acceptance of oneself and others, increased verbalisation and expression of feelings and thoughts, which in turn leads to increased understanding and integration of acknowledged aspects of oneself and relationships.

Membership

As I was able to hold two workshops, I can compare the experiences. One man and eight women came to the first group, and seven women for the second. I was concerned about the only father, who was also a black person amongst white women. He earned his membership the hardest way, by sharing with the mothers his account of caring for even the most intimate aspects of his daughter's care. He had also given up work to assist his wife, as their daughter needed help night and day. It has been my experience with other parent groups, that mothers have believed that fathers do not feel, or act, in the same way toward their disabled child. This particular father gained the respect of these mothers, and destroyed some of their assumptions.

There were some serious membership difficulties and losses in the second group. One Asian woman spoke very little English, and eventually ceased coming. At first, the other mothers gave her time and made sure she understood, but they soon forgot to wait for her in their urgent desire to discuss their own matters. The Greek mother in this same group managed with limited language. I can only conclude that language is only one factor in limiting group belonging. Different levels of cognitive ability and insight did not unduly affect a member's comfort, though strong use of denial may separate members out.

The second group also lost one mother who had to return to her country of origin, and another who, having missed two sessions, felt she had missed too much to return. We were thus mostly only five for the second group, and this did affect group dynamics enormously, as the group process became more vulnerable to domination by a needy member, and less rich overall.

Each group contained one person who acted as a catalyst for the emotions of the group, and thereby drew the groups into more painful feelings. This person was the most needy and most vulnerable. There was also one woman in each group who had an older child, and they were seen as wiser by virtue of longer experience. They were able to challenge denial by the parents of younger children.

Leadership

I had decided that it was preferable to be a sole leader than to work with someone I did not know and who did not share my theoretical base, which was the only possibility available. I felt that a group of eight was a maximum number for one leader and the first group was usually this number. The flipchart stand became my co-leader, on which I wrote up what the parents were discussing, a form of validating, summarising and recording their thoughts. Conversation did not pause while I was writing.

In each group, one parent became self-appointed co-leader for practical purposes. One woman in the first group who had been my client formerly, was protective of me, and provided cakes on the last session. I did feel exhausted and had to find support outside when sessions had been very emotional, but I was unable to find professional supervision, which would have been desirable. I made comprehensive notes after each session, and this became a process of reflection.

My leadership was directive in the first few sessions, keeping the group to the agreed agenda but allowing diversion if the group was discussing feelings and pertinent issues. The second group became self-directing earlier than the first.

Content

In the first session of each group, we looked at all the possible issues of growing up which concerned parents. From these I selected topics for the subsequent groups, and we did on the whole cover what we planned. Little time was spent on getting to know each other individually, though rules and boundaries were explored.

In the first group, we looked at the rights of any young person then examined the differences for a person with special needs. The second session was focused on naming sexual parts and on masturbation as a topic. The group all found this very difficult, but my intention was to loosen up their inhibitions about discussing sexuality. Masturbation was of importance to these parents, and one mother courageously shared problems of managing her severely disabled teenage son. Resistance to my agenda in this session may have even united the parents.

The next session worked on acceptable and unacceptable behaviour for an adolescent, particularly regarding sexuality, and the parents were able to draw up a comprehensive list of golden rules and strategies for coping with these issues. (It was enlightening to do a similar exercise with the staff at the school, who came up with a shorter list, and asked how the parents might implement these strategies. I was able to tell them that the parents had in fact done better than the staff! The parents enjoyed outdoing the 'professionals'.)

As we only had six sessions with the first group, we always felt there was not enough time, but I did attempt a review in the fifth session. I found I could only give a handout about the law as it relates to a person with learning disability, rather than have a full-scale discussion. In the last session we focused on taking away an exercise for action:

> My son/ daughter understands well/ needs to know and understand...
> How will he/she learn what he/ she need to know, Who can help them...
> How does he/she learn best...
> What makes it difficult for my son/ daughter to learn...

The group took away an evaluation form, and I was able to give them a copy of all the work we had done together.

The second group covered much the same topics, but as a result of the discomfort felt by the first group about explicit sexual discussion, the second session focused on body changes. It felt like we had far more time with eight planned sessions, and I was much more able to take time to have the parents look back at their own childhood and adolescence, and their early experiences with their special needs child. We looked at difficult times and stages, and at the parents' emotional responses, also society's reactions. We took one example of difficult behaviour, and explored what this meant existentially to the person and to the carer, how to deal with it, who to share it with, and the special ingredients of difficult behaviour. Finally we discussed issues of safety, but the parents did not raise issues of sexual dangers. Evaluation forms again were taken away and a copy of our work given out.

Alongside these agreed topics, members brought live issues to the group. When someone was brave enough to do so, the session was more valuable, and they were free to spend as much time as they liked on these issues.

Stages

Both groups went very quickly through Tuckman's (1965) *Forming* stage, and this must be in large part due to the fact that they shared common experience. *Norming* came easily, and there was very little *Storming*. The second group, by virtue of its membership, stormed until the numbers settled down, and then there was absolute commitment. The groups *performed* for the majority of their life, and both resisted ending. I colluded with them in this, as the material they brought was so powerful that it seemed less important to help them focus on the ending of the groups. There was only one occasion when the sessions over-ran, and I left them all to talk.

Ending was more or less ignored.

In both groups the third session was the most emotional and powerful. One mother had had to face a decision about surgery for her son, just prior to the session, and this brought her ambivalent feelings about his death to the surface. Another mother acted as the pressure point for the group, and left the room in tears. All of us had gone down the same intensely sad tunnel, and I too was near tears. The catalyst returned to the group and we all explored these common feelings, making them bearable by so doing. In the other group, one woman's husband had a sudden heart attack, and she used the group for support during this very difficult time.

Both events somehow highlighted the intensity of the experiences that this group of people have to go through, and were prompted basically by the subject of death, and involved ambivalent feelings. The strain of caring for someone who may die, and whom you may have wished dead to avoid any further pain, is a conflict I have experienced, and one I could relate to. Both times I wondered if anyone would return after the expression of such unbearable pain, but the fourth sessions for both groups were the best attended, and this session moved both groups on to a higher level of performance.

Themes and atmosphere

There were almost no periods of silence in either group's life. The atmosphere was intimate, warm and intense, often sad and usually emotional. 'I felt absolutely gutted after last week' one mother said in the fourth session. All members expressed the opinion that there was something unique about the groups. Themes of isolation, loss, loneliness, guilt, support or lack of it, and fears of the future were expressed. Denial regarding their children's sexuality was almost universal. In each group, the members used the experience of a parent whose child was a bit older, and thus had been through that stage ahead of the others.

The 'curative' factors in group therapy

Yalom's (1975) curative factors are particularly relevant to these two groups, and to previous groups of parents with which I have been involved. If 'cohesiveness in group therapy is the analogue of relationship in individual therapy', then this is the greatest of curative factors. Universality - the sharing of an experience - is also important, and the instillation of hope. Without exception, I have found that parents from these groups say that they do not feel they have the worst problem. Finding out about other people's suffering allows them the possibility of hope, that they will survive and that their problems are not so bad. 'Completely opened my eyes to other's problems - made me aware and realise how lucky I am' (parent).

So why was it that this set of people developed an intense degree of cohesion in such a short space of time? After all, in terms of ideal group dynamics, there were many drawbacks to the scope of these two groups. A single leader without supervision is not advisable. Managing emotion and doing a practical task at the same time was very trying. One person in each group being quite different by race or sex could have led to isolation or scapegoating but did not. If anything, the person in each group who used denial as their most usual defence, was isolated. The early depth of expressed emotion could have frightened everyone away, exposed painful issues which could not be tolerated. The use of the groups by one member to share current problems, not the expressed purpose of the groups, could have proved destructive. The volume of the material could have overwhelmed. The denial of sexuality and deeply rooted related issues could have blocked everything else, but this did not happen.

I have concluded that the following aspects may have influenced cohesiveness in these groups:

1. Parents of a disabled child join a set of people who feel as handicapped as their children. Membership of this group was placed upon them, it was not requested or acquired through achievement. Society isolates those who are different, this is society's way of protecting itself. 'Mental handicap', or whatever label you use, is a taboo subject, and we still as a society find it difficult to address. This group of parents when together share the same feeling of stigma, and gain strength through their common bonds. One parent said that for them ' the emergence of a real support group and feeling free to discuss mental handicap problems with people who are also interested - not just being tolerant or sympathetic', was the thing she most valued. One common theme is feeling let down by the 'professionals', and of having little faith in their advice or assistance. I am sure this is a function of being part of a 'handicapped' group, turning the tables and shutting out those given a more skilled status.
2. As a social worker or facilitator in previous groups, I had received the message from parents that 'You cannot understand', as I did not have a disabled child. Two years before these workshops took place, I had spent a year with my son on a children's cancer ward. I experienced exactly what these parents had told me about, the development of a 'them and us' syndrome. I too had found myself a member of a group to which I had never requested membership. It felt like I had caught the wrong train and got off at the wrong station. People did not know how to cope with me and the burden of pain which I bore. What I felt was that the professionals had no comprehension of the degree of pain which I suffered as a parent of a child with special needs, and the year of chronic illness and stress. However, during these workshops, no one suggested that I did not understand, and I feel that there must have been a subtle change in the quality of my empathy. In the third sessions, when fear of death - or fear of killing - was the theme, the sadness was unbearable, and I was able to contain that depth of pain only with great effort. Having survived along with others in the groups, we were all stronger and more

cohesive. Also, the fact that I was a sole leader, may have prevented the sub-grouping which can occur between leaders and group members, another 'them and us' situation.

3. This set of parents came to the workshops at a time in their child's life which was critical, as I have explained above. Whether conscious or unconscious, there was a tremendous motivation to explore and thereby deal with the issues of growing up for a child with special needs. 'I hoped to gain more insight in understanding and helping my son' (parent). Those who came, wanted to be there. After the third session, the one father took me aside to say how much he appreciated the workshop, even after the explosion of emotion.
4. The workshops were convened for such a short time that all the time was precious. I am sure this affected members' degree of commitment and the intensity within the sessions. No time should be wasted.
5. There is something about the quality of interaction and the absence of competition which is very different in this group of parents. Whereas a group of parents of 'normal' children would be scoring off each other, these parents never compete for the most difficult problems, and they all feel they are better off than the next person. I found this to be true even in a cancer ward. Only one parent in all those I met in a year, would complain that she was having the worst time. The absence of competition must lead to a greater cohesion. Parents did challenge each other, particularly over denial of sexuality, but with an implicit sensitivity and understanding of how far to go, and of what other people's boundaries were.
6. The expression of raw emotions, both negative and positive, were a feature of these groups. It was safe to say 'what I've never said before to anyone' (parent). Members risked themselves, because they knew the others had experienced at least some of their hidden feelings. One parent said ' the comradeship and frankness of feelings ' was what she liked best about the sessions. The group for her 'made me very aware of myself, face hidden feelings about my experiences as a mother, and as a person. It opened my eyes to other problems and others' problems'. Another mother said 'the manner in which matters were discussed, in confidence, the understanding of the other mothers, the warmth and the views expressed by each one' were the most important things for her in the sessions. No one forced anyone else to divulge painful and intense

feelings that they did not want to divulge, but the quality of cohesiveness permitted this to happen.

7. None of the parents felt they had had adequate support. This group was a completely different experience for all but one who had been in one of my previous groups. Because of all the factors mentioned above, these groups offered a unique opportunity.

Conclusion

It could be argued that an attempt to address very painful issues is not worthwhile if the experience is too short. Too much is left undone. But if a group can achieve a high degree of cohesiveness in a very short time, then much can be gained. Both sets of parents achieved a greater understanding of the problems confronting them with their adolescent children. They came away with a belief that they had the capacity to deal with issues, and to place them in the arena of the behaviour of 'normal' adolescence. Whilst denial existed regarding their children's sexuality, there was an acknowledgement of the special needs child's limitations. This was far greater than the understanding I encountered around the same time, in a training session with a set of foster parents of children with special needs, who denied any differences.

On an emotional level, expressing feelings in a supportive group and with people who could truly empathise, allowed people to confront their fears, and by doing so, they became more manageable. By feeling the pain of the losses their children's adolescence presents for them, they could begin to accept the reality of the losses, adjust to living with them, and move forward in a positive way.

It would have been helpful to have had outside evaluation, or even feedback from a supervisor. But it is important to point out that the second workshop came into being because of positive feedback from the first one. There is of course evaluation by the parents themselves. One mother related how the group had 'set off a process she had never before undertaken - grieving for my son and his disability' (he is 18). For another, 'the workshop had occurred at the right time, opened up areas I had defended against and new ones I had not considered'. For several it opened up a support link, and they planned to meet or talked on the telephone.

Many of the parents felt that they needed an ongoing support group, and I believe that short-term groups like these are a good introduction to membership of a support group. I do feel however, that support groups need objectives and an expressed purpose. They also need a facilitator to contain, as I had had to do, overwhelming group emotions. It is important for such a facilitator to have come to terms with their own life experiences before handling similar ones which other people have.

Except for the three members who dropped out in the second group, attendance was consistently good. Commitment was high, members came on time and looked happy to be there. There was a tangible warmth and caring attitude amongst the members.

The general feeling at the end was expressed by many on the evaluation form: when the workshop finishes 'I am going to miss it and feel a little lost'. For me, I felt privileged to share this experience and to learn.

I also regretted having begun a process which then had no formal support to continue. Parent support groups do not exist in this area.

References

Brown, D. and Pedder, J. (1979) *Introduction to Psychotherapy*. Tavistock Publications.

Sinason, V. (1992) *Mental Handicap and the Human Condition*. Free Association Books.

Tuckman, B. (1965) 'Developmental sequences in small groups', *Psychological Bulletin*, 63(6).

Worden, W. (1983) *Grief Counselling and Grief Therapy*. Tavistock Publications.

Yalom, I. (1975) *The Theory and Practice of Group Psychotherapy*. New York: Basic Books Inc.

GROUPWORK WITH DEAF PEOPLE

KAVITA KOHLI

This paper is based on my own experience and involvement with an Asian Deaf Women's Group in Leicester. The study examines the value and the problems encountered of developing groupwork with deaf people.
This study has shown that when an individual is profoundly deaf, he/she has far more to contend with than just the physical limitations of his/her deafness. Negative attitudes will all have major effect(s) on the deaf individual which will leave them in a socially disadvantaged position.
The available literature and my experience have pointed to the benefits of groupwork as a method of social work which is useful in reducing the negative impact of attitudes. Also it gives an increased insight into personal difficulties and improvement in interpersonal functioning. It is able to offer deaf people opportunities to challenge for demands and changes in the hearing society's treatment of them.

Introduction

When I first entered the social work profession four years ago, I came into contact with a social worker with deaf people who made a profound impact on my life. Prior to this I had no idea of the existence of such a service.

This contact led me to receiving vital and long overdue services from which I have benefited tremendously. It also made me examine all my experience as regards my own deafness. I realised that a part of me - my being black and deaf - had prevented me from fully developing the characteristics of a positive identity. I have had to allay unfounded fears about my ability to pursue a full and normal life. I have experienced differing degrees of stigma and isolation arising both from cultural factors and deafness, but fortunately I have been able to use these experiences to enable others.

Feeling a lack of fulfilment with the 'hearing' world, I decided to meet other people with the same disability. I felt particularly inclined to pursue some kind of involvement in a voluntary capacity with Asian deaf people. I contacted Leicester Centre for Deaf People. They identified a group of profoundly deaf Asian women who were severely isolated by reasons of both deafness and cultural factors. Given my relevant experience and interest, the Centre offered me the opportunity of doing groupwork with them. I felt this provided the ideal opportunity and setting in which to pursue my interest and this was to become the basis from which I could in future commit myself to a greater level of personal involvement. Simultaneously I began to do some introductory reading about groupwork and deaf people respectively. Groupwork is viewed as an important and effective social work strategy in helping people to deal with their problems. I found there was a lot of information about groupwork with a variety of client groups except with deaf people. In fact very little research has been undertaken and there is a marked lack of knowledge in this area.

This study begins with a brief introduction to define deafness. It focuses attention on the nature and effects of profound deafness and the additional difficulties faced by Asian deaf people. This study will argue that social factors are as central to the experience of deafness as is the disability itself. It will show that independent of any role an individual may assume, deafness results from a combination of the individual's deafness and society's response to it.

The second section represents my review of the literature. I visited the library at the Royal Institute for the Deaf in London. I found only four articles about groupwork with deaf people mostly based in the USA. These provided a base and some insight into the value of groupwork with deaf people. A further section describes a group I ran in Leicester.

The final section aims to offer a critique of the value of groupwork and the problems of developing groupwork with deaf people. This will be illustrated by the findings of my personal enquiry which involved interviewing a number of groupworkers, and a summary of the literature. Included in this section is the need for social workers to understand the importance of this area of work as an effective method of working with deaf individuals in a social work setting.

In pursuing this study, I have found limitations. There was a lack of literature and despite the advertisements I placed in *Community Care* (1990) and the *British Deaf News* (a national magazine by the deaf for the deaf) requesting information about any groupwork with deaf people, I did not receive much response. It would appear groupwork with deaf people is a very new thing in this country.

What is deafness?

Deafness is a blanket term used to describe many types of hearing loss. It is important then to begin with a description of deafness and attempt to cover the different types of deafness which exist. Hynes (1987, p.2) states that 'deafness is primarily a communication handicap. In our society, the majority of communication is based on auditory language, language which every deaf person, to some degree is handicapped in acquiring and/or using. The degree to which each individual is thus handicapped will depend on a number of factors. These include the type and degree of loss, the age of onset, the way in which the person is educated and the person's own and family's attitude to deafness.'

Of particular importance is whether the deafness occurs pre- or post-lingually, i.e whether the person became deaf at birth or at an age prior to the development of speech and language, or following the development of spontaneous acquisition of speech and language. Consequently the categories of deafness for people may be: profoundly, pre- and post-lingually, partially, adventitiously, severely, traumatically, acquired and hard of hearing (normally applied to elderly people).

The effects of profound deafness

The focus of attention in this study is primarily on deaf individuals who use manual communication i.e the profoundly, pre- or post-lingually deaf, as they cannot communicate fluently by aural/oral language. Their main communication is sign language, a visual gestural language. Also because of the complexity of this disability and I shall draw some general characteristics about this group.

Shearer (1981) wrote:

> A disability is something that has to be taken as given, but a handicap is something that is imposed on that disability to make it more limiting than it must necessarily be.

Although deafness may present some deep and complex difficulties, the problems deaf people face are not inherent in deafness itself but are related to feelings, attitudes and barriers that increase the effects of this disability i.e. turn it into a problem of living and that puts a person at a disadvantage.

Possible psychological consequences

Deafness may have psychological consequences. Deaf people, like everybody else, understand their own identity largely from the behaviour of others towards them.

Deafness is the disability least well understood by the hearing society as it is not visible and hence it is often misinterpreted, ignored or, even worse, misconstrued.

The hearing society's attitude towards the usage of sign language has had a major impact on deaf people, as sign language is not given a place of dignity. As a result deaf people encounter prejudice and a lack of understanding.

Deaf people have their own language, culture and community, and thus they see themselves not simply as a disabled group, but as a cultural linguistic minority.

The deaf community is made up of the mutual association of deaf people. It is described as revealing strengths in common life experiences, shared beliefs, identity and values, language traditions and art forms. Its membership offers the chance to create a positive self-image which is often disallowed by hearing values. (Ladd, 1991).

British Sign Language (BSL) is the national language of deaf people with its own grammar and syntax. It is a visual language. The signs have both concrete and abstract meanings. The use of spatial-relation, direction, orientation and movement of hands as well as facial expressions and body shift, make up the grammar of BSL (Miles, 1988).

The struggle of BSL is central to the history of the Deaf Community. In 1880 at the Milan Conference, hearing educationalists banned the use of sign language in education. Deaf teachers were removed as they were seen as subversive influences on deaf children in that they continued to use BSL. Oralism was brought in. This system maintains that spoken language should be the medium of education of deaf children. In the mid 1970s, various research studies revealed that oralism was failing deaf children who were leaving school unable to read or speak/communicate adequately. Educational policy was reviewed and sign language was bought back into the education of deaf children. (Gregory et al., 1991). It is important to say that BSL has not been given official recognition in the UK as compared to our European counterparts. Hence, the suppression of sign language still continues in some educational establishments.

As a result of their affliction, deaf people were, and continue to be, denied access to many social and educational experiences which build up confidence, and develop knowledge and skills. Such attitudes can reinforce negative experiences and can affect the development of self-esteem and isolate deaf people. Family acceptance of the deaf individual and personal adjustments may also be predicative factors of low self-esteem. This can have a knock-on effect on a deaf person's psychological make up. Whilst some deaf people may feel as described above, I do not wish to give an impression that all deaf people have psychological problems, any more than the rest of society.

Black deaf people

Taylor's (1986) article 'Deaf people, ethnic minorities and social policy' draws a comparison between deaf people and ethnic minorities in that there has been a lack of legislation and funding by government for deaf people as opposed to for ethnic minorities.

Taylor has failed to grasp the specific conditions surrounding the black experience of life in Britain. Black deaf people are doubly disadvantaged in that they face invariable institutional and cultural racism in all aspects of their lives both from the wider society and the established white deaf community.

Anderson and Bowe (1972) illustrate the problem of racism in the general field of deafness as:

> ...the black deaf have been overlooked. It is a cause for concern that extensive apathy and indifference continue to exist among professionals and laymen (sic) alike with respect to the gross under-education, mass under-employment and severe social isolation of blacks who are deaf.

Coincidently I undertook a pilot research study in my summer vacation, July 1990 looking into the needs of Asian deaf people in Leicester. One of the major outcomes of this study was that existing social services provision is not conducive to the cultural needs of Asian deaf people. The majority of Asian deaf people interviewed indicated a strong need for support, counselling and recreational and social activities in group settings to enhance their group identity.

A summary of literature on groupwork with deaf people

Below are some issues about groupwork with deaf people emerging from a literature search.

Jane Ford (1985) describes working with a group of deaf adolescent girls. Their basic problem concerned their relationships. They had difficulties in forming and maintaining close relationships with each other. This caused problems for them both at home and school with symptoms such as temper tantrums, arguments with peers and scapegoating of the weakest members of the peer group, causing considerable unhappiness and unrest. Groupwork took place with a planned series of activities and events using outside speakers, role-play, drama etc.

Allen Sussman (1974) working in a community mental health centre in New York, initiated and piloted an experimental group therapy programme for a special group of eight severely handicapped deaf adults who were socially disadvantaged late adolescents. Some were diagnosed as having minimal brain dysfunction with attendant behaviour disorder, serious interpersonal relationship problems and overall poor life adjustment patterns. All had extremely poor communication skills and limited facility with sign language. Groupwork took place involving considerable role-playing and reverse role-playing.

James Collins (1971), National Institute for the Deaf (NTID) New York, used group counselling techniques with students who enrolled for further education at a New York school for the deaf. Prior to commencing their education, an eight week programme was set up to help those students who tended to exhibit behaviour that was somewhat immature when compared with their hearing peers, had a lack of experience which often manifested itself through immaturity, and who had a lack of clear-cut goals.

Martin Sternberg (1971), Director of Communication Skills Centre, New York Society for the Deaf, describes group counselling with non-communicating deaf people, those that are severely limited, or even have non-existent functional communicative ability.

A groupwork practice example

There follows a summary chart of my groupwork at Leicester Centre for Deaf People (Kohli, 1990).

Group Name	Asian Women's Deaf Group, Leicester
Group for whom, and why?	To provide opportunities for social/educational development, improve communication skills and recreational activities for profoundly deaf Asian women appropriate to their cultural needs. The need for this group was identified by social workers for deaf people as the women were severely isolated by reasons of both deafness and cultural factors.

Aims of this group	To encourage members to value and respect themselves. To give members space to develop their abilities and potential in areas that interest them. To encourage members to think about their own needs and explore constructive and creative ways of meeting them. To encourage members to develop and value their friendship network. To provide assistance/support to be self-determining and understand any discrimination/prejudice which members may encounter.
Who has set these aims?	Myself with prior agreement of members.
Activities undertaken to achieve these aims	Informal and structured group discussions/activities on a variety of topics (that concern women in all areas of life) that demand an open exchange of information, ideas and possible responses. A wide variety of board games and role-playing exercises as a way of learning/improving social skills. Literacy and numeracy skills are incorporated in all activities using visual/audio means. Asian festivals are celebrated and outings are organised covering both Asian and English arts. A communication class is provided alongside to help members to learn BSL skills (once a month).
Groupworker's style	Eclectic. Promoting and facilitating discussion, encouraging initiative, self-determination, self-expression. Being non-judgemental. Offering support and being sensitive to each member's needs.
Any difficulties that may concern	Variation in communication abilities: some members lack knowledge of their own language,

or affect group functioning	English, and have limited BSL skills. A lot of usage of personal gesture which is not always easy to decipher. Some members are intellectually impeded.
How are issues of racism, sexism and disablism tackled?	These issues are brought into almost every area as they affect the very core of members identity. All members readily share their life experiences and at some point(s) have suffered from ostracism, disadvantage and discrimination. As a group we plan strategies of how to deal with such issues.
Resources available	Use of room(s) at Leicester Centre for Deaf People including kitchen facilities, TV and video equipment. Use of dark room for photography, large hall for exhibitions or sport, flipcharts, transport facilities to collect and return members to and from their homes, also used for outings. We have received an Urban Aid grant to develop this group and subsidise its activities.
Groupworker's best asset(s)	Being a severely deaf Asian woman myself, I am able to relate immediately to members. Also able to communicate trilingually, speak an Asian language, English and use BSL. Awareness of Asian cultures, knowledge of implications of deafness. Use of own life experiences constructively to enable others. Full understanding of institutional and cultural racism. Resourceful, enthusiastic, energetic and patient.
Evaluation	At the end of each session, all members are involved in the process of evaluating so that they take the responsibility for planning ahead.
Recording	I am responsible to the Principal of the Centre. I provide progress reports on a monthly basis and seek consultation regularly. Also influence policy in social work department relating to deaf Asian peoples' needs.

Advantages of groupwork	Personal development and enhanced self-confidence. Establishment of a positive identity. Increased participation and competence in social interaction. Isolation dramatically reduced. Provision of social and educational opportunities. Growing capacity for sharing, coping, evaluating and planning. Growing capacity for learning and maturing. Increased independence and self-responsibility. Improved communication skills. Increased capacity for self-determination. Efficient use of social work time.
Disadvantages of groupwork	Because of variation in communication abilities, the group has split into two sub-groups, each having clear and distinct needs. Running the group single-handedly, I often find it exhausting. Unable to give enough individual attention as requested by members.
Changes that may assist	A co-worker - Asian female, deaf or hearing. Regular communication classes.
Additional	Group commenced in January 1990. It has a total of ten women, age range between 18-40, most of them are in the younger age bracket. Group meets three times a month, each session lasts for two and a half hours.

A critique of groupwork with deaf people

In offering a critique of the value of this groupwork and the problems of developing groupwork with deaf people, I will examine the response to groupwork provision provided by my personal practice and the available literature, and analyse the significant findings. At the end of this section I will highlight the relevance of groupwork provision in the social work setting.

The value of groupwork with deaf people

Improving and facilitating communication

Due to lack of or limited use of BSL in school and often at home, deaf people experiencing this system are denied active participation in group and learning situations. Groupwork offers members much freedom and scope for expressing and thinking for themselves by conversing in methods natural to them.

Aiding social learning and personal growth

Lack of social and personal skills can have enormous influence on a person's feelings about themself. A significant part of our identity comes from what we are seen to do. Deaf people often experience a sense of rejection and condescension by the attitude and behaviour of others. They can internalise much of this stigmatisation inflicted on them. Groupwork offers opportunities to find ways of coping, changing attitudes, feelings and behaviour through social interaction, role-modelling, reinforcement, feedback and by sharing a range of ideas (Brown, 1986).

Enhanced self-confidence and self-esteem

This is closely related to the above section. Deaf people frequently feel inadequate and inferior to hearing people. They have low self-esteem and lack confidence. Because of this their level of functioning is also reduced. The members of the groups in the personal enquiry, through their involvement in groupwork experienced a sense of identity and belonging. The members were helped to deal with their negative emotions in the following ways:

1. by providing contact with others in the group who were experiencing similar encounters;
2. by providing reassurance and support to each other;
3. by encouraging them in the decision-making processes;
4. by involving them in the planning of group activities;
5. by assisting them to discover their strengths, resources and skills.

This gave the members a sense of achievement within the group as this fostered the growth of self-esteem and increased confidence.

Isolation reduced

Deaf people by their conditions of deafness and their mode of communication are likely to have less human contact. Additionally they are vulnerable to predicaments like mental illness, learning difficulties etc, and if they are from an ethnic minority group, they are likely to lead more isolated lives. This decreases their self-esteem. Heap (1979, p.74) affirms that 'the isolated client is caught in a descending spiral of self-reinforcing social failure, which inevitably influences both the individual's mental and physical health'.

Developing recreational and educational interests and skills

Restraints on the deaf person's ability do not come from mental constraints but from their experiences in life i.e. skills are only learnt if the opportunities have been offered. Those with poor intellectual ability are doubly disadvantaged and move into adulthood with severe disadvantages which significantly impinge on their capacities to live fulfilled lives.

The groupwork in my personal practice showed that interests such as latent talents, cultural interests, hobbies etc were promoted and developed within the group. Apart from the interests being a means of self-expression, they encouraged participation and provided a strong motivation to communicate. These opportunities gave way to discovery of hidden skills and ideas within the group.

Race, culture and gender: groupwork with Asian deaf women

In this society, minority groups experience extreme discrimination. Women in minority groups are usually disadvantaged, as I found was the case in my groupwork with Asian deaf women. Their oppression is compounded by such factors as race, ethnic origin and gender. One of the main underlying reasons for the establishment of this group was that existing groups (mainly consisting of people from the white deaf community) did not always provide a supportive setting for Asian deaf women.

In the earlier stages of my groupwork, discussions took place on what it felt like to be an Asian deaf women in this society. The members felt that in white deaf groups, deafness was the only issue. Issues such as power and oppression which are central to race, culture, gender and other forms of social difference were evaded or ignored.

Szircom and Dyson (1987, p.2) in their book *Greater Expectations* (a source book for working with women) state that 'experience has shown that one of the most effective ways of working towards personal and social change for women is to work together in women only groups'.

In my groupwork with Asian deaf women, not only do they share similar aims and provide positive support to one another, they are able to share experiences relating to deafness, gender, race and culture which are usually denied to them in mixed groups. Hanmer and Statham (1988, p.78) affirm this by stating:

> ...because of racism, black women may find it easier to speak frankly in groups where both cultural differences and racism are fully appreciated and it is important that these opportunities are available since black women may feel comfortable in certain neighbourhoods where people of their communities congregate and where culturally relevant services are available...

As a groupworker with Asian deaf women, my work has centred around building their confidence and discussion of values (this is a major focus) which are integral to positive self-esteem and affirmation of the Asian woman's cultural identity.

Empowerment

Up to now, the value of groupwork with deaf people has been explored through several ways. All this gives rise to some kind of constructive involvement in empowering members so that it facilitates change both individually and collectively.

Sussman (1974) in his groupwork with severely handicapped (sic) deaf adults, reports that at the end of the 28 group sessions, most of the members secured employment or educational training.

On a wider scale, the identity and cohesion of the Asian Deaf Women's Group has highlighted the lack of services for Asian deaf people. I came to realise increasingly the extent of unmet need within my group. There was a lack of awareness and knowledge among group members about the existing Social Services provision for deaf people. The members who did have contact with Social Services felt the service was culturally inappropriate as it did not recognise Asian deaf people as a distinct group with their own unique needs. These concerns resulted in a pilot survey being undertaken into the needs of Asian deaf people in Leicester. The results of this survey have assisted Social Services in making an application for Section 11 funding. Although this is helpful, the concept of Section 11 funding is inappropriate. Such programmes should be financed from the mainstream budgets.

Effective use of social work time and effort

Sternberg (1971) in his group counselling with deaf people states that 'there is nothing that can be accomplished in individual counselling that cannot be duplicated more efficiently both in time and money through the group process'. There is a likelihood that once groupwork is established in an agency, it will be relatively economical in terms of social work either in the short-term or long-term. The groupworkers that I interviewed found that some of their members will always require some individual contact with the social worker. However they emphasised that by working in groups, their dependency levels are reduced in that it may avert members from requiring one to one work or other extra support alongside one to one work.

As a groupworker with Asian deaf women, I came to realise that traditional casework tends to isolate people from the community. The members requested that the establishment of their group be publicised so that other Asian deaf women could join and benefit from it.

Problems of developing groupwork with deaf people

Communication difficulties

The lack of communication skills and the variation of communication abilities have implications for smooth group functioning. Many of the members have a poor standard of English and limited BSL skills. They use home-made sign language or personal gestures, and these are not always easy to decipher. One of the main reasons cited for the lack of effective communication is that the use of BSL has been suppressed in Britain.

Lack of individual attention

A common problem identified in my experience was that the workers were unable to provide exclusive attention as requested by individual members. There were times when members could not always cope with sharing in a group setting. This also raises the issue of confidentiality and whether it can be maintained in groups.

Black/ethnic minority deaf peoples' needs

All groupwork which is undertaken must tackle racist assumptions and stereotyping. As Muston and Weinstein (1988, p.31) in their article on Race and Groupwork state 'if groupwork is not offering an effective, culturally sensitive service to members from the various minority ethnic groups, it is in danger of becoming quite marginalised both professionally and politically'.

Resources

Any form of groupwork requires resources. It is necessary for groups to have access to certain physical resources such as accommodation, equipment, catering facilities, transport, financial assistance etc, if they are to function effectively.

In my groupwork with Asian deaf women, a great deal of time, effort and involvement was spent in setting up and running sub-groups, each with clear and distinct needs. Without the availability of a co-worker I was unable to cater fully for their needs.

Relevance to social work

The information on groupwork with deaf people from the available literature and my own practice has recognised and established that the value of groupwork outweighs the problems of developing groupwork with deaf people. It clearly shows that groupwork is useful and helpful for deaf people for a number of reasons. It helps to raise a positive self-concept and improves ability to cope with the effects of deafness. Group counselling and using methods such as social skills and assertiveness training further assists them in their development.

Social workers clearly have a role to use groupwork as a preventive way of working. It should be linked to team discussions and research, whereby identifying need based on knowledge of local networks, client opinion and services provided by other agencies.

Social work agencies must offer groupwork as an alternative. Also they must provide social workers with the necessary training to gain skills and knowledge that is required within this work. Finally they must create the space to allow social workers to explore and carry out groupwork.

Social work agencies are still some way off and need to develop groupwork as an effective provision of service. In particular I feel the isolated situation of black deaf people is virtually ignored by social workers. They are not aware of issues such as racism, and much work needs to be done by way of training and developing awareness strategies. They will also need to challenge their own values and the practices they carry out.

My personal view of being a groupworker who happens to be deaf is that groupwork offers a rich variety of learning opportunities and there is much educational and social potential yet to be explored. It enables deaf people to gain maximum satisfaction without undermining their deafness and differences, leading to greater self-advocacy. If groupwork is anything, it is, as Brown (1986, p.11) affirms, 'democratic, self-determining and it gives more power to the people we are working with'.

References

Anderson, G. and Bowe, F. (1972) 'Racism within the deaf community', *American Annuals of the Deaf.*

Brown, A. (1986) *Groupwork*. Gower.

Collins, J. (1971) chapter in Schein, J.D. and Naiman D.W. (eds.) *The Use of Groupwork Techniques with Deaf Persons.* Deafness Research and Training Center, New York University, School of Education.

Community Care (1990) 'Services for deaf people', 26 April.

Ford, J. (1985) 'Working in groups', *Journal of National Council of Social Workers with the Deaf,* Bristol, 1(4), p.10.

Gregory, S. and Silo, J. (1991) *Deaf People in Hearing World, Unit 5.* The Open University.

Hanmer, J. and Statham, D. (1988) *Women and Social Work*. BASW.

Heap, K. (1979) *Process and Action in Work with Groups*. Pergamon Press.

Hynes, D. (1987) *Social Work with Deaf People.* Social Work Monographs.

Kohli, K. (1990) *A Survey into the Needs of Asian People with an Hearing Impairment and their Carers.* Leicester Centre for Deaf People.

Ladd, P. (1991) *Deaf People as a Minority Group.* The Open University.

Miles, D. (1988) *British Sign Language*. BBC Books.

Muston, R. and Weinstein, J. (1988) 'Race and Groupwork, some experiences in practice and training', *Groupwork*, 1, pp.30-40

Shearer, A. (1981) *Disability, Whose Handicap?* Blackwell.

Sternberg, M. (1971) chapter in Schein, J.D. and Naiman D.W. (ed.) *The Use of Groupwork Techniques with Deaf Persons.* Deafness Research and Training Center, New York University, School of Education.

Sussman, A.E. (1974) 'Group therapy with severely handicapped deaf adults', *Journal of Rehabilitation of the Deaf*, USA, 8(1), p.122.

Szircom, T. and Dyson, S. (1987) *Greater Expectations*. Ebenezer Bayliss.

Taylor, G. (1986) 'Deaf people, ethnic minorities and social policy', *Journal of National Council of Social Workers with the Deaf.*

Bibligraphy

Deaf People from Ethnic Minority Groups (1987) *Report* of a seminar in London. RNID.

Dominelli, L. (1988) *Anti-Racist Social Work*. BASW.

Etherington, S. (ed.) (1990) *A World Apart? Deafness and Social Policy*. Reed Business.

Freeman, R., Carbin, C. and Boese, R. (1981) *Can't Your Child Hear?* London: Croom Helm.

Higgins, P. (1980) *Outsiders in a Hearing World*. Sage.
Preston-Shoot, M. (1987) *Effective Groupwork*. BASW/Macmillan.
Preston-Shoot, M. (1987) 'Groupwork presents its challenges and its rewards for those with the right initiatives', *Social Work Today*, 9 March, p.12.
Schein, J.D. and Naiman, D.W. (1971) *The Use of Groupwork Techniques with Deaf Persons*. Deafness Research and Training Centre, New York University School of Education.
Topliss, E. (1982) *Social Responses to Handicap*. Longman.

Combining activities and growth games: a systems approach

Oded Manor and Miriam Dumbleton

Activities and growth games are often offered to groups, but they do not always achieve their purpose. Some failures may be explained within the systems approach which suggests an essential difference between the two. Activities are relevant when more ordered predictable responses are helpful. Growth games are called for when creative chaos is needed. An example of one session is used to show how such a systems view can enable workers to decide when to offer growth games and when activities are helpful so that the group's development is enhanced; enabling it to fluctuate between chaos and order constructively.

The problem: when fun fails

Groupworkers often choose activities, games, or exercises according to their personal preferences rather than to enhance the processes. They are then puzzled by the members' reactions. By drawing on the systems approach, we shall define these forms of play more clearly, taking into account the different dynamics built into each. We hope that this discussion will help workers select activities and growth games in a way that is more clearly related to the group's developmental needs.

As play is the subject of this paper, let us begin with a game. Our first example is a group for children who were about to enter secondary school and who had been identified by their teachers either as too withdrawn or as particularly aggressive. The teachers were concerned that these children might find the transition to the new school unusually difficult. Therefore, a time limited small group was offered, to run for seven months. Four boys and four girls were invited. They were told that the group was for 'doing things together' which could help them cope better at school. By 'doing things' the workers meant that free play and activities would be offered to the members. There were a number of reasons for this. Drawing on the work of Winnicott play was seen as a means for the 'search for self' (Winnicott, 1971, pp.53-64). While children play, they often freely and spontaneously express their feelings or attribute them to play

Groupwork Vol. 6(3), 1993, pp.248-265

materials. The worker can then respond to these forms of free association by reflecting them back to the children so that they can make sense of their expressions as part of their 'self'. As Axline (1969, p.15) put it, the worker 'recognises and clarifies the expressed emotionalised attitudes by a reflection of what the client has expressed'. In more technical terms, the approach was similar to what West (1990) called 'focused therapeutic play'.

Rose and Edelson (1987) have summarised other reasons: play and activities are attractive to young people and so easily make sense to them. They suggest that these methods also provide opportunities to observe the members' interacting with others. These methods can be used to reveal members' skills and to practice them as well as to offer new roles and leadership opportunities (Rose and Edleson, 1987, pp.239-240). The workers thought that these aims could be pursued in the group since they saw it as a social microcosm, where:

> A freely interactive group, with few structural restrictions, will, in time, develop into a social microcosm of the participant members...given time, every patient will begin to be himself (sic), to interact with the group members as he interacts with others in his social sphere (Yalom, 1970, p.24).

It was expected that as the group develops through its phases (Levine, 1979, pp.65-89), each member would respond to the others in the ways she or he knew, and so could be helped to choose other, more enabling, ways of relating to others.

The group had been meeting weekly for more than five months and had successfully negotiated the expected developmental phases. Quite suddenly, six weeks before the end of the group, unexpected chaos emerged: some children used abusive language, some just sat quietly, while others threw play materials all over the room. The workers expressed extreme worries in supervision. They felt it was important to bring the group back to its collaborative orderly state, and so decided to suggest to the children that together they construct a big house out of cardboard boxes. The workers surmised that this house could be used by the children to express their feelings about ending the group as well as going to their future school. Their supervisor agreed.

However, after the following session, the workers returned to supervision even more confused and dispirited. They described the session as a 'total failure' and the children as 'just awful'. Instead of the mature collaboration they had aimed for, some children had withdrawn into silence while others had been throwing cardboard boxes all over the room while hurling insults at the workers who could not make sense of what had happened. The workers felt that the chaos did not serve any purpose, but was simply destructive. Clearly a new approach was needed as the previous plan was such a failure; but what should it be? After some discussion the supervisor, in what, at that time, could be described only as a leap of imagination, said: 'You know what? Perhaps we are forcing them to build before they destroy. Perhaps that is exactly what they cannot do. What if we reversed the order?' And so a very different suggestion emerged.

It was agreed that the workers would bring a huge pile of empty cardboard boxes to the next session. After clearing the room of every hard object in order to make it safe, they would pile the boxes in a huge heap in the middle of the room. When the children came in the workers would not say much but would just let them look. At an opportune moment the workers would yell: 'go get them!' and then encourage the children to jump on the heap ravaging each and every box until all were destroyed. Only then would the workers gather the group and raise questions such as 'what are we wrecking now?'. In the following supervision session the workers described their amazement. The children 'had gone wild', jumping and yelling with released excitement. Yet the workers could also see how the children had been very careful not to harm each other or any valuable object in the room. The children had destroyed the boxes as before, but this felt very different. When the chaos gradually subsided the children talked spontaneously about how much they would miss the group, and of their fear of moving to the secondary school. Yes, it was chaotic, but this chaos seemed creative; it led to constructive results and ended of its own volition.

Why was the first session a failure and the second so constructive? Answering this question calls for a closer look at the similarities and the differences between the two interventions. Clearly, in both cases the workers suggested that group members do something; that is, motor activities were involved. Both included the use of materials; the cardboard boxes, and in a very general sense, the theme of the two was the same: ending the group.

What were the differences? One intervention aimed at 'constructive' collaboration and the other endorsed 'destructive' behaviour. Knowing the children, the workers did not believe that they simply liked the latter and disliked the former. They were puzzled as to why the group needed the destructive behaviour first. We think that answers can be found by integrating ideas from quite a number of different sources within the systems point of view.

Major concepts: activities, growth games, group development, and fluctuations in groups

We make sense of the children's different responses within the systems approach (Durkin, 1981). This strand is not to be confused with the social systems approach (Pincus and Minahan, 1973; Chetkov-Yanoov, 1992) which dealt only with equilibrium in systems. The present stance examines also instability and transformation, and can be allied to the 'second cybernetics' (Hoffman, 1981, pp.50-52; pp.339-349). We do not have the space to explain all the possible connections here. Instead, we aim to show how useful it can be to be aware of the different dynamics which are emphasised in activities as compared to growth games.

Firstly, we shall explore this possibility. Then we shall expand our discussion to consider how the fluctuation between chaos and order can be regarded as an important feature of group development. The benefits of this theoretical development will be demonstrated in a practice example at the end.

Let us begin with activities.

Activities elaborate order

Constructing a house out of cardboard boxes can be described as an 'activity'. Following VanderVen (1985, pp.155-156) an activity can be defined as the use of an already accepted sequence of behaviour to help group members further understand their relationships with one another, and increase their competence in handling these relationships, within an agreed set of rules.

In our example, constructing the house was expected to serve all these three aims. At their age the children were already familiar with this game and how to go about it; for them, it was an activity. With the rules being so informal, Vinter's (1974) 'institutional control' was low. As the children could choose the type, and the shape, of the house, 'prescriptiveness' was low too. Further drawing on Vinter (1974); enough 'physical movement' and 'interactiveness' were involved to give room for the release of strong feelings. So, while building the house, the children could freely add their own associations related to their experiences of 'a home', 'our own place', 'being taken care of' and the like. Interacting around the theme of a house was a potential source of free association and discussion about the home this group had been for them on the one hand, and the unknown home which the new school was going to be. In this way the children could increase their understanding of the changes involved. In addition, the 'level of competence required' (Vinter, 1974) was low, encouraging collaboration. By collaborating in the construction of the house, the children could learn that having a home meant coordinating their individual activities with those of others. So, their competence in collaborating could have increased.

Altogether, the choice of this particular activity seems to have been appropriate. What then was wrong?

Many social groupworkers have described the use of activities in detail (Heap, 1979; Middleman, 1983; VanderVen, 1985; Vinter, 1974). Vinter (1974) was the first to show how to incorporate them so that the group reached a desired level of interaction, by focusing our attention on the aspects that predict the group's responses. Phillips (1989) offered a comprehensive review of the applications of Vinter's ideas, pointing out that he put an emphasis on the amount of interaction rather than on its quality. Perhaps a certain quality was missing from the chosen activity?

From the systems point of view, the quality of interactions is not simply a matter of personal taste. When we use activities, specific and discrete goals are usually identified in advance (Phillips, 1989, pp.49-50). By pursuing these goals, activities contribute mainly to increased understanding of, and competence in, applying certain rules. Rules tell us how to play: which moves are acceptable and which ones are not. These constraints lead to experiencing the boundaries of this particular form of play. So, by introducing these limits, activities lead the group towards a pre-determined pattern of interaction. The pattern may be of parallel moves as in swimming, it may resemble an alternating sequence, as in musical chairs, but whatever form it takes, a predictable pattern will always emerge out of activities. This effect is similar to the consequences of 'negative feedback' within the systems approach (Simon et al., 1985, pp.155-158). Indeed, the more predictable are the effects of activities the more they enable the group to pursue a desired range of interaction; in systems terms, a 'homeostasis'. During homeostasis, we feel that our relationships are 'as they should be', or 'normal'. In other words, while homeostasis is sustained, we experience patterning: an increased sense of order.

Growth games enable creative chaos

The second session involved a very different workers' response. Rather than attempting to modify behaviour, it encouraged the children to exaggerate the disturbing ones. The workers' supervisor suggested that rather than trying to restore collaborative behaviour, the children should first be encouraged to destroy the boxes. Contrary to what could be called 'common sense', the disturbing behaviour (termed 'deviation' in the systems approach) was not suppressed, but rather intensified. Along similar lines, a whole range of games was developed in encounter groups, and called 'growth games' (Lewis and Streitfield, 1970). It can be shown that safely intensifying disturbing experiences is the hallmark of growth games, since pure growth games are characterised by isolating an element of the group's dynamics and charging it with positive connotations; that is, drawing out the enabling aspects. This element is then intensified. Again, many groupworkers resort to growth games these days (Brandes and Phillips, 1977). William Schutz (1967) was probably the first to suggest a coherent conceptual scheme which showed how to apply growth games with reference to three group phases: inclusion, control, and affection. At each point, the growth game should intensify the dynamics of the particular phase.

In our second example, destroying the materials disturbed the desired pattern of collaboration, yet it was that very disturbance which was fully accepted and then persistently intensified. Such an amplification increases the sense of chaos in the system as long as this system is not guided towards a specific goal. This is very similar to effecting 'positive feedback' within the systems approach (Hoffman, 1981, pp.50-51). It seems to us that the workers' second response involved such intensifying of the disturbance.

Indeed, like other 'second order changes', growth games tend to increase the sense of chaos for a while. The ensuing chaotic experiences can lead to a revision of the roles, rules, and underlying principles governing the system (Hoffman, 1981; Simon et al., 1985, pp.33-34).

However, most people will not tolerate the sometimes violent eruption of chaos for very long. Quite soon they will want to know what is happening; that is, find a way of making the experience meaningful.

In the first example, the workers misjudged the meaning of the children's behaviour. They did not consider why the children were destroying the boxes, but interpreted their behaviour as defiance and sheer destructiveness. However, once the workers considered that the children's behaviour was actually an expression of how they felt, the workers changed their perception, and consequently their response. By emptying the room and putting the cardboard boxes in the middle, the workers communicated acceptance of the children's own interpretation: 'you do need to destroy, we accept this, and we shall let you do it safely'. By doing this, the workers conveyed a new connection between the children's need to destroy, their fear of the risk, and the workers acceptance. Within the systems approach, when such a message is verbalised, 'meta communication' is formed (Simon et al., 1985, pp.164-168). Indeed, the children and the workers had then to talk about this unusual experience. A time for reflection was needed for chaos to lead to constructive solutions, and to expand the meaning. Reflection can help the group cope with the fluctuations between the patterning of interactions and intensifying behaviours that disturb the pattern.

Groups development and fluctuation in groups

We have explored how the use of activities elaborates the group's sense of order and enhances its continuity. We have also suggested that growth games can be used to enable creative chaos as a step towards transformational change. Most systems need continuous changes as well as transformation . How do they go about it? From research we know that interactions oscillate all the time (Davis, 1982; McGrath, 1988, pp.151-181), and this seems to be true for small groups too (LaCoursiere, 1980). These oscillations have been explained in a number of ways (Breunlin, 1989; Wilden, 1980, p.368). One of them is that they fluctuate between phases and crises.

Both sessions took into account the ending of the group. How did they differ? We have found Levine's (1979) theory of group development particularly useful in explaining this. Levine suggests that a successful group passes through four phases: the 'parallel phase', the 'inclusion phase', the 'mutuality phase', and the 'termination phase'. The movement from one phase to another is brought about by crises. These he calls the 'authority crisis' the 'intimacy crisis' and the 'separation crisis'. Levine's (1979. p.73) understanding of phases leads to seeing them as periods during which the members are working out the implications of the direction they have already chosen. In doing this, the members increase their competence in their preferred sphere. Such periods usually involve an increased sense of order. Step-by-step changes can then be planned and carried out incrementally while the group's norms, roles, and rules remain unaltered. As suggested before, such incremental changes can be pursued while interactions are relatively more patterned; that is, while activities are offered.

In contrast, Levine's (1979, p.73) 'crises' can be seen as the points at which a previous sense of order has collapsed, and the group members are busy choosing a new direction for their involvement in the group. These are disturbing times of upheaval, bringing about an increased sense of chaos. In our previous example, we showed how instead of moving against the tide, the workers used a growth game that actually intensified the very disturbance presented by the children. Yet, their intensification was safe, and it allowed for reflection at thé end. This is what we mean by creative (rather than random) chaos. Growth games, which enhance such a change, seem relevant to the group during crises.

Of course the difference between the two is only a matter of degree. Elements of both phases and crises are present throughout the life of the group, but each has a tendency to become more apparent at different points of the group's development.

With this added understanding, the children's behaviour makes more sense. The children were not simply 'awful'. Disrupting the activity was perhaps their way of saying that there was no point in the activity of building the symbolic house: the real one was about to collapse. Their dynamics were at a crisis rather than at a phase. The workers' second intervention, offered through a growth game, charged destruction with positive connotations and enabled a crisis to erupt safely. Levine called this 'the separation crisis'. Only when group members had been through this crisis were they able to come to terms with feelings of loss. During the first session, this crisis had been suppressed and had not been given a chance to be expressed. This had led to the children's random and destructive chaos. Yet, when the problematic behaviour was seen by the workers as a valuable experience, and was allowed to erupt safely, it led to a helpful resolution. Now each child could learn about coping with the end of relationships (the Termination phase).

The relative difference between phases and crises has more general implications. Since this difference is only a matter of degree, the worker may well have to respond to each during one and the same session. This they can do by conceiving of the session as a wave. Let us see how.

The session as a wave

Valuable as their ideas are, neither Schutz nor Vinter tell us exactly how to order and pace various responses within each session. Ross and Thorpe (1988) drew on Schutz's ideas to do this, but their ideas apply only to what we call activities, and, as the authors suggest, do not add up to a clear theory. A systems understanding seems to offer this by suggesting the appearance of a wave.

In groupwork practice the wave was most clearly identified in Blatner's (1973) psychodrama curve, which we have translated into systems terms. Blatner suggested that each group session should begin with a 'warm-up' period during which the sense of what is to happen is elicited. The step of warm-up is usually rather orderly involving relatively little chaos. Following the warm-up, 'action' is facilitated, at times to complete catharsis, and it is then that chaos reaches its peak. However, members should never be left 'hanging' there. A period of 'integration' should always follow, to allow the processing of the experience in a more orderly fashion at the end (Blatner, 1973, pp.74-76). So, a wave appears: flowing from order to chaos and back to order again.

We suggest that when using non-verbal methods such as activities and growth games it is helpful to respect the same dynamics. This will mean that during the warm-up the worker will help the group elaborate its own sense of order. Such a sense of order can be enhanced by offering activities. During the action the worker may enable some degree of creative chaos. For creative (rather than random) chaos to arise, growth games seem most suitable. Then, for Integration, a sense of order has to re-surface. Since the sense of order is facilitated more easily through activities, integration can be comfortably reached by offering them. Figure 1 shows these connections graphically.

Figure 1
The flow of a single wave

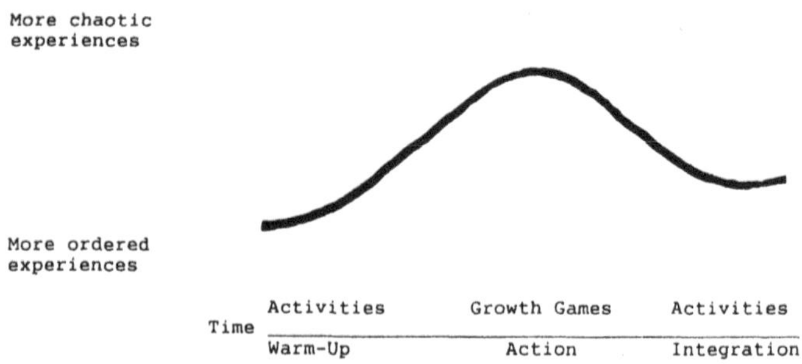

However, to regard a session as a smooth wave would be an over-simplification, and would not allow group members breathing spaces where they can make the transitions between chaos and order. So, a good session should follow the flow of a wave, but this wave should, so-to-speak, breathe: it should have intermittent periods for reflection among the members while the wave fluctuates. Let us see all these ideas in a practice example.

Combining activities and growth games: an example

The group which will serve as an example, was set up for ten women with learning difficulties, who had minimal verbal ability but who were physically able. The group members had been prepared by the groupworker beforehand (Manor, 1988). Therefore, the worker already knew of their abilities, limitations, and interests. The major purpose of the group was to increase self-awareness, confidence, and communication skills among the members. The choice of methods was based on the same view of the group as a microcosm of the members' relationships, as with the children's group.

We have chosen Levine's initial parallel phase (Levine, 1979, pp.90-118) to show how to combine activities and growth games in view of the ideas presented here. Levine suggests that during the parallel phase group members relate chiefly to the groupworker because they are still unsure how far they can trust one another. However, although group members are primarily concerned with whether they can trust the worker, they realise that if they are to benefit from what other members may have to offer, they will have to feel safe enough to relinquish some of their personal autonomy. How can the worker let the group explore both needs? In systems terms, the way to do this would be to facilitate a wave. The wave can begin by settling the group at a comfortable ordered level of homeostasis, using an activity. The worker can then invite some exploration of uncertainty with two growth games which safely intensify the disturbing experiences. The session can end by consolidating the newly found order (the new homeostasis) with another activity, and so increasing patterning of the interactions again. However, in practice, this is not likely to be so simple.

Firstly, there are times when neither a pure growth game nor an activity seems appropriate. This happens when the members are coping with the simultaneous impact of both a phase and a crisis. Because such intense ambivalence occurs often, we have introduced what we call 'a modified growth game'. In this game a disturbance is intensified, but patterning is retained too. Secondly, if group members are to assimilate any of the experiences; both those of activities and of growth games, they need periods of reflection between them. This is why the introduction of either an activity or a growth game is always followed by gathering the group together in a circle. Sitting in a circle enables members to see one another and share their reflection; and so, expand the meaning of their experiences.

The session

The session was held in a mid-size room with a carpet and a few windows high up which were unlikely to prove hazardous if the games became vigorous. Adjacent to the room was a kitchen supplied with urn, mugs, and tins of biscuits. Participants had been told to wear comfortable loose-fitting clothes which would not inhibit their movements.

The names game; an activity

The worker began the first session with an introductions game which aimed to recognise the individual importance of each group member without being too challenging. As each member entered the room she was asked to join the circle sitting on the floor. When all participants were present each was asked to say her name. If a member spoke quietly the worker said: 'I cannot hear you because you are speaking very quietly'. If there was no response, the worker raised her voice and said more loudly: 'Try saying your name loudly so we can all hear you'. If the participant talked too loudly the worker did the opposite; that is, repeated the member's name more quietly. This was an activity in that it resembled a socially established sequence of behaviour: the host (worker) introduced the newcomers (new members) to one another. Drawing on Vinter's scheme (Vinter, 1974), this was a highly prescribed activity in which institutional control was also high. The intention was to engender a feeling of safety and containment among the members by emphasising the centrality of the leader. The worker decided where each member was to sit and whether she spoke too loudly or too softly. Physical movement was kept to a minimum to encourage control and enable participants to acclimatise themselves to being in the group without having, at this early stage, to communicate with one another. Competence required was minimal too so as not to emphasize differences in ability and lead to competition among participants, which could have emphasised power differences prematurely. The structure of interaction was parallel: each member relating to the worker on her own so that the holding function of the leader was established first. In terms of our 'wave', this was a warm-up activity. The worker had a clear aim in her mind and offered incremental steps which brought the members to this level of involvement. From a systems point of view, patterning was emphasised.

The animals game; a growth game

Following the first activity was a growth game. The game was designed to let the members themselves explore how close they wanted to be to the others. The worker did not have a desired level of closeness in mind. Rather, she wanted the members to find the distance for themselves. The worker anticipated the fears the members might experience during the parallel phase. She knew that these fears were often that their need for autonomy would not be recognised on the one hand, and on the other that their wish to belong to the group would be ignored, but the worker did not have the solution. Any 'change of directionality' (Levine, 1979, p.73) had to come from the members. Since the worker expected group members to think that the norm was to move closer to the others, she considered moving further apart to be necessarily disturbing. Therefore, the worker improvised the intensification of such a disturbance. The worker simply said:

> In the beginning it is difficult to know where we are in this new group. Let's find out. Go anywhere in the room where you feel comfortable. You may stand on the table, hide underneath, stay in the middle near me, curl up, or stand up with your arms out; whatever may show how you feel now.

Some did not move, while others went rushing around looking for something on which to climb. As the worker invited group members to express their dilemmas physically, each was encouraged to exaggerate how she felt within the group while, at the same time, each member's sense of autonomy was emphasised. This first section of the growth game helped members to intensify unexpected and potentially disturbing behaviour. Of course, the worker made comments all along helping the member make sense of this unusual experience, thus enhancing reflection. However, reflection was more directly encouraged in the second part of the game. When the members found their spaces the worker stood in the centre of the room and said:

> Quite often, when we come to a new group, we feel strange: almost as if suddenly we don't know who we are. Well, I'm feeling a bit like this right now, but that's OK too. Let's find out how we all feel. I actually feel like a giraffe who likes to see what everyone is doing. I'm a big giraffe. What about you?

This contribution introduced the associated verbal level which was necessary for fully expanding the meaning of such experiences. The worker then went to each woman in turn encouraging her to say what animal she might be, and whether it was big or small. Some did not speak at all while others needed to be restrained from acting their animals in vivo. In this game the worker used metaphors to draw out the meaning of the previous game; that is, she enhanced reflection more directly.

This second section served two purposes. The first was to help members positively assert their autonomous individuality through exaggerating it by imagining themselves as 'strange' animals. So, a disturbance was safely intensified. The second purpose was to elicit verbal descriptions of these differences in order to find the connections among them: reflection was enhanced. When this third step was over the group was asked to sit in a circle once more and was offered a short period for further reflection.

The falling game; a modified growth game

All the same, the worker knew that many group members feared closeness with their peers without first ensuring that she protected all of them. She expected that the members would wish to go on exploring what would be her role when they began to trust one another. For further free exploration an activity seemed relatively restrictive. More open seemed to be another growth game, improvising yet again a new dilemma in action. So, each member was encouraged by the worker to fall into her arms. This acknowledged the continuous need for the worker's centrality at that point of the group's life. It demonstrated the validity of the members' need to trust her before they could begin to trust one another. Each member could choose where to stand; some stood very close to the worker afraid to take the risk, while others tested her by standing so far away that they could not be caught. This game also gave each woman an opportunity to respond according to how each felt individually. Then, when members showed that they could trust the worker in this way, the game was expanded encouraging the members to trust one another. The worker herself divided the women into pairs rather than leaving each member to choose a partner, and so discouraged potential competition. She then invited them to take turns in falling into each other's arms. In this version of the trust game the disturbing experience was the members' fear of trusting one another, and this disturbing experience was actually intensified. Yet, because of the potential intensity of the theme of trust, and because it was enacted physically, the worker did not let this growth game freely run its course. The worker monitored the experiences and made sure no one was hurt. In this she introduced more patterning; encouraging members to catch and fall within pre-determined bounds of safety. Some members refused to play, indicating that they did not yet trust members enough or that they felt excluded. Such inactivity was regarded as a form of communication too and was accepted as equally valid.

This modified growth game incorporated some elements of activities. At the beginning of this step the worker was central, but the game also represented her giving more responsibility to group members, and therefore, giving up some of her power. In Vinter's terms the game was highly prescriptive as each member in turn was encouraged by the worker to fall into her arms. However, as basic trust in the worker was established, Prescriptiveness was lowered and each pair was given the freedom to find its own way. Yet, in this game interactiveness continued to be low since interaction was mostly parallel: that is, in pairs. This had further minimised the potential for competition.

Drinking tea; an activity

Drinking tea may seem a trivial matter to some, but only to those who belittle the impact of non-verbal gestures. Close observation suggests that eating and drinking may have a rather marked effect on interactions. The last step aimed to increase the level of order and stability again. So, a socially accepted sequence of behaviour: that is, an activity, was chosen rather than a growth game. The group shared several plates of biscuits and the worker made tea, handing a cup to each member who formed part of a seated circle. By handing out the drinks herself the worker maintained a high level of institutional control. Ensuring that members were sitting down meant the control was increased by keeping physical movement to a minimum. Obviously, the competence required to drink tea was low resulting in decreased competition. Interactiveness was also relatively low since it was confined to the parallel activities of eating and drinking. All these features helped to create a feeling of containment.

Only after this sequence ended did the worker begin to discuss the purpose of the group and how it might work; that is, the worker began the process of contracting (Croxton, 1974; Preston-Shoot, 1988).

For the purpose of this paper the period before contracting is the essential one. Let us look now at the dynamics of that very beginning in more general terms.

Fluctuations of the wave

The whole sequence can be represented as the fluctuations of a single wave, as in Figure 2.

Figure 2
Fluctuation of the session as a wave

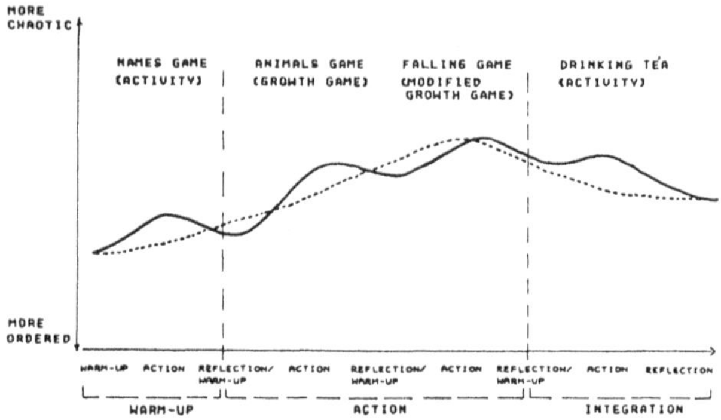

Overall, the session can be visualised as a wave which is indicated by the broken line. Within this wave, there are fluctuations marked by the continuous line.

Each growth game or activity began with the women sitting in a circle. Sitting like this provided space where the women could reflect on the experience they had just had, and prepare them for the next part of the session. It is these 'breathing spaces' which created the fluctuations of the wave. These dips in the wave were interspersed with the little bursts which provided the core parts of each growth game or activity.

The warm-up part of the session comprised of an activity which increased patterning of the interactions. It invited relatively little potential for chaos. This ordered affair settled the group at a stable level. The action part of the session was taken up by two growth games. The first involved intensifying disturbing possibilities in order to explore members' feelings about being in the group, and provided the potential for sharing their uncertainty. This was followed by a modified growth game in which other disturbing experiences were safely intensified, to enable the members to explore the dilemma of relating to one another while retaining the worker's concern for them. However, this particular growth game had such potential for chaos that measures were needed to restrict it. Therefore, elements characteristic of activities were introduced; patterning the interactions sufficiently to make them safe. We called this combination 'a modified growth game' to suggest that the difference between growth games and activities is a matter of degree. This modified growth game provided the peak of the wave as the potential for chaos was the highest.

The last part of the session was deliberately an extremely conventional activity where the potential for chaos was negligible while order could be easily enhanced. This was the Integration part of the session, enabling the group to reach a new sense of order through very patterned interaction which prepared them for the contracting work which followed.

Summary

We began with an example of workers' failure to order their responses to a group of children. The discussion which followed suggested that a systems understanding of the dynamics of activities as different from that of growth games might have prevented that failure. Activities seemed to meet the group's need to elaborate an already achieved sense of its direction and order, but this was not what the children in our first example needed. These children probably needed first to get down to basics again and explore what direction to take. In the terms suggested here; their 'wave' was not at a phase, but in a crisis. The children needed the peak of chaos so they could go through the separation crisis safely. Only then could they settle at the trough of a newly found order; that is, enter the phase of termination. Such a peak could be offered to them more safely through a growth game rather than an activity. A systems understanding of the differences led to describing the combination of phases and crises as 'a fluctuating wave'. This fluctuating wave had, so to speak, four layers, which corresponded to each other in this way:

Order	-	Chaos	-	Order
Patterning	-	Intensifying a disturbance	-	Patterning
Warm-up	-	Action	-	Integration
Activities	-	Growth games	-	Activities

The wave flowed by reflecting upon the connections among these layers.

A different example of enabling a group of women to fluctuate over such a wave was then offered. We hope that the generality of these ideas may encourage workers to offer more than their personal recipes when they combine activities and growth games in their work with other groups. Ah, and don't forget: if it isn't fun at all, it probably isn't working.

Note

This paper originated from an essay Miriam Dumbleton submitted as part of her post-graduate Diploma in Social Work studies at Middlesex University. The preparation of that essay was tutored by Oded Manor.

References

Axline, V.M. (1969) *Play Therapy*. New York: Ballantine Books.

Blatner, H.A. (1973) *Acting In: Practical Applications of Psychodramatic Methods*. New York: Springer Pub. Co.

Brandes, D. and Phillips, H. (1977) *Gamesters' Handbook*. London: Hutchison

Breunlin, D.C. (1989) 'Clinical implications of oscillation theory' in Ramsey, C. (ed.) *The Science of Family Medicine*. New York: Guilford Press, pp.135-149.

Chetkov-Yanoov, B. (1992) *Social Work Practice: A Systems Approach*. New York: The Howarth Press.

Croxton, T.A. (1974) 'The therapeutic contract in social treatment' in Glasser, P., Sarri, R. and Vinter, R. (eds.) *Individual Change through Small Groups*. New York: The Free Press, pp.169-185.

Davis, M. (1982) *Interaction Rhythms*. New York: Human Sciences Press.

Durkin, J.E. (ed.) (1981) *Living Groups: Group Psychotherapy and General Systems Theory*. New York: Brunner/Mazel.

Heap, K. (1979) *Process and Action in Work with Groups*. Oxford: Pergamon Press.

Hoffman, L. (1981) *Foundations of Family Therapy*. New York: Basic Books Inc.

LaCoursiere, R.B. (1980) *The Life Cycle of Groups*. New York: Human Science Press.

Lewis, H.R. and Streitfeld, H.S. (1970) *Growth Games*. London: Souvenir Press.

Levine, B. (1979) *Group Psychotherapy*. Englewood Cliffs, N.J.: Prentice Hall.

McGrath, J.E. (1988) (ed.) *The Social Psychology of Time*. London: Sage Pub.

Manor, O. (1988) 'Preparing the client for social groupwork: an illustrated framework', *Groupwork*, 1(2), pp.100-114.

Middleman, R. (ed.) (1983) *Activities and Action in Groupwork*. New York: The Howarth Press.

Phillips, J. (1989) 'Targeted activities in group contexts.' *Groupwork*, 2(1), pp.48-57.

Pincus, A. and Minahan, A. (1973) *Social Work Practice*. Itasca, Illinois; F.E. Peacock Pub.

Preston-Shoot, M. (1988) 'Using contracts in groupwork', *Groupwork*, 2(1), pp.36-47.

Rose, S.D. and Edleson, J.L. (1987) *Working with Children and Adolescents in Groups*. London: Jossey-Bass Pub.

Ross,S. and Thorpe, A. (1988) 'Programming skills in social groupwork', *Groupwork*, 1(2), pp.135-146.

Schutz, W.C. (1967) *Joy: Expanding Human Awareness*. London: Souvenir Press.

Simon, F.B., Stierlin, H. and Wynne, L.C. (1985) *The Language of Family Therapy*. New York: Family Process Press.

VanderVen, K.D. (1985) 'Activity programming: Its developmental and therapeutic role in group care' in Fulcher, L.C. and Ainsworth, F. (eds.) *Group Care Practice with Children*. London: Tavistock Pub, pp.155-186.

Reviews

A Workbook of Group Analytic Interventions
D. KENNARD, J. ROBERTS AND A. WINTER
London, Routledge, 1993, price £35.00 (hbk) £12.99 (pbk)
ISBN 0 415 08783 X (hbk) 0 415 08784 8 (pbk)

Here is a little gem. This short book provides a fascinating read, if tantalising at times, in which we are given 'fly-on-the-wall' glimpses of experienced group analysts in action. The authors, all group analysts themselves, present the findings from a research project at the Institute of Group Analysis, in which respondents were faced with eight hypothetical situations derived from real-life incidents arising in small psychotherapy groups. These situations were presented to them in brief (described in about 200 words each), and they were asked to complete a questionnaire as to what they thought was happening in each situation and why, to outline what they would do or say (if anything), and to give their reasons for their interventions. The situations range from the mundane, such as the problem of prolonged 'turn-taking' in the group, through the awkward challenge, when group members bring wine and mince pies to a pre-Christmas session, and even to one situation of physical danger when a borderline patient produces a razor blade and threatens to 'carve up' the therapist. The authors analyse the responses given by those completing the questionnaire and present them in eight chapters, framed within a few brief chapters on intervention and interpretation, including some discussion of a categorisation of types of intervention, plus a very brief resume of theoretical approaches to group psychotherapy.

The value of the material presented is very great, providing a most detailed insight into what experienced therapists say they would do in a number of difficult circumstances - of course there is no knowing what they might actually do or say, but this does not detract from the value of the book. What is most striking throughout the book is the huge range of types of response which these therapists - many of them leading lights at the Institute - make to the same situation, and the fact that what appears to explain these differences is only partly to do with theoretical considerations, and very largely to do with personal style. Thus, alongside the majority of respondents whose approach to most situations matches the approved style described by David Kennard as 'relaxed, empathic and encouraging', we also meet therapists who indulge themselves in whimsical and enigmatic metaphors, those who bark at their groups with fearsomely frank interpretations, and those on the other hand who consume themselves with angst and self-blame when confronted with those unexpected mince pies. Should we be concerned or should we perhaps be delighted to find such variations within the practice of what is claimed as 'the group analytic method'?

Indeed, does a group analytic method emerge from the material presented? One unfortunate consequence of the methodology of the research project, of selecting a number of critical moments and analysing these in isolation from each other, is that the book risks creating an impression of group analysis as episodic rather than ongoing. Malcolm Pines' chapter on interpretation helpfully counteracts this impression, and several of the respondents consistently refer to the need to consider issues such as the stage of the group's development, but it might have been very productive if we could have followed some of the therapists through from one scene to the next. Thus we might have learned whether, for example, the male therapist who is so clumsy in situation 4 is the same one still lumbering over people's emotional corns in situation 5, and whether the female therapist who is so profound and sensitive in one of the situations is the same one who crops up again with similar skill in several other places.

The lack of such a perspective also prevents us from discovering whether anything can be generalised about, for instance, the personal styles of male and female therapists (there do seem to be some stark differences revealed here), or about the connection between personal style and theoretical allegiance. I do hope the authors will return to issues such as these, since the data which they have assembled is presumably capable of much further analysis. The absence of a longitudinal perspective also prevents us from achieving real clarity about the central concern of the book: is there such a thing as the 'group analytic method' which can be clearly distinguished from other methods of group psychotherapy? Or is there simply an 'approach' - a way of thinking and feeling, located within an Institute with eminent founders, and promulgated through a training course and growing library of publications? We do learn in passing about some particular components of the group analytic method such as 'therapeutic abstinence within the communication field of the group' (this in the context of the discussion of the mince pies), and the chapters on theory and method do include some helpful signposts, but the book would still have benefited from a rather fuller account of the principles and practice of group analysis. As it turns out, the categorisation of interventions proposed in the introductory and concluding chapters figures very little in the detailed discussion of the responses to the situations, although what is discussed in these chapters is consistently interesting, and very rich material for training purposes.

To those closely involved in the IGA, of course, the book will have the added interest that they will be able to try to spot the personal style of the therapists - the rest of us will never know. The authors themselves are faced with the related problem as to how critically they will comment on their colleagues' work: in general, they are perhaps clearer in endorsing what they consider good practice than in criticising potentially damaging interventions.

The book is primarily intended as a training tool and it will certainly be a useful resource to set alongside related tools such as the concept of the 'critical incident' (Cohen and Smith, 1976) and the 'trigger' videotape. Indeed in the training context I can envisage situations such as these being usefully presented on videotape for 'live' and immediate response by trainees, rather than on paper, where, as the authors concede, respondents have the luxury of time to think. On the other hand, in the context of training I would be somewhat concerned by the resolute avoidance in the text of issues of gender and 'race'. For example, the only group member given a physical description in the situations as presented by these male therapists is the 'attractive young woman' in situation 4, and the only mention of racism is to decry those 'inexperienced' therapists who may give it inappropriate attention. This last comment is disappointingly dismissive in a book of such subtlety and depth, and it could have been very instructive to explore the range of responses which the subjects themselves might have made to group situations in which ethnic, religious or gender differences appeared to be significant.

On reflection, the image which this book conjures up for me is not so much of a little gem as of a small treasure box washed up on the shore: it has many compartments, each crammed with a mixture of the sparkling and the everyday, with a few oddities which are puzzling, and one or two which are quite alarming. I would love to have found a perfect string of pearls, but this was not the point, and what I did find was enthralling.

Adrian Ward, Director of Social Work Studies, University of Reading.

Reference

Cohen, A.M. and Smith, R.D. (1976) *The Critical Incident in Growth Groups*. La Jolla, California; University Associates.

Art Therapy and Dramatherapy Masks of the Soul
SUE JENNINGS AND ASE MINDE
Jessica Kingsley Publishers, 1993, price £22.50
ISBN 1 85302 027 3 (hbk)

This is a fascinating and unusual book, in both content and style. It is written with refreshing honesty and transparency, and gives considerable insight into the authors' lives as well as their work.

The book describes the way in which one art therapist and one dramatherapist (both pioneers in their own fields) have collaborated over a period of ten years. This collaboration has taken place not only over the 'divide of mistrust' between different disciplines, but also across national boundaries, between Britain and Norway.

Many co-authored books have fairly obvious 'division of labour', and Sue Jennings and Ase Minde could have taken this route. Although both have their own introductory chapters to explain their backgrounds - Sue Jennings in dramatherapy in Britain, Ase Minde in art therapy in Norway - they also demonstrate and model other ways of collaboration.

Most chapters, at some point, include dialogues between the authors, and these are invaluable in showing how they develop their initial ideas together. The dialogues also clarify where they have different but complementary perspectives on the same issue, by virtue of their different backgrounds and personalities. The chapter called 'The fertile relationship' expands this theme in some detail.

The authors also demonstrate their collaboration in their descriptions of workshops, both their preparations and the way they run them. Readers can see how the two disciplines interweave to achieve something far greater than either discipline on its own. The authors also feel that, far from losing their identities through this cooperation, they become 'more themselves' as a result.

Weaving is only one of many resonant metaphors in the book. Both authors draw on a vast 'storehouse' of therapeutic and artistic experience, including acting, knowledge of literature, stories and myths, several years in a Malaysian rain forest, psychotherapy, working with textiles and textures, travel to the United States, and bringing up families.

Another of their metaphors, which I found very fruitful, is that of therapy as the 'art of navigation'. Their work with metaphors encourages patients and clients to explore their lives through metaphors and myths, and to make the connections with their own lives themselves.

Some people find myths and metaphors 'airy-fairy' and somewhat removed from everyday life and psychological problems. The clinical examples, given all through the text at appropriate points, show how myths and metaphors relate to people's everyday concerns. Art therapy and dramatherapy based on stories can help people to express what cannot be expressed in any other way.

The examples are drawn from clinical work in the psychiatric field, and also from the many joint workshops run for professional people, in the UK, Norway and elsewhere.

Work with both individuals and groups is included. The groupwork is well described, so that readers can both learn what structures are used - and why - and also 'get a feel' for what is going on. Several group workshops are described in considerable detail, with full programmes.

There is a view in the world of therapy, that work with clients is concerned chiefly with reducing defences, and working through their problems, sometimes by re-living them. Sue Jennings and Ase Minde believe that there are occasions when people need their defences, and can work with them more creatively using story and metaphor, involving an expansion of imagination rather than the reductive approach of psychoanalysis. Thus, rather than searching for 'the key', they would help individuals to explore, through art and drama, a variety of keys, with different meanings and possibilities.

The authors use the concept of 'theatrical distancing' to show that using the arts as a parallel frame of reference can, paradoxically, enable people to approach more closely otherwise unassailable problems.

Although there is a lot in this book about therapy, the authors obviously find the links with the arts more creative than the links with psychoanalysis. So there are only two mentions of Freud, but many quotations from Shakespeare, Ibsen and Rilke; and references to paintings and sculpture by Botticelli, Munch and Moore. The only exception to this trend is the inclusion of several lengthy passages from Winnicott, the 'patron saint' of arts therapists.

Some art forms used by the authors are seen by them as belonging both to art therapy and dramatherapy - such as sand play and mask-making. The chapter on body work also involves some very unusual approaches which result from the confluence of the two disciplines.

The final chapters include several descriptions of joint workshops, centred round different themes, such as a fascinating series on 'Doors'. The way these workshops are developed is a tribute to the authors' experience and skill, and their ability to work together. Their honesty about difficulties makes the accounts more authentic.

The book is illustrated with black-and-white photographs of art therapy work, and one or two drama events. There are also some light-hearted drawings by Gro Finne, produced specially for the book. However, several of the illustrations have no captions, and their connection to the text was not always clear to me. The pictures were at their most powerful when they faced the relevant text.

There are a few places where the text is slightly difficult to follow, or suffers discontinuities, and there are several irritating discrepancies and mistakes, especially in the references. The book ends somewhat abruptly, albeit on a 'high note' - I would have liked it rounded off with some personal comments from the authors, on completion of their 'magnum opus'. I am sure there were comments to be made, and it would have been more in keeping with their process-oriented style.

Apart from these minor criticisms, the book is highly readable and easy to understand by interested lay people, as well as those with experience. It will be of interest to anyone working in a therapeutic setting with individuals or groups, and especially those wishing to explore the use of art, drama, story and metaphor. It will also be extremely illuminating for anyone already working across disciplines or contemplating doing so.

This is the first book, as far as I know, which details close collaboration between art therapy and dramatherapy. The authors have been very open about their work and methods, and their experience and wisdom comes through. They have created an interesting and readable book which is more than a text, it is a work of art - and (depending on your choice of metaphor) it both provides a feast and fires the imagination.

Marian Liebmann, Art Therapist/Probation Officer/Mediation Worker

Fritz Perls
PETRUSKA CLARKSON AND JENNIFER MACKEWN
London, Sage, 1993
Price: £9.95 ISBN: 0 8039 8453 7 (pbk)
Price: £19.95 ISBN: 0 8039 8452 9 (hbk)

This book appears in the series on key figures in counselling and psychotherapy published by Sage and edited by Windy Dryden. Other titles include Sigmund Freud, Carl Rogers and Eric Berne. I hope there will be more. The editor is to be congratulated on the clarity with which he has encouraged his authors to write within a clear framework which speaks to and makes the series readable to both newcomers to the field as well as experienced and critical therapists and counsellors.

He is perhaps more to be congratulated for his choice of authors. Once more in this volume we find a book written by experienced therapists whom the reader can sense have lived with, fought with, breathed, slept and dreamed with Gestalt therapy over a long period of time. Both authors are Gestalt therapists. However if readers are expecting a single minded partisan adulation of the hero and founder of a popular form of therapy, they had better forget it.

What is striking about the book is the depth of research and scholarship that has gone into the creation of this volume. There is not only a search and review of the original documents and books written by Perls along with his collaborators since the 1940s, there is the search for oral history in the recorded views of colleagues with whom the authors have had first or second hand contact, as well as a critical analysis of their relationships and the way parts of their theories became neglected not least by Perls himself. Not only does this provide a rich range of views, a thorough review of the literature and a critical evaluation of Perls as a man and as a therapist, it also illustrates perhaps one of the man's greatest determinations which was to make himself and his work publicly known to a wide range of people. He is clearly painted as a man who liked to create controversy, and one, whose bequest for his followers to lay claim to, was to sort out the difference between his personal style and the inspiration of the ideas that shaped his work and that in turn he re-created and shaped himself. This book is a genuine and valuable contribution to this process.

The five chapters, in common with other books in the series follow a clear format in the theme of each chapter: 1 - The life of Fritz Perls; 2 - Major contributions to theory; 3 - Major contributions to practice; 4 - Criticisms and rebuttals; 5 - The overall influence of Fritz Perls.

The first chapter provides a vivid summary of the psychological uncertainties in Perls early life that provided conflicted attachments to father, mother, family, national, cultural and religious roots. In the years before the last war life for Atheistic Berlin Jews was anything but rooted. The authors indicate some of the consequences in his dominating and controlling as well as rebellious style of work. If personal life lacked secure attachments so did geographical and professional roots. The story illustrates a not uncommon picture for many in the developing field of psychoanalysis of Jews dispersed searching for a home, frustrated with the institutions that they encountered, often warring to find a home, and a way of working, that Perls found first in South Africa, then in the USA. This nomadic life-style, the author's trace into Perls highly individualised and workshop style that has left to later Gestalt therapists the task of re-finding the context, community and group as agents of development and change. Perls infamous Gestalt 'prayer' - 'You are you and I am I/If by chance we find each other, it's beautiful./If not it cannot be helped' - becomes highlighted as other denying.

The chapters on theory and practice provide a summary and a critique of Perls thinking and therapy. The wide range of theories used to support his ideas indicate the breadth of the man's resources and curiosity, but perhaps also leave the reader bombarded by such a wide sweep of perspectives that it is sometimes difficult to see where learning might have happened from the client directly. Perhaps holistic and integrating theories inevitably run this risk. Many encounters are reported verbatim to illustrate well ideas of Perls, yet nowhere are there case studies from which conclusions are drawn. This seems not to have been Perls style.

Perhaps more interesting and valuable is the chapter on criticisms and rebuttals. The authors report selected criticisms both from within Gestalt therapy and from outside. They carefully sift the evidence, evaluate its competence and sympathy to Perls and evaluate the judgements made. This chapter is a model of psychotherapy scholarship. I wish others in the field would resist the temptation to rubbish or idealise views according to whether they fit their own views. Not in this chapter, nor in the final one do the authors confuse the criticisms of the man with criticisms of his ideas and work - again such a common trap in the psychotherapy world. Perhaps I can do no better than to quote their conclusions:

> Some of these criticisms we have found to be fully justified, as for example the accusation that Perls behaved unethically by having sexual contact with clients and the charge that Perls made grandiose claims for Gestalt and for himself. Some of the criticisms - such as that Perls caused pain, that he sometimes played down verbal explanations and that he used techniques and gimmicks - we have found to be partially justified. Other criticisms of Perls we have shown to be one-sided and misrepresentative of Perls as a whole, if taken out of context. We have tried to contextualise the criticisms which fall into this category - as for instance Perls' anti-intellectual stance, his view of maturity and his attitude towards support and responsibility. Finally, some of the criticisms seem to us to be entirely unjustified and based on gossip, prejudice or gossip, prejudice or a very partial understanding of Perls. Unjustified criticisms of Perls include the suggestion that Perls minimised the past and that Perls had no theory of transference (p.154).

On a personal and professional level I was interested to read the book at this stage in my work as in the last year I have been asked to offer psychotherapy to no fewer than six clients who formerly worked with Gestalt therapists. It is clear to me that each received much from their therapists yet three areas of their criticisms and disappointments were only partly echoed in the book. Each seems to have roots in Perls' approach.

On is that Gestalt therapists, in the name of being authentic and offering contact to clients, disclose their own often undigested responses in a way that has inhibited clients from bringing crucial unresolved personal feeling or complexes to their therapist, as the message was received that it would not be approved of or welcome.

A second criticism has been the failure of Gestalt therapists to keep boundaries, and a sense that the power balance disadvantaged the client in such a directive therapy.

The third criticism was that Gestalt therapists have used Perls' idea of the need to complete situations in a way that over manages regressions and can create the fantasy that deep rooted emotional patterning can be overcome by catharsis that resolves it. At one level clients risk being persuaded that all is resolved when it isn't, at another that unresolved regressions overwhelm later.

I raise these issues not to vaunt my own analytic approach in relation to Gestalt - heavens knows many clients are driven into Gestalt therapy because of the seemingly dead impassiveness of their analytic psychotherapists which can be equally self-negating - but rather to promote the dialogue which the authors have embarked upon. In this context the account of developments in Gestalt since Perls go some way to addressing these criticisms and are to be welcomed.

I recommend this volume as a valuable contribution to some hard thinking that is much needed in the era of psychotherapy where first generation reactions to Freud are now being re-evaluated and where psychotherapists have now their own UK register recognising professionally trained psychotherapists as a step towards becoming a profession that cannot be practised by anyone who has attended a few workshops or courses.

Rick Morgan-Jones.

NOTES ON CONTRIBUTORS

Dorothy Atkinson is a Senior Lecturer in the School of Health, Welfare and Community Education, Open University. Her background is in social work, and social work education, and includes several years experience of working with people with learning disabilities. Her Open University work has been primarily in the learning disability field.

Miriam Dumbleton is Care Manager for the London Borough of Westminster Social Services, with a special interest in mental health, groupwork and counselling. She graduated in literature in 1982, and had worked in residential and day care with people with learning difficulties before completing her post-graduate Diploma in Social Work (CQSW) at Middlesex University in 1991. She has since worked in a Family Service Unit and a mental health centre.

Helen Gobat qualified as a social worker in Australia in 1969, and has worked in various fields, interrupted by a spell in the Caribbean producing a family. She moved into the field of learning disability in the early 1980s, prompted by the experience of having a sister-in-law with a disability. She is currently studying a 'psychotherapeutic approach to mental handicap' at the Tavistock. Helen now works as an independent social worker, attempting to meet emotional needs of people with a learning disability, their families and caregivers, as she fears these needs are being overlooked in the huge organisational changes in the statutory services.

David Henchman and Susan Walton are Probation Officers who work for Avon Probation Service. They are experienced groupworkers whose current thinking is informed by their extensive work with people who have committed offences of a violent and sexual nature. In addition to their joint work David has run the Ross and Fabiano Reasoning and Rehabilitation Programme and Sue is an established Practice Teacher of Social Workers and has lectured at Bath University.

Kavita Kohli is an Asian deaf woman. This paper is an extract from her Study of Groupwork with Deaf People which was written during her final year of CQSW. Kavita is a social worker with deaf people in a local authority, Hounslow Social Services Department.

Oded Manor is Principal Lecturer in Social Work at Middlesex University, London. He qualified as a social worker (Goldsmiths' College), and a counsellor (South West College) after completing a BA (Jerusalem) and a PhD (London School of Economics) in the social sciences. Having practised and supervised groupwork and family work for several years, he now concentrates on teaching and research while still serving as a consultant. Oded has published widely both in Britain and the USA.

Olive Otway is Admissions Tutor and Lecturer in Social Work, University of Keele. She has worked as a Senior Practitioner Social Worker and has run a range of groups including groups for children who have been abused and women of children who have been abused.

NOTES FOR CONTRIBUTORS

Articles are welcome from all who have an interest in work with groups (whether as practitioner, trainer, researcher, user or consultant) and who wish to contribute to the development of groupwork theory and practice.

Types of Articles

The journal will publish two main types of articles:

i. PRACTICE-BASED PAPERS

These articles will be based directly on groupwork practice experience, but written in a way which is evaluative as well as descriptive. We recognise that many practitioners may not be familiar with writing for journals, and we wish to suggest the following guidelines to assist in this process:

(a) A brief summary of the contents of the article (100-150 words), drawing attention to any particular theme or emphasis.

(b) Background to the group, the context, e.g. agency setting, type of group, workers and members; group aims and objectives; and the theoretical/philosophical perspectives i.e. any particular principles or values central to the approach taken.

(c) A brief review of the group, content, methods and process.

(d) Outcome and analysis, specific topics of interest relevant to the focus of the article, e.g. key issues arising from this piece of practice; and evaluation of the group drawing out learning points for other practitioners.

ii. THEORY-BUILDING PAPERS

Each issue will carry several theoretical papers ranging over groupwork concepts, theory, research, issues and values. Papers on the following topics would be especially welcomed:

(a) The current 'state of the art' of groupwork.

(b) Papers analysing the significance for the groupwork process of race, gender, class, culture and other social factors.

(c) Papers analysing key group concepts and issues.

(d) Papers from different countries, sharing current developments and theoretical concerns and preoccupations likely to be significant for groupwork practice in Britain and elsewhere.

(e) New sources of research evidence.

(f) Groupwork training and skill development, consultation/supervision.

Length of papers

The normal range will be 2,500-4,000 words, with practice accounts normally not longer than 3,000 words. Exceptionally, longer articles will be accepted and there will be a place for briefer contributions on new developments, responses to previous articles and other material of special interest.

Form of Submission

Articles should be submitted in one of two ways:

i. typed on A4 paper, 3 copies, double-spaced with wide margins

ii. on computer disc. Authors who have prepared their material by word processor are asked to provide a copy of the computer file on disk. Most Macintosh, IBM-PC compatible and Amstrad word processing programs can be read.

References

These should be quoted in the text by giving in brackets the author's name and year of publication. They should then be listed in alphabetical order at the end of the article as follows.

Books - author's surname, initials, date, title of book, place of publication, publisher's name, page if relevant.

Articles - author's surname, initials, date, title of article, title of journal, volume and number. Only those references which occur in the text should be listed. Where appropriate, additional resources may be listed separately as further reading.

Assessment for publication

Articles submitted will normally be passed to members of the journal's panel of assessors, and decisions as to publication made by the editors in the light of the assessors' comments.

Enquiries

Allan Brown, Dept of Social Work, University of Bristol, 8 Woodland Road, Bristol BS8 1TN. Tel: 0272-303030, ext.853/Nano McCaughan, 12 Barr Beacons, Canonbie Road, London SE23. Tel: 081 699 8438

Appendix: Contents of *Groupwork* Volumes I-13

Volume 1 (ISBN 9781861770554)
Groupwork practice with hard to reach clients: A modality of choice Lawrence Shulman
The worker and the group process: A dilemma revisited Ken Heap
Race and groupwork: Some experiences in practice and training Ros Muston and Jeremy Weinstein
A group for white women with black children Clare Rhule
Structured activities with adolescent boys Rod Craig
Supporting voices: Groupwork with people suffering from schizophrenia Lynda Randall and Wendy Walker
Groupwork books published in Britain 1980-86 Harold Marchant
Swimming upstream: Articles on groupwork in social work journals 1986-87 Nano McCaughan
Preparing the client for social groupwork: An illustrated framework Oded Manor
Groups for older people in residential and day-care: The other groupworkers Lorraine Bernard, John Burton, Phyllis Kyne and June Simon
'But I don't want to lead a group!' Some common problems of social workers leading groups Ken Reid
Programming skills in social groupwork. Sue Ross and Andy Thorpe
A model for evaluating groupwork Michael Preston-shoot
Groupwork as the method of choice with black children in white foster homes Audrey Mullender
Short term groupwork in the treatment of chronic sorrow. A Norwegian experience Gerd Kramm Engebrigtsen and Ken Heap
Revisiting open groups Michael Henry
Social action groupwork as negotiation: Contradictions in the process of empowerment Eamonn Keenan and John Pinkerton
'Nowt to do and always getting into trouble'. The Bulwell Neighbourhood Project: A social action response Bill Badham, Michael Bente and Pauline Hall
A team development exercise John Taylor, Di Miles and John Eastgate
'The brothers and sisters group': A group for siblings of children with physical disabilities Anne Badger
Groupwork with adolescents: Abstracts Alison Skinner

Volume 2 (ISBN 9781861770561)
Challenging familiar assumptions: Preparing for and initiating a self-directed group Audrey Mullender and David Ward
Doing something with our lives when we're inside: Self-directive groupwork in a youth custody centre. Bill Badham (Ed.). Bob Blatchford, Steph Mcartney and Malcolm Nicholas
Using contracts in groupwork Michael Preston-shoot
Targeted activities in group contexts: The analysis of activities to meet consumer need Julie Phillips
Designing cancer groups for maximum effectiveness Barry M. Daste
Decision-making in therapeutic groups Marian F. Fatout
Confronting human finitude. Groupwork with people with AIDS George S. Getzel and Kevin F. Mahony
Organising accountability for social groupwork: More choices Oded Manor
A group for black and white sexually abused children Marie Lebacq and Zaffira Shah
Learning about groupwork. Jenny Lumley and Harold Marchant
Establishing a feminist model of groupwork in the Probation Service Tara Mistry
A way forward: A group for refugee women Rachel Tribe and Jane Shackman
Searching the literature on women's groups Cathrine Fitzgerald
Open grief groups: the resolution of complicated loss Marianne Davidsen-Nielsen and Nini Leick
Groupwork with the spouses of seriously ill patients Janine Favier
Supportive groupwork for dialysis patients Lizzie Bollmann
Supportive groupwork with young arthritic mothers Amy Østertun Geirdal
Staff development through groupwork in Polish

community agencies: 'The Centres Of Culture' Jerzy Szmagalski
Self-help groups as basic care in psychotherapy and social work Jürgen Matzat
Family group treatment in drug abuse Anna Casanova Torras
Groupwork As Early Intervention In High Risk Families Rigmor Grette Moe

Volume 3 (ISBN 9781861770578)
Social work with groups in multicultural contexts Kenneth L. Chau
Siblings in groups: Children of separated/divorced parents Sandra Regan and Jan Young
Groupwork techniques in a residential primary school for emotionally disturbed boys Peter Clarke and Amanda Aimable
The role of groupwork in research with people with learning difficulties Jan Walmsley
Groupwork training: A case study Andrew Kerslake
Beulah Rothman: An appreciation Oded Manor
Starting the journey: Enhancing the therapeutic elements of groupwork for adolescent female child sexual abuse victims Eileen Craig
Evaluating success in groupwork: Why not measure the obvious? Anne Peake and Olive Otway
Investigating groupwork: A Case study using a group approach in the initial stages of child sexual abuse investigation Sarah Allum
The Forgotten parent: Groupwork with mothers of sexually abused children Helen Masson and Marcus Erooga
Work with male sex offenders in groups Malcolm Cowburn
Protection, control, treatment: Groupwork with child sexual abuse perpetrators Marcus Erooga, Paul Clark and Mai Bentley
Group treatment for women sex offenders against children Sharon Barnett. Francesca Corder and Derek Jehu
Selected article abstracts on child sexual abuse and groupwork Julia Cramp and Helen Armstrong
Self help groups: A minefield for professionals Ulla Habermann
Facing the challenge of developing group services for high risk families Alice Home and Lise Darveau-Fournier
Groupwork with parents of sleepless children Rona Robertson
Culture' groups in prison Graham Towl
Groupwork with a difference: The group 'mosaic' in residential day centre settings Allan Brown
Groupwork in residential settings for elderly people Audrey Mullender

Volume 4 (ISBN 9781861770585)
Empowerment through mutual aid groups: A practice grounded conceptual framework Judith AB. Lee
Making authority accountable: The experience of a statutory based women's group Helen Bodinham and Jeremy Weinstein
Towards a model of social groupwork practice with marginalised populations Margot Breton
Working creatively with children Eugene Clerkin and Belinda Knaggs
The termination phase in groupwork: Tasks for the groupworker Sue Ross
Miami, October 1990 Oded Manor and Dave Ward
Black/white co-working in groups Tara Mistry And Allan Brown
Groupwork and oral history: Raising the consciousness of young people during social transition Sandra Drower
The use of photographs as a projective and facilitative technique in groups Merav DeVere And Ossi Rhonne
Facilitation in self-directed groupwork Dave Ward and Audrey Mullender
Evaluative study of groupwork for stress and anxiety Rhona Birrell Weisen
A long-term support group for chronic schizophrenic outpatients: A quantitative and qualitative evaluation Julie Cwikel And Adina Oron
Using groups in working with offenders:
A survey of groupwork in the Probation Service of England and Wales Brian Caddick
A Miskin Model of groupwork with women offenders Marion jones, Mary Mordecai, Frances Rutter and Linda Thomas
Evolution and accountability Ten years of groups in a day centre for offenders
Judith Earnshaw
The Telford Motoring Offenders Education Project Kathryn Hutchins
Groupwork in the Luton Probation And Bail Hostel Catherine Mulvie
The Newcastle intensive probation programme A centralised approach to groupwork Jane Mackintosh

Meeting prisoners' needs through groupwork Mike Ashe
Groupwork in the Probation Service: Care or control in the 1990s Paul Senior
Selected abstracts on groupwork with offenders John Hodge
Derek Carter 1934-1991

Volume 5 (ISBN 9781861770592)
Groupwork from across the Atlantic: Its identity and diffusion Catherine Pappell
Groupwork in Europe: Past, Present, Future Ken Heap, Diakonhjemmet School of Social Work, Oslo
The groupwork consultant's role in facilitating work groups Alan Turkie, Independent
Evaluation For The Improvement Of Groupwork Practice Kenneth H Gordon, School of Social Work, King's College, Western Ontario
Groupwork in a residential home for older people: Building on the positive aspects of group living Gun Lewis, Officer in Charge
Groupwork with Youth Gangs in Hong Kong T Wing Lo, City Polytechnic, Hong Kong
On empowerment, partnership and authority in groupwork practice: A training contribution Michael Preston-Shoot, School of Social Work, University of Manchester
Groupwork with involuntary clients: Remotivating strategies Cyrus S Behroozi, Indiana University School of Social Work
Handling conflict: Groupwork with violent offenders Rob Canton, Carolyn Mack and Jeff Smith, Nottinghamshire Probation
The dream in groupwork practice Iain Edgar, Dept of Social Work, University of Northumbria
Support groups for older people: Is homogeneity or heterogeneity the answer? Susan Rice and Catherine Goodman, Dept of Social Work, California State University, Long Beach
The group turns inward: A consideration of some group phenomena as reflective of the Northern Irish situation Jarlath Benson, Psychotherapeutic Groupworker, Belfast
Groupwork with bereaved children Nuala Harmey and Bernie Price, Medical Social Work, Temple Street Children's Hospital, Dublin
Reminiscence groupwork with older people Faith Gibson, Dept of Social Work, University of Ulster, Coleraine
Social workers and psychologists as facilitators of groupwork with adults with a learning difficulty: A survey of current practice Heno Schonfield and Mary C Morrissey, Senior Social Workers, Dublin
Groupwork with teenage cancer patients Nicola Martin Medical Social Worker in Oncology, and Eddie O'Neill, Paediatric Oncology Social Worker, Mater Hospital, Dublin
Bereaved by suicide: Setting up an 'ideal' therapy group in a real world Imogen O'Connor, Therapist, Dublin Rape Crisis Centre

Volume 6 (ISBN 9781861770608)
Groupwork versus *casework in a group* Roselle Kurland and Robert Salmon, Hunter School of Social Work, New York
Why groupwork is not put into practice: Reflections on the social work scene in Denmark Ulla Habermann, Director, Volunteer Centre, Denmark
Away with the experts? Self-help groupwork in Germany Jürgen Matzat, Psychologist, Klinik für Psychosomatik und Psychotherapie, Justus-Liebig-Universität, Gießen
Groupwork with siblings of children with special needs: A pilot study Georgina Ferraro and Julie Tucker, Senior Family Project Workers
Neutralisation of group control in youth gangs T Wing Lo, City Polytechnic, Hong Kong
The large group: The heart of the system in group care Adrian Ward, Dept of Social Work, University of Reading
Working with a family group of bereaved children Sheila Finlayson, Child Advisory Social Work Service, City of Birmingham Education Dept
A comparative study of four family bereavement groups Estelle Hopmeyer, and Annette Werk, McGill School of Social Work, Montréal
An asian mothers' group Lynne Muir Director, MEd Programme in Community Education and Hardev Notta, Acorns Hospice for Children, Birmingham
A Cruse family circle Joyce Rimmer, Birmingham Cruse
Coping with trauma Frank Parkinson, former Army chaplain
From group meeting to therapeutic group Bernadette Duffy. Social Care Worker, Dublin and Brian McCarthy, Lecturer in Psychology, Dublin Institute of Technology
Group therapy with adults with learning difficulties who have committed sexual offences Elisabeth

Cormack, Young People's Centre , Northern Ireland
Critical incident analysis and its application in groupwork David Henchman and Susan Walton, Avon Probation Service
Life history work with a group of people with learning disabilities Dorothy Atkinson, School of Health, Welfare and Community Education, Open University
Art therapy: Creative groupwork for women. Olive Otway, Lecturer in Social Work, University of Keele
Groupwork with parents of learning disabled adolescents. Helen Gobat, Independent Social Worker
Groupwork with deaf people. Kavita Kohli, Social Worker, Hounslow Social Services s
Combining activities and growth games: A systems approach Oded Manor, Middlesex University, and Miriam Dumbleton, Care Manager, Westminster Social Services

Volume 7 (ISBN 9781861770615)
The linguistic and cultural barriers to cross-national groupwork Paul Taylor, Lecturer in Community Education, University of Tours, France
Partnership in training and practice with refugees Jill Reynolds, School of Health, Welfare and Community Education, Open University and Jane Shackman, Social Worker, The Medical Foundation for Care of Victims of Torture
Men working with men in groups: masculinity and crime John Benstead, Gloucester Probation, Allan Brown, School of Social Work, Bristol University, Carlton Forbes, and Rick Wall, Avon Probation Centre
Working *with religious communities* Geraldine Grindley, Dublin City University
Issues of empowerment: Anti-oppressive groupwork by disabled people in Ireland Maire Ni Chorcora and Eddie Jennings, DET and Nuala Lordan, Dept of Applied Social Studies, University College Cork
A Psychotherapeutic group for boys who have been sexually abused Gary Dixon formerly South London FSU and Michelle Phillips, Clinical Nurse Specialist, Camberwell Child Guidance Centre
Groupwork and black women: Viewing networks as groups Marcia Francis-Spence Centre for Applied Social Studies, University of Durham
Staying alive in difficult times: The experience of groupwork with mothers of children who have been sexually abused Deb Dobbin and Sarah Evans, Independent Social Workers
A time for women: An account of a group for women on an out of city housing development in Leicester Claire Wintram, Independent Trainer, Kerry Chamberlain, National Health Service Administrator, Marlene Kuhn, Midwife and Jo Smith, Woman with a Disability active in support and campaign groups , Leicester
Groupwork for mental health: Providers utilising the enchanted self concept Barbara Becker Holstein, Psychologist, Long Branch, New Jersey, and Doreen Laperdon-Addison, Movement Educator and Professional Dancer
Promoting positive images:. The role of groupwork in promoting women managers within organisations Judy Fawcett, Independent Consultant and Trainer
Using a facilitated self help group for women whose children have been sexually abused Olive Otway, Dept of Social Work, Keele University, and Anne Peak, Principal Psychologist, Oxfordshire
'All I've got in my purse is mothballs' the social action women's group Sandra Butler, Dept of Social Work, University of Nottingham
Silence in working across difference: Groupwork in a youth and community work training context Janet Batsleer, Youth and Community Work Section, Manchester Metropolitan University
Ourselves and others Helen Gobat, Independent Social Worker
Groupwork with young mothers Caroline Norman, Project Worker, St Gabriels Family Centre, Brighton
Groupwork for parents of young people in trouble: A proposal Mark Drakeford, Dept of Applied Social Studies, University of Wales, Swansea
A dramatic view of groupwork Jeremy Weinstein, Dept of Social Work, South Bank University
Anger management groupwork with prisoners: An empirical evaluation Graham J Towl and Polly Dexter, Forensic Psychologists, HM Prison Service

Volume 8 (ISBN 9781861770622)
'Cycling Over Everest' Groupwork with depressed women Pamela Trevithick, Dept of Social Work, Bristol University
Groupwork in Croatia: Experiences with older refugees Marina Adjukovic, School of Social Work, University of Zagreb, Milena Cevcizovic

and Ksenija Kontak, Psychologists, Society for Psychological Assistance, Croatia

Group dialogue within prisons Peter Garrett, Centre for Action Research in Professional Practice, School of Management, University of Bath

Establishing community meetings in a children's home Adrian Ward, Dept of Social Work, University of Reading

Groups for children who have lived with domestic violence: Learning from North America Audrey Mullender, Centre for Applied Social Studies, University of Durham

Facilitating enquiry and action learning groups for social work education Hilary Burgess and Imogen Taylor, School for Policy Studies, University of Bristol

Developing critical conversations about practice Mark K Smith, Research Fellow and Tutor, YMCA George Williams College

Dialogue and reparation in the large whole group Alan Turkie, Independent and Lecturer in Youth and Community Work, Goldsmiths' College

Using groupwork methods in social work education Margaret O'Dee, Social Work Studies, Salford University

An outdoor treatment programme for a group of first year sixth formers Derrick Rowland Coverdale consultant

A Strategy for groupwork education and training in a social work agency Mark Doel, University of Sheffield and Catherine Sawdon, Training Officer, Wakefield Social Services

Managing the tension between being task-centred and being anti-oppressive Marcia Francis Spence and Beverley Prevatt-Goldstein, Centre for Applied Social Studies, University of Durham

Teachers, learning, ego and groups Leslie Silverlock and Marion Silverlock 'Groups Work'

Creative short term group therapy in a managed care environment Barry M Daste, Louisiana State University School of Social Work

Groupwork to facilitate family reconstitution: A social work response Jan Hadlow, Keynes College

Social groupwork practice in Hong Kong: Application of western ideas in an asian population Debbie O B Lam, University of Hong Kong

Time and space to grieve: A bereavement group for children Sister Margaret Pennels, Northampton General Hospital NHS Trust

An integrated feminist-socioeducational model: Groupwork with nurses in Hong Kong Elaine Au Liu, City University of Hong Kong

Volume 9 (ISBN 9781861770639)

Living with loss: A bereavement support group Sheila Thompson, School of Social Work, McGill University

A collaborative group approach for urban parents Mary McKernan McKay, Teresa Garcia, Joseph Scally and Lori Martinez, Institute for Juvenile Research, University of Illinois, Chicago

Groupwork with male 'domestic' abusers: Models and dilemmas Audrey Mullender, Professor in Social Work, University of Warwick

'Without the group, I'd still be eating half the Co-op': An example of groupwork with women who use food Jill Ball and Annemarie Norman, , Northern Initiative on Women and Food, Newcastle

The use of sculpt in social groupwork education Nuala Lordan, University College, Cork

Groupwork into the future: Some personal reflections Allan Brown, formerly University of Bristol

Ethical issues in practice: Participatory social research and groups George Taylor, Dept of Social and Community Studies, De Montfort University

Enhancing research usefulness with adapted focus groups Alice M. Home, Professor of Social Work, University of Ottawa

Focus groups and familiar social work skills: Their contribution to practitioner research Pat Walton, Lecturer in Post-Qualifying Studies (Child Care)

Focusing on groups in social policy research Paul Swift, Project Researcher, School for Policy Studies, University of Bristol

Exploitation or empowerment? Gaining access to young people's reflections on crime prevention Strategies Alan France, Research Fellow, University of Warwick University

A youth and community work approach to practitioner research into sensitive issues Steve Kenny, Dept of Applied Community Studies, Manchester Metropolitan University

Black community members-as-researchers: Working with community groups in the research process Simon Dyson and Mark Harrison, Director, Centre for Social Action, de Montfort University,

Empowering research process: Using groups in research to empower the people Asnarulkhadi

Abu-Samah, Doctoral student, University of Nottingham

Storming as transformation: A case study of group relationships Oded Manor, Middlesex University

An art therapy group for young people with eating difficulties Janet Fitzsimmons, Social Worker and Rosemary Levy, Art Therapist, Barnet Social Services Children and Families Health related Social Work Team

Intervention in the decision-making of youth gangs Francis W L Lee, Dept of Social Work, Chinese University of Hong Kong, T. Wing Lo and Dennis S W Wong, Dept of Applied Social Studies, City University of Hong Kong

Support groups for families of confused elders: Issues surrounding open peer-led groups Elizabeth Hughes Schneewind, Independent Social Worker

Drama and groupwork: Overcoming the 'double whammy' Philip Moore, Actor and Groupworker, Cumbria Probation

Psychosocial assistance to refugee and displaced women in Croatia Nina Pecnik, School of Social Work, University of Zagreb and Mira Miskulin, Programme for Refugee Women, 'Sunflower' Centre for Grassroots Relief, Zagreb

Volume 10 (ISBN 9781861770646)

Teleconferencing group counselling: Pre-group public phase Sandra Regan, Senior Lecturer in Groupwork, School of Social Work, University of New South Wales,

Suddenly the light went on: Using groupwork to empower returning students Roni Berger, Assistant Professor, School of Social Work, Adelphi University

A group's journey through separation and loss: Therapeutic groupwork with children as a social work intervention Maria Neary and Geraldine Brandon, Thamesmead Family Service Unit

Implementing a novel groupwork model: Application of an innovation-developmental process Jerome R. Kolbo, University of S Mississippi, Kimberly Horn, W Virginia University and Elizabeth Randall, University of S Mississippi

Applying a strengths, competence and empowerment model Anna Nosko, Family Services Association of Toronto and Margot Breton, University of Toronto

Effective groupwork packages and the importance of process David Henchman and Susan Walton, Freelance Trainers and Probation Officers

Using the sensory orientation group with a frail elder population Norma Thomas, Professor, Center for Social Work, Widener University, Pennsylvania and Suzanne Coleman, Social Worker, Bryn Mawr Terrace Nursing Home, Pennsylvania

Research into practice does go: Integrating research within programme development Rob Harry, Staff Dev't Manager, Patricia Heggarty, Probation Officer, Cathy Lisles, Freelance Researcher, Richard Thurston, Research Mgr, Mid-Glams Probation and Maurice Vanstone, Lecturer, University of Wales, Swansea

Brief group therapy and the use of metaphor Christian C Sunderland, Clinical Social Worker, Cardston Clinic, Alberta

We'd like you to come back Hilary Hopkin, Social Worker, Royal Liverpool University Hospital

The use of music in group work with out-patient alcoholic couples: A pilot investigation Wilfred A Gallant, Assoc. Professor of Social Work, Melanie D Galant, Research Asst Human Services Research Unit, Kevin M Gorey, Assoc. Professor of Social Work, Michael J Holosko, Professor of Social Work and Sammi Siegel, Director of Music Therapy, University of Windsor, Ontario

Exploring worker responses to critical incidents Marian F Fatout, Professor, School of Social Work, Louisiana State University, Baton Rouge

A Critical analysis of a support and clinical supervision group for interpreters working with refugees located in Britain Rachel Tribe, Senior Lecturer, Psychology Dept, University of East London, Romford

Feminist groupwork with lesbian survivors of incest Patricia A Groves, Director of Social Work Program and Connie Schondel, formerly Associate Professor, , University of Toledo, Ohio

Don't worry, it's just a stage he's going through: A reappraisal of the stage theory of group work as applied to an open model treatment group for men who abuse women Tom Caplan, Adj. Professor and Director, and Harle Thomas, Clinical and Groupworker, McGill University Domestic Violence Clinic

Active learning programmes to promote cognitive change Siu-Kau Cheung, Principal Lecturer,

Division of Social Studies, City University of Hong Kong

Volume 11 (ISBN 9781861770653)
Crossing bridges: Groupwork in Guyana Judith A B Lee, Professor, Dept of Social Work, Florida Gulf Coast University
Working with polarities, roles and timespirits: A process oriented approach to emotions in the Group Bogna Szymkiewicz-Komalska, Asst Professor, Inst of Applied Social Sciences, Warsaw University
It ain't (just) what you do: It's the way that you do it: Working towards effective practice in probation groupwork Alan Hayden, Jonathan Hopkinson, Janeen Sengendo and Elisabeth von Rabenau, Probation Officers, Cambridgeshire Probation
A Group intervention for children of incarcerated parents: Initial blunders and subsequent solutions David W Springer, Asst Professor, Elizabeth C Pomeroy, Asst Professor and Toni Johnson, Doctoral Student, School of Social Work, University of Texas, Austin
Expressing our anger: Hindrance or help in groupwork with adolescents? Andrew Malekoff, Director or Program Development, North Shore Child and Family Guidance Center, Roslyn Heights, New York
Technical errors or missed alternatives: An interview with Catherine Pappell
Groupwork with the mothers of teenage mothers Catherine Dennison, Research Psychologist and Helen Ingledew, Family Centre Worker, Trust for the Study of Adolescence
Men united: Fathers' voices Jennie Fleming, Research Fellow, Centre for Social Action, de Montfort University and Zbyszek Luczynski, Broader Initiatives Development Worker, Nottingham City Council
Parent education groups: Using cultural literature during engagement phase Gwenelle Styles O'Neal, Assoc Professor of Social Work, West Chester University, Pennsylvania and Janis Coombs Reid, Vice President of Academic Affairs, Atlanta Metropolitan College, Georgia
Action methods and interpersonal processes in groups: An exploration of psychodramatic concepts Annie Huntington, Lecturer, Dept of Social Work, Salford University
Building solutions in groupwork with parents John Sharry, Senior Social Worker, Dept of Child and Family Psychiatry, Mater Hospital, Dublin
Crossing the great gap: Groupwork for personal growth John Rowan, Group and Individual Psychotherapist
When actions speak louder: Groupwork in occupational therapy Linda Finlay, Associate Lecturer in Social Psychology, the Open University, Leeds
Help as mutual aid: Groupwork in mental health Oded Manor, Principal Lecturer in Social Work, School of Social Science, Middlesex University
No Group is an island: Groupwork in a social work agency Mark Doel, Professor of Social Work School of Social Work and RNIB Rehabilitation Studies, University of Central England and Catherine Sawdon, Training Officer, Wakefield Social Services
Breaking the culture of silence: Groupwork and community development Jacky Drysdale, Lecturer in Social Work and Rod Purcell, Lecturer in Community Development and Adult Education, University of Glasgow
Values as Context: Groupwork and social action Mark Harrison, Director, Centre for Social Action and Dave Ward, Professor and Head, Dept of Social and Community Studies, De Montfort University

Volume 12 (ISBN 9781861770660)
Punishment and the question of ownership: Groupwork in the criminal justice system Liz Dixon, Senior Lecturer in Criminal Justice Studies, University of Hertfordshire and Probation Officer, ILPS
Picking up the Pieces: Groupwork in Palliative Care Pam Firth, Senior Social Worker/Head of Family Support, Isabel Hospice, Welwyn Garden City
Developing the professionals: Groupwork for health promotion Ellen E Reverand, Senior Manager (Learning and Professional Development) and Louis B Levy, Acting Director, Health First, London
Learning beyond the classroom: A role for groupwork? Marion Silverlock, Education and Training Consultant, Somerset
Evolving the curriculum: Groupwork and community based learning Lynne Muir, Course Director, MA in Community Based Learning. , Centre for Education Development, Coventry
Using workshops on loss for adults with learning

disabilities Sue Read, Vicky Papakosta-Harvey and Sal Bower
Groupwork with schizophrenia: Clinical aspects Susan E. Mason, Associate Professor of Social Work, Wurzweiler School of Social Work, Yeshiva University, New York
Multi-family group interventions with schizophrenia Jane Hanvey Phillips, Doctoral Candidate, and Jacqueline Corcoran, Assistant Professor, School of Social Work, University of Texas, Arlington
The mixed-based nature of self-help groups in Finland Marianne Nylund, Researcher, Doctor of Social Sciences, Dept of Social Policy, University of Helsinky
Teenagers' experiences of a health promotion project Frances Maggs-Rapport, Senior Research Fellow, Mary Seacole Research Centre, De Montfort University
Working with natural groups of youth-at-risk: An RGC approach Francis Wing-lin Lee Assistant Professor, Dept of Social Work, University of Hong Kong
The strengths perspective in reminiscence groupwork with depressed older adults Alison C. Rishty Advanced Standing MSW Candidate in Clinical Practice, Columbia University
Using fieldwork experience as a tool for teaching: A multi-layered approach Barbara Worden, Assoc. Professor of Social Work, Southern Conecticut State University

Volume 13 (ISBN 9781861770677)
Using technologies in groupwork . Part I: Face-to-face groups, and *Part II: Technology-based groups* Paul R. Smokowski, Director of Distance Education, Maeda Galinsky, Kenan Distinguished Professor, School of Social Work, University of North Carolina at Chapel Hill, and Kristin Harlow, Social Work Practitioner
Researching our own practice: Single system design for groupwork Paul Johnson, Asst Professor, Dept of Social Work, University of S. Maine. Aaron Beckerman, Professor Emeritus and Charles Auerbach, Professor, Wurzweiler School of Social Work, Yeshiva University
Facilitating group beginnings. I: A practice model, and *Part II: From basic to working engagement* Alf Lizzio, Lecturer, and Keithia Wilson, Senior Lecturer, School of Applied Psychology, Griffiths University, Brisbane
To share or not to share: Dilemmas of facilitators who share the problem of group members Marian Maram, Assistant Director of Field Education, and Susan Rice, Professor and Undergraduate Program Coordinator, Dept of Social Work, California State University, Long Beach
In their own voices: Play activities and art with traumatised children Bruce St. Thomas, Psychotherapist/Art Therapist, Westbrook Street Psychotherapy Associates, Portland, and Paul Johnson, Assistant Professor, Dept of Social Work, University of S. Maine
Groupwork with children and adolescents using lifegames Isabelle C. Streng, Chartered Clinical Psychologist, Erasmus Medical Centre, Rotterdam, The Netherlands
Closing a cultural divide: Enhancing mutual aid while working with groups in Hong Kong Fanny L.W.C. Liu, Senior Lecturer, Division of Social Studies, City University of Hong Kong
Strengths and weaknesses of self-help groups in mental health: The case of Grow Kam-shing Yip, Associate Professor, Dept of Applied Social Studies, Hong Kong Polytechnic University
Using groupwork in community mental health: Practitioners' views Ben Papps, Lecturer in Clinical Psychology, Institute of Psychiatry, London., Oded Manor, Principal Lecturer in Social Work, Middlesex University and Jerome Carson, Senior Lecturer in Clinical Psychology, Institute of Psychiatry, London
Hearing voices: Learning to engage the group Terry Conway, Senior Social Worker, Kneesworth House Hospital, Royston
An isle full of noises: Enhancing mental health through the Music Workshop Project Tony Gillam, Early Interventions Team Leader, Merdian Family Interventions Programme, South Worcestershire Early Interventions Service
Henderson Hospital: Greater than the sum of its sub-groups Dr Kingsley Norton, Director, Henderson Hospital and Reader in Psychotherapy, St George's Hospital Medical School
Groupwork fit for purpose? An inclusive framework for mental health Oded Manor, Principal Lecturer in Social Work, School of Health and Social Sciences, Middlesex University

Authors' professional affiliations are those at the time of original publication

www.ingramcontent.com/pod-product-compliance
Lightning Source LLC
LaVergne TN
LVHW101443200926
848483LV00001B/30